This book is the culmination of Ana-Mar
1891 *Aphasia* monograph. Although its sci
ago by neurologists, the monograph was curiously orpnaneu by 11cuu ...
this book, Rizzuto demonstrates with definitive authority its seminal importance
for psychoanalysis. Although not her main intention, she simultaneously opens
new lines of interdisciplinary enquiry regarding some contemporary neuropsy-
chological topics, such as the role of declarative memory (Freud's 'word presentations') and episodic recall (Freud's 'scenes') in reflexive consciousness.

— *Mark Solms*, Professor in Neuropsychology and
Chair of the Research Committee of the IPA

Rizzuto's accurate, precise and inspired analysis of Freud's *On Aphasia* is the scarlet
thread that runs through the whole book, weaving interconnections with some
of the problems facing psychoanalysis today. The title *Freud and the Spoken Word* is
essential for defining the field of research not about language but about the individual and unrepeatable linguistic act of the speaker.

The author lists not only the prominent qualities of Freud's theories but also
its limitations: the lack of an agent, of the addressee, and affect as a dischargeable
quantity. Rizzuto's important book addresses their relevance to psychoanalysis.

— *Professor Jorge Canestri*, MD, Training analyst,
Italian Psychoanalytical Association

FREUD AND THE SPOKEN WORD

There is extensive literature on Freud and language; however, there is very little that looks at Freud's use of the spoken word. In *Freud and the Spoken Word: Speech as a key to the unconscious*, Ana-María Rizzuto contends that Freud's focus on the intrapsychic function and meaning of patients' words allowed him to use the new psychoanalytic method of talking to gain access to unconscious psychic life. In creating the first 'talking therapy', Freud began a movement that still underpins how psychoanalysts understand and use the spoken word in clinical treatment and advance psychoanalytic theory. With careful and critical reference to Freud's own work, this book draws out conclusions on the nature of verbal exchanges between analyst and patient.

Ana-María Rizzuto begins with a close look at Freud's early monograph *On Aphasia*, suggesting that Freud was motivated by his need to understand the disturbed speech phenomena observed in three of the patients described in *Studies on Hysteria*. She then turns to an examination of how Freud integrated the spoken word into his theories as well as how he actually talked with his patients, looking again at the *Studies on Hysteria* and continuing with the Dora case, the Rat Man, and the Wolf Man. In these chapters, the author interprets how Freud's report of his own words shed light on the varying relationships he had with his patients, when and how he was able to follow his own recommendations for treatment and when another factor (therapeutic zeal, or the wish to prove a theory) appeared to interfere in the communication between the two parties in the analysis.

Freud and the Spoken Word examines Freud's work with a critical eye. The book explores his contribution in relation to the spoken word, enhances its significance, and challenges its shortcomings. It is written for psychoanalysts, psychotherapists, Freud's scholars, and academics interested in his views on the words spoken in life and in psychoanalysis.

Argentine-born **Ana-María Rizzuto** trained in psychoanalysis in Boston and was for forty years in the PINE Psychoanalytic Center Faculty and is Training and Supervisory Analyst Emerita. She has made significant contributions to the psychoanalysis of religious experience and has written in national and international journals about the significance of words in the clinical situation. She has written three books and lectured about her work in North America, Latin America, Europe, and Japan.

FREUD AND THE SPOKEN WORD

Speech as a key to the unconscious

Ana-María Rizzuto

Routledge
Taylor & Francis Group

LONDON AND NEW YORK

First published 2015
by Routledge
27 Church Road, Hove, East Sussex, BN3 2FA

And by Routledge
711 Third Avenue, New York, NY 10017

Routledge is an imprint of the Taylor & Francis Group, an informa business

© 2015 Ana-María Rizzuto

The right of Ana-María Rizzuto to be identified as author of this work
has been asserted by her in accordance with sections 77 and 78 of the
Copyright, Designs and Patents Act 1988.

British Library Cataloguing in Publication Data
A catalogue record for this book is available from the British Library

Library of Congress Cataloging-in-Publication Data
Rizzuto, Ana-Maria.
   Freud and the spoken word : speech as a key to the unconscious /
Ana-Maria Rizzuto.
      pages cm
   1. Freud, Sigmund, 1856–1939.   2. Psychoanalysis.
3. Psycholinguistics.   4. Subconsciousness.   I. Title.
   BF173.F85R558 2015
   150.19′52092—dc23
   2014049103

ISBN: 978-1-138-85810-7 (hbk)
ISBN: 978-1-138-85811-4 (pbk)
ISBN: 978-1-315-71820-0 (ebk)

Typeset in Bembo
by Apex CoVantage, LLC

Printed and bound in the United States of America by Publishers Graphics,
LLC on sustainably sourced paper.

CONTENTS

ACKNOWLEDGMENTS

I owe deep gratitude to all the patients who taught me and at times *forced* me to listen to them and to learn to speak to them.

I thank my colleagues Jacqueline Amati-Mehler, Bonnie E. Litowitz, and Cordelia Schmidt-Hellerau for reading chapters of the first draft of the book and making most valuable suggestions.

I specially thank the candidate members of the 2011 Fall Advanced Seminar of the PINE Psychoanalytic Center in Boston for agreeing to discuss the first draft of the book. Their questions, challenges, and comments were most valuable to me.

I also owe much to my editor Deborah Schneider, who with resolute determination and a deep sense of how language conveys meaning, reviewed my clumsy English sentences and gave them more elegant form.

I am deeply indebted to my husband Agustín Aoki, who with great patience gave me continuous encouragement and support in both good times and bad times.

PREFACE

When Freud demonstrated that the ego is no master in its own house, he prided himself on having inflicted a third blow to humankind's naive self-love. Copernicus's cosmic revolution had removed us from the center of the universe. Darwin's biological discoveries narrowed the gulf between human beings and the animal kingdom. Now Freud's psychological investigations proved that a person's conscious awareness leaves out core aspects of psychic life. He demonstrated the existence of unconscious mental processes and was firm in his belief that "the unconscious is the true psychical reality" (Freud 1900, 613).

Freud had every right to be proud of his discovery, but he omitted to mention another revolution that is as significant as the other three: he created a new way for people to speak and to listen to each other, a key approach that opened the up-to-then closed doors of unconscious mental processes. The change he introduced involved directing his patients' attention to *perceive* their private mentation while he focused on the *intrapsychic* functions of the representations that emerged when he insisted that they describe them with words. By listening to the patient's words in this manner a psychoanalyst could progressively access the psychic realities whose unconscious activity condition the analysand's illness.

Freud transformed the exchange of words between people from an ordinary conversation into an exploratory tool to uncover their private histories, stories, fantasies, and the narrative of their psychic itinerary; he also transformed it into a therapeutic instrument to undo the pathogenic effect of unacceptable mental processes. He had the *courage* to introduce the spoken word as a medical procedure not only comparable to but remarkably more efficient than the psychiatric treatments of the day.

Much has been written about Freud and language culminating in John Forrester's conclusion that "language is the central concern of psychoanalysis" (Forrester 1980, x). If by language we understand a community's use of agreed-upon sounds, words, and linguistic functions present in a particular culture, I cannot fully accept such a statement. My detailed reading of Freud, starting with his collaboration with his senior colleague Josef Breuer, has convinced me that he focused on the "talking cure," the spoken language between himself and his patients. He concerned himself with the work of contemporaneous philologists only to the extent that it provided confirmation for his clinical findings and theories.

It is true that Freud did not use the expression "spoken word." But it is also true that in *On Aphasia: A Critical Study* (Freud 1891), he created a "speech apparatus" whose key function was the production of *spontaneous* speech. The monograph's focus appears to be the neural pathology of aphasias, and, in fact, Freud's masterful examination of existing theories and "speech apparatuses" of his eminent contemporaneous neurologists led him to reject their theories and schemas and present his own conception of aphasias, theoretical apparatus, and conclusions. His core thesis affirms that all aphasias result from disruption of associations. In *verbal aphasia* the associations between the single elements of the word representation are disturbed by neural lesions. In *asymbolic aphasia*, a new category he created, the associative link between the word and the object-representation is disrupted by *functional* processes. Freud considers that such a link is the "weakest point" (p. 83) of the speech function. In his later theorizing it would become the place used by pathological motives to repress disturbing representations but also the avenue to restitute their original integrity by the mediation of speech.

Freud's stated motive for writing the monograph was an invitation to present his views on aphasia. He produced a neurological description of its pathology with an admirable analysis of all the available data that led him to disprove the validity of his fellow neurologists' models and to create his own. He went beyond the study of aphasic conditions, however. The model apparatus he created offers a description of the foundations of the speech function in all people, including the source of our need to speak.

This expansion of his theorizing did not come from Freud the neurologist but from the already deeply involved psychotherapist who needed to understand the *functional* pathology of speech and other symptoms present in the lady patients he was treating at the time. Josef Breuer had also described his patient Fräulein Anna O. to him. Breuer and Freud had undertaken to treat them by using the *empirically* determined therapeutic effect of verbal exchanges between patient and doctor. The evidence of his psychological interest in words in the monograph comes from the title of his core diagram in the book (see illustration in Chapter 2): *Psychological Diagram of the Word-Presentation (Wortvorstellung)*. He had moved from basic neurology and its aphasic pathology to the *functional* organization in the mind of the words we use.

In *On Aphasia* Freud presents the foundational principles that undergird all representational processes. Some of them are neurologically obvious but others result from Freud's creative theorizing or his inferences from clinical observations. I list here those already present in the monograph that would frame *all* of his later theories and technique. Bodily sensory *perception* of reality is the *exclusive* foundation of psychic life. There is no direct registration of what is perceived; the sensory information undergoes several changes in *meaning (Deutung)* on its way from the sensory periphery of the body to the cerebral cortex. They result from synaptic associative processes that take place in gray nuclei along its path. Thus, in Freud's view, *to perceive is to associate*, a single process. The convergence in the cortex of several percepts – visual, tactile, acoustic, and others leads to the formation of object-representations, which portray the individual's bodily and associatively organized *internal* percept of objects. These processes leave behind a neural documentation of their formation by creating not only *physiological correlates* but *facilitations* that will permit *conscious* revival of the original registration at a later time. Whenever the previously established cortical state is stimulated: ". . . the psychical (*das Psychische*) emerges anew as a *remembered image (Erinnerungsbild)*" (1891, p. 58). Freud is talking about the *internal* revival of representations. The neural registrations are indestructible, they are paths that have been laid down and that remain functionally available thus creating the conditions for Freud's later conception of obligatory psychic *determinism*. The mind expands its object-representations, however, by adding new sensory and associative perceptions to them. This apparently dry notion of revival of "the psychical" and its expansion introduce the two key theoretical elements for psychoanalytic technique: perception of the internal imagery and its pathogenic and therapeutic elaboration.

The object-representations remain in the mind ready to be reawakened by a proper stimulus. To be articulated into speech their visual component must *stimulate* the sound image (*Bild*) of the word-representation. The latter originates in the *perception and registration* of the words other people use to relate to us and the world. The word-presentation also forms a complex of associations of sound and kinaesthetic images (*Bild*) early in life and of printed or scripted images later in life. It is this link between the visual image and the sound image that is so fragile in psychopathology. When it is functionally – not anatomically – disrupted, we have an *asymbolic aphasia*, that is, the inability to make the internal presentation accessible to the *intentional* speech of the person. Much later in his theorizing, when describing the concept of repression, Freud would consider that this defensive function consists in creating a *gap* in consciousness by depriving unpleasant representations of access to awareness, a condition that depends on their being linked to words. In brief, representational gaps create pathology while verbal *translation* of the repressed representations makes them consciously available and restores the ego's integrity.

The listing of these foundational concepts in *On Aphasia* indicates that *Freud's essential theoretical and technical edifice is built upon the structure and functional organization of the speech apparatus.* Furthermore, beyond the study of neural processes Freud used direct observation and introspection to explore how we use words. He observed his *divided attention* when proofreading, noting that he could not attend to the comprehension of the text when checking grammar and spelling. Such a discovery, directly linked to what he had already documented in his clinical work, became the foundation of his evolving technique. He *distracted* his patients from their guarded attitude toward painful internal processes – representations – by using hypnosis, and later pressure on their foreheads, insisting that they *look* into what came to their minds, and finally by requiring free association. Later, he called such procedures a *trick* to divert the patient's attention from controlling the emergence of the pathogenic material.

In the monograph Freud introduced the basic terminology for his future theories. Beyond the already mentioned representation, association, divided attention, complex, connection, facilitations, physiological correlate, self-observation, the impulse to speak and spontaneous speech, as already mentioned, he first used terms there that he later elaborated into full concepts: cathexis, memory-image, and transference. Still later Freud enlarged the meaning of these concepts and added several other significant theoretical notions such as affect, the division of the mind into conscious and unconscious, the structural theory, and others. Nevertheless, I believe it is accurate to say that *the speech apparatus model remained the foundation of his later efforts to articulate the interdigitation between unconscious and conscious processes in his theories and technique.*

Freud concludes the monograph with the recommendation that we concern ourselves with the functional states of the speech apparatus. He himself did precisely that for the rest of his life: he attended to every nuance of his patients' speech; he theorized about what he heard; he created mental structures to find a location for the different components of representations and words; in brief, he created psychoanalysis in all its astonishing complexity. Yet, he refused to include *On Aphasia* in his psychoanalytic publications claiming that it pertained solely to his neurological work; he mentioned it only once on passing in *Studies on Hysteria*. In 1957 James Strachey, the editor and translator of the *Standard Edition*, found such similarity between some concepts in *The Unconscious* and the monograph that he added pages 74 to 81 of the original German edition as "Appendix C" to Freud's original text. Freud did not make the connection.

Freud repeats in the monograph: "All stimuli to spontaneous speech arise from object associations" (1891, E. p. 79; G. p. 81),[1] which he links to the "activities of the rest of the cortex" (E. p. 90; G. p. 92). This is not a demonstrable neurological fact but a *clinical* observation about what prompts people to talk or even to avoid talking. Freud's assertion about the "rest of the cortex" goes beyond the registered representations of a discrete isolated object as it appears in his diagram. It connects representations to other cortical activities such as recollections of events, scenes, and experiences that hold the power to find and stimulate the sound component of a word presentation when *we want* to speak. If we are able to do it we simply speak meaningfully. If we fail and the stimulation exercised by the object-representation cannot establish the link, we suffer from *asymbolic aphasia*. Freud does not mention internal conflict in the monograph or the compensatory symptoms stemming from the failure to process the representational stimulation. Later in his theorizing he would consider that painful affects prompt patients to avoid giving words to them. He never established a connection between the two conceptions but the notion that representations call for expression is ever present in his theorizing about the relation between conscious and unconscious processes. In fact, the failure to express in words the stimulation of representations makes them pathogenic and keeps them unconscious. Clinically, Freud documented in his early work that only the *full* examination of an avoided representation will bring about the necessary symptomatic change because the patient has accepted it as his own.

There is another observation to be made. Freud never again used the term (re)-presentation until 1915 in *The Unconscious*, the only other Freudian text where we find it as a concept. In the rest of his clinical and theoretical papers he prevalently uses *scene*, event, or other equivalent. It is as though, in working with patients, he found the term 'representation' too narrow to apply to the wealth of scenes or stories (remembered or imagined) that appeared in their minds and prompted them either to talk or to avoid talking. The term *scene* is not listed in the index of the *Standard Edition* and has not received the attention it deserves as the heir – as I propose – to (re)presentation.

In the monograph Freud says that the *visual* component of an object-representation is the predominant link to the sound of words to form a meaningful expression. This assertion, which appears purely theoretical, in fact underlays Freud's technical approach to access the internal reality of his patients, from the *Studies on Hysteria* to his last publication, *Construction in Analysis*. Seeing what came to mind (*Einfäll*, in German) constitutes the critical first step to assist the patient to give words to them. Early in his work Freud insistently asked: "What have you seen?" Furthermore, even though he never says it, he seems to have taken for granted that his *order* to the patient to look inside would bring up precisely *the one* correct *Einfäll* linked to the pathology from within a vast representational realm. The *tacit* assumption is that such a particular representation and its associations are ready with "stimulation" to make themselves available, which, in fact they are, as we know from our clinical work. Freud claims that once the troubling scenes have been fully described they never reappear in the treatment.

What is then the value of words? In *On Aphasia* Freud says: "The word acquires its meaning (*Bedeutung*) through its connection (*Verknüpfung*) with the object representation (*Objektvorstellung*)" (1891, E. p. 77; G. p. 79, my translation). It must be noticed that the word does not impose its own meaning but *acquires* it from the internal representation, what I described above as the *intrapsychic* meaning of words. Internal representations bestow personal meaning upon ordinary words as illustrated by Freud's shocking metaphor about his task – which he saw as using his interpretations to extract "the pure metal of the repressed thoughts from the ore of the unintentional ideas" (Freud 1904, 252). The words and associations called "ore" are to be explored until the repressed representation, the "pure metal," is found by means of interpretations capable of restoring the "initial organization" of what has been repressed, thus integrating the psychic word into the person's conscious mind.

Freud also conceived of his technique of interpretation as a *translation*, a term he had not used in *On Aphasia*. In the monograph he described the change of meaning that occurs as percepts ascend through synapses on the way to the cortex and are enriched by associations. In his December 6, 1896, letter to his colleague Wilhelm Fliess Freud links explicitly such conception in *On Aphasia* to the reorganization of memory when "fresh circumstances" call for a "rearrangement" – a "retranscription" of representations (Freud 1985, 207). I am assuming that the analyst's interpretation 'translates' for the patient the last organization of such a percept, one so disturbing that he had to repress it. The evolution of the concept does not detract from its early meaning and the conclusion that emerges from Freud's entire work: *speech about psychic life is always a translation. We live in translation.*

What happens to the words we encounter in the language of our culture, the only ones we have to speak with in life and in analysis? Freud simply says "words are a *plastic material* with which one can do all kinds of things" (Freud 1905, 34, my italics) from aptly describing internal and external perceptions in everyday life and in the analytic process to becoming intentionally or unconsciously deceptive, false, misleading, or distracting; they may hide or reveal double meanings, or express something other than what the speaker intended. In fact, we can be sure of what a word means to us – and this is one of *Freud's core contributions* – only when we have managed to link it to our internal representation that contributed to its formation. Otherwise, the word may keep its *linguistic referential meaning* without revealing its true conscious *and* unconscious motivation.

There are other detectable influences of *On Aphasia* in Freud's work that the reader will find in the chapters that follow. Yet, beyond these contributions to Freud's creation of psychoanalysis the monograph also marred it in significant aspects. The apparatus had neither an agent to organize its functions nor a subject to experience the feelings so critical for psychic life. Furthermore, Freud says nothing about speech being addressed to others. These omissions contributed to Freud's "one person" psychology and led him to conceive of affect in *The Project* as a quantity that needed to be discharged. In all his efforts, Freud was unable to offer a viable integration of representations, words, and affects.

I disagree with Freud's rejection of his early masterpiece. Taking his advice, I have examined all I could find in his writings about his rich, almost inexhaustible, ways of exploring the psychic function of the spoken word, since it is the only tool we have to articulate the unconscious representational reality in which we live. I constantly have found in his works the *tacit* but omnipresent influence of the concepts he presented in *On Aphasia*. It is my goal in this study to make these concepts and their influence explicit as well as to elucidate the impressive psychic variations Freud unveiled in the words we use innocently, unaware of their true meaning.

In brief, in this book I explore in detail Freud's second revolution: how by using the spoken word in an original and therapeutically effective manner he uncovered the true psychic reality of our unknown representational unconscious.

I hope my readers will find a new key to ponder Freud's work. I further hope it may serve as a useful companion to Freud's texts to explore his understanding of the contributions words offer to our psychic life.

Note

1 From now on, when the English translation does not do justice to Freud's original German I cite them indicating G. for the original version and E. for Stengel's English translation. G. presents my own translation and frequently lists the original German term in parentheses. When the English edition is correct I cite it directly.

  For other Freudian texts in the following chapters I use the *Gesammelte Werke*, S. Fisher Verlag, Frankfurt am Main, 1952–1968.

References

Forrester, John. *Language and the Origins of Psychoanalysis*. New York: Columbia University Press, 1980.

Freud, Sigmund. *The Complete Letters of Sigmund Freud to Wilhelm Fliess 1887–1904*. Trans. and ed. Jeffrey Moussaieff Masson. Cambridge, MA: Belknap Press of Harvard University Press, 1985.

———. Freud's Psycho-Analytic Procedure. Vol. 7 of *Standard Edition*, 247–54. London: Hogarth Press, 1904.

———. *The Interpretation of Dreams*. Vols. 4–5 of *Standard Edition*. London: Hogarth Press, 1900.

———. *Jokes and Their Relation to the Unconscious*. Vol. 8 of *Standard Edition*. London: Hogarth Press, 1905.

———. *On Aphasia: A Critical Study*. Trans. Erwin Stengel. 1953. New York: International Universities Press, 1891.

———. *Zur Auffassung der Aphasien. Eine Kritische Studie*. Leipzig: Franz Deuticke, 1891.

1
INTRODUCTION
Freud, psychoanalysis, and the spoken word

In his essay *The Question of Lay Analysis*, Freud describes an imaginary conversation with an "Impartial Person" who wants to know what an analyst does to help a patient other doctors have been unable to heal. The answer is brief and to the point: "*Nothing* takes place between them *except* that they talk to each other" (Freud 1926, 187) (my italics).[1] When his interlocutor shows some contempt to his response, Freud continues: "Do not let us despise the *word*. After all it is a powerful instrument; it is the means by which we convey our feeling to one another, our method of influencing people. Words can do unspeakable good and cause terrible wounds" (pp. 187–88).

This book is about the '*except*' of that '*nothing*' except talking with one another. It is about Freud's deceptively simple sentence specifying the treatment a patient undergoes: "[The analyst] gets him to talk, listens to him, talks to him in his turn and gets him to listen" (p. 187), a description that encompasses the entire process of carrying out an analysis. For the patient and the analyst talking and listening are the *only instruments* they have in their efforts to elucidate the sources of the analysand's suffering and symptoms.

Freud defends the function of the spoken word as a powerful instrument for change, but clarifies that the effect of analytic exchanges is not based on any magic power words might be thought to have; the treatment consists rather of a continuous process of listening and talking that may last a long time. Today, regardless of the development of many different psychoanalytic schools and theoretical approaches that have emerged since Freud's time, we observe that all psychoanalysts use the spoken word as their *only instrument* to access the analysand's private reality. This obvious fact contrasts with the limited attention most practicing analysts and theoreticians have paid to the contribution the spoken word brings to the unfolding of the analysis and the transformations it elicits in both analysand and analyst (Litowitz 2011). I believe it is time for us to give our full attention to the function of the spoken word in our clinical work and in our theorizing. Although the task is a vast one I decided to start at the beginning and read the entire corpus of Freud's writings with the goal of grasping how he defines the many complex functions we perform by employing the spoken word. As far as I know, no other analyst or scholar has carried out this exploration. The closest approach is the scholarly examination that John Forrester, a philosopher of science at King's College Cambridge presented in his book *Language and the Origins of Psychoanalysis* (Forrester 1980). This work focuses primarily on *language* and the connections between the psychoanalytic understanding of neurosis as propositional structures based on Forrester's conviction that "language is the central concern of psychoanalysis" (p. x). I disagree and in what follows replace this principle with my own conviction that the central concern of psychoanalysis is spoken words and what they are capable of revealing about the private unconscious life of a person.

The words patient and analyst exchange with each other differ from ordinary conversation. The analyst aims at assisting the patient to give words to the unconscious representations that would remain unknown to him though they constitute the core of his psychic life. They must be articulated into personally experienced *living words* capable of bringing back to psychic life the moments felt to be unbearable and hence repressed. They become the indispensable referent to open up the closed area of unconscious processes. In ordinary spoken exchanges the most frequent referents are either actual realities or consciously known psychic processes. In both instances, analytic or ordinary conversation, the structures of language *mediate* the process of achieving understanding between two interlocutors while accessing meaning remains a psychical event between two people beyond the mediation of language.

My analytic training went no further than mentioning Anna O's name for her treatment with Breuer, the "talking cure." We took it for granted that patient and analyst speak to each other but did not explore the changes introduced in ordinary speech necessary to achieve our goals. The reader may ask what prompted me to focus on speech in the analytic situation. The answer is complex and requires that I describe my journey as an analyst.

I was born in Argentina, grew up in Córdoba, a university city, and was trained as a teacher before entering medical school. In the 1960s I taught child and adolescent development at the university. In 1963 the dean of the local Roman Catholic seminary asked me to teach a course to his advanced students about the psychological foundations of belief and pastoral care, focusing on belief in God and the internal struggles and consolations that people experience in relating to the divinity. The literature on the subject was scanty; the course had never been taught before. I collected what was written on the subject in several academic disciplines and ended by focusing on Freud and Jung as the authors who had carried out a serious exploration of the subject. Soon I came to see that Jung's complex symbolic and archetypal elaborations were fascinating but far removed from the concrete experiences of ordinary people. Freud won me over with his brilliant clinical elaboration of the role of the parents in the formation of the God-representation.

The child, Freud proposed, uses his experiences with his parents (in his appraisal the father in the first place) to *represent* an *invisible God* by linking the divinity to the parental representations, including the affects and convictions the child associates with his imagos of them. This is how I came to be interested in Freud's notion of object-representations.

I used the course to learn about the local children's conceptions of their God. The seminarians were teaching catechism classes to youngsters in the latency stage and I asked them to take notes about what their pupils asked or said during class in relation to their own experiences. After listening to the words of many children I became hooked on the representational mind, in particular one capable of representing and *relating* to a non-visible and non-directly experiential being called God. A researcher was born in me at that point and I decided to dedicate my available time to study Freud's ideas on internal representations and, most important, to carry out comprehensive clinical research to see if I could prove whether Freud was right or wrong.

In 1965 I immigrated to the United States and settled in Boston the following year. There I began my research in earnest. I published my first paper, *Freud, God, the Devil, and the Theory of Object Representation* (Rizzuto 1976). My book *The Birth of the Living God: A Psychoanalytic Study* (Rizzuto 1979) presented the results of a comprehensive and thoroughly documented study of a large number of patients and their dealings with God. The book starts with a disclaimer: "This is not a book on religion. It is a clinical study of the possible origins of the individual's private representation of God and its subsequent elaborations." The second chapter offers an enlarged revision of Freud's theory of object-representation in relation to the divinity; the fourth chapter, "The Representation of Objects and Human Psychic Functioning," reviews the existing psychoanalytic literature on the subject up to 1979 and presents my own ideas.

The endless hours spent talking and taping the patient's words on the subject and the much longer time spent in reflecting upon them (it took me ten years to elaborate what I had learned) opened my eyes to an obvious fact: the only access to parental or divine representation is the patient's own words. I formulated truly unusual incomplete statements such as "What I like the most about God . . ." or "I feel that what God expects from me is . . ." The responses I heard as my subjects completed the sentences – deeply felt and sometimes carefully, sometimes hesitantly presented – articulated their relationship to a personal God they had never experienced except in the recesses of their representational mind. Now I was hooked again, this time on the power of words to grasp and bring to light the private or hidden realities of human experiences.

In the meantime I had become a psychoanalyst and was seeing several patients in analysis. It so happened that at one point I had four analytic patients who suffered from eating disorders. Working with these patients alerted me to their peculiar manner of talking without talking about themselves. Pierre Marty and Michel de M'Uzan in Paris had described such a phenomenon as *pensée opératoire*, while in Boston in 1973 Peter Sifneos introduced the term alexithymia, a name derived from Greek meaning "no words for feelings." These other authors from the field of psychosomatics did not consider the dynamic motivations present in the patient's difficulties in articulating their experiences in words. Meanwhile, my patients were conveying to me some of their feelings about words. A young anorexic woman almost chanted a mantra in response to my words saying, "Those are only words. They do not mean anything to me." Similarly a woman in her forties with a twenty-year history of binging and vomiting explained repeatedly with patient impatience, "This is like a play. You say your part and I say mine. But we don't mean anything." These patients taught me much about their conditions and showed me that a significant part of their pathology stemmed from emotional deprivation in their early relationships and in particular from disaffected patterns of communication in the family. My first task thus consisted in helping them to explore the parental imagos of their childhood so that they could learn to talk about themselves with me and published what I had learned (Rizzuto 1988).

Now, to fully deserve my name as a practitioner of the "talking cure," I had to wrestle with words and their complexities. Somehow I learned of Freud's pre-analytic publication about words, his 1891 monograph entitled *Zur Auffassung der Aphasien. Eine kritische Studie* (Freud 1891). I read the 1953 English translation (Freud 1891) and felt I was not grasping what Freud was saying. I decided if I were going to understand it properly I had to study the original German. The Boston Psychoanalytic Society and Institute allowed me to make a photocopy of the original edition in its library. Tackling Freud's German text was no easy task. He wrote it for the neurologists of the time who were immersed in the task of creating neural models for the function of speech and its most blatant pathology, aphasia. While Freud's monograph was carefully organized and tightly reasoned, the technical vocabulary presented a steep learning curve. Nevertheless I was determined to understand what Freud had said to override most of his fellow theorizers. I needed colored pencils, tracking lines, cross references, and other technical aids to finally understand what he was saying. Once I did, however, I became a devotee of the monograph, greatly appreciative of the richness of its concepts and the many original ideas it offered in relation to object-representations and the neural/psychical structure of the spoken word. I published my detailed analysis of several aspects of it in five papers: "A Hypothesis about Freud's Motive for Writing the Monograph *On Aphasia*" (Rizzuto 1989); "A Proto-Dictionary of Psychoanalysis" (Rizzuto 1990a); The Origins of Freud's Concept of Object Representation ('*Objektvorstellung*') in His Monograph *On Aphasia*: Its Theoretical and Technical Importance" (Rizzuto 1990b); "Freud's Theoretical and Technical Models in *Studies on Hysteria*" (Rizzuto 1992); and "Freud's Speech Apparatus and Spontaneous Speech" (Rizzuto 1993a).

Freud presented a conclusion in the monograph: "All stimulations to *speak spontaneously* come from the region of the object associations" (1891, G. p. 81; E. p. 79, my translation, my italics). It was just what Freud and I needed to connect internal representations with spoken words. From this moment on my analytic listening was always on the alert, waiting for such connections in the material as I was hearing it. As usual, my patients were my teachers. One taught me about the psychical significance of pronouns and I wrote "First Person Personal Pronouns and Their Psychic Referents" (Rizzuto 1993b). Other patients educated me about their surprising metaphors and I shared what I had learned in "Metaphors of a Bodily Mind" (Rizzuto 2001). Then I felt the need to integrate the developmental point of view and affect with my knowledge about words and representations and the analytic process. I wrote two papers on the subject: "Speech Events, Language Development and the Clinical Situation" (Rizzuto 2002), and "Psychoanalysis: The Transformation of the Subject by the Spoken Word" (Rizzuto 2003).

When I presented my ideas about the *spoken word* the discussants talked about *linguistics* and the contribution it makes to psychoanalysis. I was aware that the psychoanalytic literature up to that time contained few articles dealing with the function of words, although some had appeared in the mid-1990s that focused on this topic. It became clear to me that Jacques Lacan had preempted the field, dividing those working in it into his eager followers and his determined opponents. Lacan had presented his landmark paper "The Function and Field of Speech and Language and Psychoanalysis" to the Congress held at the Rome Institute of Psychology in September 26–27, 1953. It was published in *La Psychanalyse* (Lacan 1956). Lacan had been influenced by Roman Jakobson, a structural linguist, and by Ferdinand de Saussure.

It was Lacan's original intention to return to Freud's work, revive the best of his theorizing, and go on from there to offer a new understanding of the function of language in psychoanalysis. Soon, however, the evolution of his own ideas led him to frame a conception of the unconscious that differed from Freud's foundational concept. Lacan "asserts the supremacy of the signifier, and argues that the signified is a mere effect of the play of signifiers," thus suggesting that the unconscious is primarily linguistic as reflected in his famous dictum that "'the unconscious is structured like a language'" (Evans 1996). By contrast, Freud's discoveries had led him to see the unconscious as the realm of representations.

Lacan lectured at the École Pratique des Hautes Études and became involved with many prominent intellectuals, academics, and students. These scholars took to Lacan's ideas and read Freud to reinterpret his work in the light of Lacanian concepts. Lacan and his followers were among the few focusing on the role language plays in psychoanalysis. He offers elaborate, abstract and, at times, algebraic formulas and theoretical constructs to elaborate on the role of language in psychoanalysis. He published only one clinical case of a paranoid woman he called "Aimée" (Lacan 1975); this was in the dissertation he submitted to obtain his doctoral degree in 1932. In his clinical lectures he discussed cases and offered clinical commentaries, while his seminars contain clinical vignettes to help the attendees grasp his concepts. (These were later published.) Lacan's contributions on the function of language in psychic life and his own conception of the unconscious as a language are rich, exceedingly complex, and presented in elliptical sentences that are difficult to grasp. It is not my aim here to evaluate Lacan and his followers' work because I wish instead to make explicit what Freud said about words. I must assert, however, that Lacan's *linguistic* approach to clinical discourse *differs* from Freud's interest in *spoken words*. Twenty years after Freud's *On Aphasia* appeared, Ferdinand de Saussure introduced the innovations about language that Lacan adopted and later modified in his own theorizing. His *Course in General Linguistics* published by his students in 1916 became the starting point of formal linguistic studies. One of the key concepts de Saussure introduces is the distinction between *la langue* – language as a formal *system* – and *parole* – that is, actual speech. Another of de Saussure's core conceptions is the linguistic unit, the sign, which is composed of two associated and mutually dependent elements. The linguistic sign links a *concept in the mind* (not a thing in reality – as other linguists had proposed), with an acoustic image. De Saussure understands the *sound-image* not only as a physical sound but as the *psychical registration* of that particular sound.

The essence of de Saussure's theory is already present in Freud in *On Aphasia* in the form of object-representation and word-representation in the mind which are linked to each other by their visual and sound images, respectively, to form the *psychically meaningful word*. It is almost certain that de Saussure knew nothing about Freud's early neurological monograph. Yet the similarity between the ideas is striking. I even wonder if Lacan knew about its existence when he began developing his theories. There were very few copies in German, the English translation appeared in 1953, and Strachey's own translation of a portion of it appeared in the *Standard Edition* as "Appendix C" to Freud's *The Unconscious* in 1957, four years after Lacan's lecture in Rome. Be that as it may, the fact is that Lacan worked with *linguistic* concepts and the many *structural* components of language to offer his own highly modified version of psychoanalysis.

Just as I started my book about God as a psychical representation by declaring that "this is not a book about religion," so now I wish to make it clear that *this book is not about language*. It is about the *words* involved in carrying out an analysis between two people, words as Freud conceived of them in his writings. He had clearly said about the analyst and analysand: "Nothing takes place between them except that they talk to each other." This point requires making a clear distinction between language and the speech that occurs between people.

Edward Sapir compared the process of a child learning to walk with its learning to talk. He concluded that walking is a biological function: a child will learn to walk in practically an identical manner in any community. Not so with language. Without a society that helps the child acquire the linguistic heritage of the group, its language, and the continuous social usage of this language, the child could not achieve the capacity to speak on its own. Speech is an acquired cultural function offered by a community to its children as its way to introduce the young person to the culture. Thus, language is the foundational component of human culture while speech is an event between people (Sapir 1921).

Language is a cultural product with a staggering structural complexity that involves the minds of all those who speak it and all the societal structures dependent on it. Language belongs to the community of speakers and the persistence of a spoken language depends on the survival of the people who speak it. When the community disappears the language becomes extinct; it has become a dead language. Even if a language is preserved in writing, we cannot know how it was pronounced, nor can we retrieve the affective components present in the spoken exchanges among the members of the extinct community. The bodily components of the pronunciation of words and the speaker's stance are critical for understanding the meanings exchanged between individuals even when they share a communal language and the culture in which they use it. Equally important is the individual's selection from equivalent terms to convey his private ideas and feelings. The conclusion seems obvious: a language is a socially integrated system regulated by complex structural and generative rules; it becomes alive and psychically meaningful only through the exchange of words among the people who live their personal and psychical lives immersed in a community and its linguistic atmosphere. In brief, the essence of language is that there are people who speak to each other.

Contemporary linguists have presented and continue to present to the scientific community an ever more refined understanding of the complexity present in human language including organizational, structural, phonetic, and pragmatic features among others. It is a magnificent contribution and must be welcomed by those who think that psychoanalysis may benefit from it. Analysts may learn much about the extraordinary richness of the simplest words; that is the kind of gain we obtain from interdisciplinary discourse. There is, however, a caveat. In order to study the structure of language it is necessary to select a particular set of words from a spoken or written context and examine them from a particular point of view. The selection process can become an object of study itself.

Speech, by contrast, *is a living process* that requires the engagement of two people carrying out the alternative and complementary functions of talking and listening. Both participants must collaborate for their speech to acquire meaning. We could freeze a moment of speech and study it from a linguistic or other point of view, but then we have objectified it and it is no longer the living exchange between persons as meaning-making people. There is value in such study but it cannot concern itself with the *existential psychological moment* occurring between individuals.

In everyday life we are all expected to be *linguistically competent*, that is, to have internalized the rules of our society's language and to use them in our speech with others. Linguistic competence can also be described as the non-conscious knowledge of a language that allows speakers to use it efficiently. Linguistic competence is a *theoretical concept* to help understand how people manage to speak well without being fully aware of it. In contrast *linguistic performance* refers to a person's actual use of language in real-life situations, including the words he says, the grammatical errors and other features that color the utterances addressed to another person.

For the establishment of an analytic process both patient and analyst must be linguistically competent. The patient's speech *performance* and his way of using the words of a shared language to participate in the analysis constitute the core elements of their work together, which is to unveil the pathogenic unconscious processes and convictions that ail him. The analyst's own speech performance *qua analyst* shapes her participation in the process.

Once I had become fully aware that psychoanalysis involves nothing but words spoken between an analyst and a patient, I was prompted to ask what Freud – the principal originator of the process – had said about words. This book is a response to that question. It is my own modest return to Freud, to his detailed examination of words, their psychic organization and use by both patient and analyst in a clinical context. Freud did not theorize much about language, although he was well informed about the language research of his day and referred to it occasionally to prove some of his *analytic* points, as when he used Karl Abel's philological paper about the antithetical meaning of primal words (Freud 1910). Instead, Freud discussed the significance of words in psychoanalysis and life frequently and from many different points of view. This fact contrasts with the absence in his writings of a systematic study of the function of words in the organization of psychic life or in the accomplishments of analytic work.

I have approached Freud's writings like a dedicated bookworm who reads attentively anything he said about words in the context of his intentions at the time he wrote each work. Here I will document what he says, examine it to the best of my ability, and take the liberty of asking him questions. I dare to extrapolate new implications from his ideas and challenge some of his conceptions while remaining within the overall context of his thinking. My intention is to engage in dialogue with Freud and Freud only, the writer, the theoretician, and the clinician whose ingenuity, imagination, and creativity led him to use spoken words with his patients to unveil *for the first time in history* the deeply hidden convolutions of their unconscious psychic lives. To all my colleagues – be they classical in their approach, Lacanian, or otherwise affiliated – and even to many linguists who have written meaningfully and significantly about language and words in psychoanalysis, I offer an apology for not dealing with their valid contributions. I do not want to be distracted from documenting Freud's texts and reflecting about them.

My central thesis is that Freud's great innovation consists in attending to the *intrapsychic function* of words and the method he established to investigate it. Freud is not referring to signifiers or signifieds but to the extremely complex interconnections between the words heard or pronounced and the sensory-based internal representations of both originating in the patient's external *and* internal experiences in real or mental life.

My first task is to address a historical question: how did psychoanalysis come into being as a method based only on spoken exchanges between patient and analyst to treat mental pathology and its psychical and physical manifestations? And a no lesser question: how did psychoanalysis come to fulfill Freud's adolescent dream of being a great man and an adventurous explorer of ignored territories? I leave the first question open at this point to attend briefly to the second. On May 1, 1873, the seventeen-year-old Freud wrote to his friend Emil Fluss: "I have decided to be a Natural Scientist. . . . I shall gain insight into the age-old dossiers of Nature, perhaps even eavesdrop on her eternal processes, and share my findings with anyone who wants to learn" (Freud 1969). "Eavesdrop" means to listen secretly to what is said in private. It is a perfect definition of what an analyst does when listening *in* the patient's words for thoughts and experiences that the patient attempts to keep secret even from himself. I claim that the progressive discoveries of psychoanalysis and their theoretical elaborations represent the fulfillment of the adolescent Freud's desire to penetrate the secrets of nature. In fact, he wrote to his friend and colleague Wilhelm Fliess on May 21, 1894, that in his monograph *On Aphasia* he had "touched upon one of the great secrets of nature" (Freud 1985, 74). There is no question that he entered by means of *eavesdropping* in a mysterious territory no one had even thought about before him: the hidden unconscious processes ever-present in psychic life (Barron et al. 1991).

My book is a response to the first question: how psychoanalysis progressively came into existence. I believe that two processes are coterminous: first, the development of psychoanalysis as a technique and a theory and second, Freud's continuous re-elaboration of the phenomena conveyed by the words he heard from his patients. I will trace chronologically and thematically Freud's persistent efforts to articulate the manner in which words lead to the revealing of a patient's internal experience, his hidden psychic life. It bears repeating that Freud never assembled all his elaborate observations and complex conclusions about the psychic services offered by words in a single unified theory. My own scrutiny of Freud's writings indicates that he dealt with new phenomena by focusing on one aspect at a time. He first observed the facts and tried to clarify and define what he had found; following this initial step he attempted to formulate theoretical and clinical explanations for the words he had heard from his patients. I am convinced that he was attending to their words and that language was present in his thinking only in the background. This assertion demands some clarification.

Freud took for granted his patients' linguistic competence, their ordinary capacity to speak about themselves and other realities. When patients consulted Freud as a physician he invited them to talk to him using everyday language and spoke to them in a similar manner. Both participants accepted that they could communicate with each other during the treatment without having to do *anything* other than *to talk*. Today it seems very obvious that such is the case. Yet this simple and quotidian approach introduced a momentous change: the spoken word became a *therapeutic tool* to heal the mind's disturbances and their psychical and somatic manifestations. It seemed like magic, Freud commented, but it was no more, and no less, than the magical powers present in the most ordinary of words. Admittedly people had attempted to cure diseases by using words in other times and circumstances. Pedro Lain Entralgo wrote a well-researched book about the use of words for healing in classical antiquity (Lain Entralgo 1970). The difference between such a use of words and Freud's lies in the cultic context of the first kind of cure. The devotees of a particular deity attended ritual ceremonies in which words mediated the healing but, in the end, it was the benevolent divinity who accomplished the cure. Something similar happens with invocations and incantations offered by shamans today. Freud, in an astonishing shift, intended his procedure to be part of modern medicine as *a scientific method that used speech to undo the pathogenic effects of psychical trauma and conflict.* The sheer power of verbal exchanges between analyst and patient brought about the desired therapeutic change.

The daring novelty of such a scientific approach can be better understood in the context of the times. In the second half of the nineteenth century extraordinary advances occurred in chemistry, pathology, physics, microbiology, pharmacology, anatomy, and other medical disciplines, including the emergence of neuroscience. The remarkable new knowledge in all these fields of science and medicine had little impact on the treatment of mental illness and its pathology, however. Mental patients with limited means languished in well-intentioned but ineffective hospitals. Richer patients paid considerable amounts of money to be treated with baths, massages, hydrotherapy, electrotherapy, and other physical procedures, but no effective attempt was made to find the etiology of their suffering. Hypnosis had been added to the medical armamentarium in the 1880s by French physicians, but only few doctors were trained to use it. Heredity, degeneracy, syphilis and other sexually transmitted infections, and fatigue were frequent explanations for psychopathology. Energized by the exponential growth of the medical disciplines, the medical profession was committed to uncovering *physical* determinants as the cause of all illnesses, including mental illness.

This was the context in which Josef Breuer and Sigmund Freud had the remarkable courage to suggest a *psychical* treatment for hysterics and other neurotics, a procedure whose only tool was the spoken word. It must be said at once that both physicians were not only deeply committed to the scientific approach of their medical community, but also well-trained scientific researchers themselves. Before writing *On Aphasia* in 1891, Freud had published more than a dozen research papers on the nervous system in recognized journals, including the prestigious British journal *Brain*. He also published clinical papers about neural conditions.

Freud's training as a scientist was impeccable. After attending Ernst Wilhelm von Brücke's lectures on "The Physiology of Voice and Speech" as a first-year medical student in 1873/1874 (Jones 1953, 36), Freud worked at the professor's prestigious physiology laboratory. The members of the laboratory followed the principles of the Helmholtz school to whose philosophy Ernst Brücke and Professor Emil Du Bois-Reymond had committed their scientific life. Du Bois wrote: "Brücke and I pledged a solemn oath. . . . : 'No other forces than the common physical-chemical ones are active within the organism. In those cases which cannot at the time be explained by these forces one has . . . to assume new forces equal in dignity to the chemical-physical forces inherent in matter, reducible to the force of attraction and repulsion'" (Jones 1953, 40–41). Freud adhered to such a creed and when confronted with his own astonishing discoveries – the eerie therapeutic power of words – he resorted to the creation of a theory based on *psychical* forces he considered "equal in dignity." In his *An Autobiographical Study* he writes about pathogenic mental processes: "I . . . was inclined to suspect the existence of an interplay of forces and the operation of intentions and purposes such as are to be observed in normal life" (Freud 1925, 23).

Freud applied his disciplined training as a scientist to make sense of his clinical discoveries in working with hysterical patients. One of the dominant interests of the time was the understanding of aphasia as a neural disorder of speech and many of the great neurologists of Europe were writing their own essays and devising diagrams to explain its pathology. Freud joined them with his monograph *On Aphasia: A Critical Study* (1891), where he presented a tightly reasoned refutation of his senior colleagues' theories and replaced them with his own theory and diagrams of the speech apparatus. The author's name appeared as "Dr. Sigm. Freud, Privatdozent for Neuropathology in the University of Vienna," that is, as a neurologist. By that point in his career, however, Freud had already been exposed to radically different approaches. He had studied with Jean-Martin Charcot in 1885 in the famous Salpêtrière Hospital in Paris and witnessed his remarkable work with hysterics responding to his verbal orders. Charcot was a neurologist and professor of anatomical pathology recognized today as the founder of modern neurology. In 1889 Freud had also gone to Nancy to visit the famous hypnotist Hyppolyte Bernheim and commented: "I was a spectator of Bernheim's astonishing experiments upon his hospital patients, and I received the profoundest impression of the possibility that there could be powerful mental processes which nevertheless remained hidden from the consciousness of men" (Freud 1925, 17). Most important, before going to Paris, Freud had heard from his senior colleague Josef Breuer about the innovative treatment of a hysterical young woman, later to be called Anna O., which "had allowed him to penetrate deeply into the causation and significance of hysterical symptoms" (ibid., p. 19). Charcot, Bernheim, and Breuer had one tool in common to achieve their surprising effects: they used words, and only words, with the patient under hypnosis.

It is impossible to think that Freud – great synthesizer that he was – did not have in mind what he had witnessed and heard when he wrote his monograph *On Aphasia*. The book follows rigorous neurological reasoning to challenge his fellow neurologist's theories and to offer his own conception of how the mind organizes words to carry out the *function of speech*. Freud concluded the monograph by rejecting the "factor of localization for aphasia" and suggesting "we should be well advised once again to concern ourselves with the *functional* states of the apparatus of speech" (p. 105, my italics). I hope that by studying what he said about words, in particular spoken words, I am following his recommendation.

The monograph presents Freud's only systematic reflections on the process of forming and organizing words in the mind and of the corporeal sensory processes that make this possible. It also offers Freud's understanding of the source of spontaneous speech. Its connection with nascent psychoanalysis becomes obvious when one discovers that a large number of the later foundational terms of psychoanalytic theory appear in *On Aphasia* for the first time. Studying this work in depth becomes essential for understanding psychoanalysis and the function of words in the analytic process.

In the chapters that follow I present Freud's 'conversations' with his patients and discuss the continuous process in which he learned, reflected, and theorized about them and their words. I have organized the material in both chronological and thematic order. As a result I will at times return to a case or concept I have already presented, look at it from a different angle, and add a new understanding. I ask the reader's patience and indulgence when he recognizes the reappearance of an issue in the text, while I hope that the new approach adds to what I have already discussed. Again I ask the reader's patience when in Chapter 7 on theory, the German words, particularly those related to affect, appear as a perhaps superfluous repetition. The fact that Freud does not always distinguish between feelings, emotions, and affect as theoretical concepts makes it necessary in my opinion to tolerate such annoyance.

I begin my journey by discussing "Breuer, Freud, the Talking Ladies, and the Monograph *On Aphasia*" (Chapter 2), where I describe the context in which the monograph was written as well as Freud's explicit and implicit goals in writing it. I present the structure and function of the speech apparatus and its connection to concepts that form the bedrock of Freud's entire psychoanalytic theory and method of accessing internal representations through the use of words. I document how Freud's first lady patients taught him how to attend to what they had to say. Frau Emmy von N. demanded to be listened to and in this manner, as he explicitly acknowledged to her daughter, she helped Freud create psychoanalysis.

In "Hysteria as Asymbolic Aphasia" (Chapter 3), I consider the impact of the monograph in creating a therapeutic model for the neurosis. Freud had committed his professional life to the use of words as a therapeutic tool to uncover the mental processes that made people ill. Working with neurotics led him to find one surprise after another. His patients' words disclosed unsuspected private dramas of psychical trauma, incompatible wishes, and intolerable feelings, in short, their conflicts with affects and thoughts they could not accept. These emerged during the treatment as a result of his insistence that they describe in words what they were *seeing* in their minds as accurately and completely as possible. They saw real or imaginary *scenes* of their past or present life. Freud wanted to integrate their rejected representations of them with meaningful words to undo their functional aphasias. As a result, he witnessed the affects they evoked in the patients and their intense struggle to disown their experiences. Confronted with these facts, he progressively modified his technique and theories.

In "The Function of the Spoken Word in *The Interpretation of Dreams*" (Chapter 4), I leave most of Freud's contributions unattended to focus on his conception of the function of words and representations in dream formation and interpretation. By requesting that the patient associate and give words to the elements of the dream Freud intended to gain access to the representational complexes, the dream thoughts, in order to progressively overcome the dream censorship. He was determined to undo the separation inflicted by the defenses upon the patient's wishful but conflicting dream thoughts by making them explicit in conscious awareness. This technique represented another way of undoing *a different variety of asymbolic aphasia* capable of revealing the patient's unconscious wishes. The patient's words describing the dream's scenes are the sole psychic avenue to reach his private dream experience. The polarities between the dream imagery and verbal representations that Freud delineated in *On Aphasia* return now in new forms to display the astonishing complexity they attain in dreaming life.

Chapter 5, "Pliable Words, Scenes, and the Unconscious," examines Freud's exploration of the function of words in ordinary life in his two essays *The Psychopathology of Everyday Life* (Freud 1901) and *Jokes and Their Relation to the Unconscious* (Freud 1905a). They offer a treasure trove to grasp Freud's detailed examination of the complex organization of spoken words, consciously and unconsciously, their unwelcome malfunction in everyday life, and their remarkable pliability when we want to make a joke to give pleasure to others. I have also included an example of Freud's use of imagery in listening to his patient Dora.

Chapter 6, "Freud's Technique: Translating Repressed Scenarios into Words," encompasses Freud's writings from his early paper *Psychical (or Mental) Treatment* published in 1890 (Freud 1890) and mistakenly dated by Strachey (Freud 1905b) to his last posthumous contribution *An Outline of Psycho-Analysis* (Freud 1940), forty-eight years later. Following him on this lengthy journey is rich and rewarding. It starts with his first assertion that "words are the essential tool of mental treatment" (p. 283) and ends with reflections on the limited power of words to open up unconscious processes that are in themselves unknowable. Yet without words there is no conscious awareness. We also learn about the ever-present tension in his theorizing between imagery and words.

Freud's technique created a new way of speaking and listening to speech. It was *the first time in history* that words were used to gain access to unconscious processes. His technical approach rests upon a few basic principles delineated in *On Aphasia* and *The Project* and their later elaboration to incorporate clinical discoveries. *Perception* of things and of internal experiences sustain the whole psychic organization. The resulting percepts that are foundational for psychic life remain unreachable unless they are described in words that make them consciously available. In other terms, words are the only instrument we have to articulate our inner life consciously or, to say it with Freud's words, to *translate* internal realities into conscious awareness. The translation is possible because words have the power to transform thoughts into *internal perceptions* that can be remembered. Freud's technical presentations constantly refer to *scenes* when dealing with actual experiences. Subtly, but persistently, it is as though he uses the term *scene* to replace *representation* in *On Aphasia*. Thus analysis becomes a process of translating unconscious scenarios into words.

In "Freud's Theories: Repression as Gaps in Consciousness and the Words to Fill Them" (Chapter 7), I start with his dogmatic assertion that the "theory of repression is the cornerstone on which the whole structure of psycho-analysis rests." Repression creates a *gap* in conscious awareness that leads to pathological manifestations. Freud's entire theoretical enterprise encompasses his efforts to create a scientific understanding of repressed phenomena and to find the structures that support them as well as the means of *translating* into conscious awareness the repressed material to undo their pathological consequences.

Freud's theories are exceedingly complex. He repeatedly subjected them to periodic revisions to integrate new discoveries, including the structural theory in *The Ego and the Id* (Freud 1923), which deserves particular attention because it integrates the spoken word into the core *structures* of the mind. Freud had noted early in his career that his case histories read like a novel. His theorizing about the ego also reads like a complex theatrical plot about seeking love. The description shows that *technical terms are insufficient to understand the need for love*, even intrapsychic love. Freud had to resort to *scenes* of human interactions to describe the exchanges among the agencies of the mind. In intrapsychic life the ego 'talks' to the id, trying to 'seduce' it by saying: "Look, you can love me too – I am so like the object" (p. 30).

In reviewing Freud's entire theoretical edifice I found that the original elements from *On Aphasia* – perception, representation, and the spoken word – offer the foundation to understand psychopathology as a repressive process that removes experiences from conscious awareness to avoid painful affects and thus creates a gap in it. Only words that describe the repressed experienced scenes and the feelings they awaken can restore the integrity of the mind.

In "How Did Freud Talk with His Patients?" (Chapter 8), I examine his three case reports to explore this topic. I attend to Freud's use of words and the context he created to entice the analysands to open their private reality to his investigation. Many valuable papers have been written about such cases to understand dynamic processes, Freud's technique, and other issues. I ask my readers' forgiveness for not discussing these contributions because I want to focus exclusively on Freud's manner of talking with his analysands. The task is difficult because all we have are Freud's *written* reports, the transcription in writing of his spoken words, and some memoirs of Freud's patients about their analysis with him. These include accounts by the analyst Abram Kardiner (Kardiner 1977) and the poet Hilda Doolittle (Doolittle 1974) who wrote about their experience of talking with Freud during the treatment.

Freud published the cases of the patients who became known as Dora, the Rat Man, and the Wolf Man. Once more, his presentations are rich in detail and reveal the extraordinary complexity of any analytic process. I have selected for our attention the type of exchanges between them, their manner of relating, their vocabulary and styles in order to attend to how Freud and each of his patients created a particular spoken atmosphere to carry out the analysis. In reading the cases we cannot fail to notice that Freud as an analyst behaved quite differently with each of them while remaining within the pre-established analytic setting.

In "Conclusions" (Chapter 9), I gather the partial findings of each chapter together in an overview and offer a summary of what we have learned in exploring Freud's theoretical, technical, and conversational understanding and use of the spoken word in creating and practicing psychoanalysis. I hope that the reader who follows me on this journey will find it helpful that I have collected so many widely dispersed Freudian texts into organized units and themes. I also hope that it may enhance my colleagues' understanding of the many functions of words during clinical work.

A central thesis emerges from this grand tour: the ever-present if tacit influence of the model of the word in *On Aphasia* as listed in the chapters: the conception of hysteria as *asymbolic aphasia*; of *defense* as the repression of painful representations by depriving them of words; of treatment as the *therapeutic joining* in conscious awareness of the rejected scene/representation with words that undo the patho-logical *gaps; of the constant dynamic tension between imagery and word*s; of the implicit but persistent substitution of the concept of representation in clinical work by that of *mental scenes*; of the indispensable concept of *translation* from one modality of registration and expression to another; of the all-encompassing role of external and internal *perception* in the organization of the mind, and other minor themes.

I hope further that my efforts to learn, to question, and to challenge some of Freud's ideas will open a fertile dialogue among colleagues in relation to the spo-ken word, our use of it with our patients, and in the elaboration of our converging and diverging theories. I would find myself greatly rewarded if I, following Freud, have argued convincingly that the spoken word is not only our tool *par excellence* but in fact the only means we have for gaining access to the hidden recesses of the unconscious mind.

Note

1 The original German says "they talk *with* each other" ("Sie *mit* einander reden," *Gesam-melte Werke*, 14, p. 213).

References

Barron, James W., R. Beaumont, G. Goldsmith, M. Good, Robert L. Pyles, Ana-María Rizzuto, and Henry F. Smith. Sigmund Freud: The Secrets of Nature and the Nature of Secrets. *International Review of Psychoanalysis* 18 (1991): 143–63.

Doolittle, Hilda. *Tribute to Freud*. 1956. Boston: David R. Godine, 1974.

Evans, Dylan. *An Introductory Dictionary of Lacanian Psychoanalysis*. London: Routledge, 1996.

Forrester, John. *Language and the Origins of Psychoanalysis*. New York: Columbia University Press, 1980.

Freud, Sigmund. The Antithetical Meaning of Primal Words. Vol. 11 of *Standard Edition*, 153–61. London: Hogarth Press, 1910.

———. An Autobiographical Study. Vol. 20 of *Standard Edition*, 1–74. London: Hogarth Press, 1925.

———. *The Complete Letters of Sigmund Freud to Wilhelm Fliess 1887–1904*. Trans. and ed. Jeffrey Moussaieff Masson. Cambridge, MA: Belknap Press of Harvard University Press, 1985.

———. The Ego and the Id. Vol. 19 of *Standard Edition*, 1–66. London: Hogarth Press, 1923.

———. *Jokes and Their Relation to the Unconscious*. Vol. 8 of *Standard Edition*. London: Hogarth Press, 1905a.

———. *On Aphasia: A Critical Study*. Trans. Erwin Stengel. 1953. New York: International Universities Press, 1891.

———. An Outline of Psycho-Analysis. Vol. 23 of *Standard Edition*. 1938, 139–207. Lon-don: Hogarth Press, 1940.

————. Psychical (or Mental) Treatment. In *Die Gesundheit*, edited by R. Kossmann and J. Weiss, 368–84. Stuttgart: Union Deutsche Verlagsgesellschaft, 1890.

————. Psychical (or Mental) Treatment. Vol. 7 of *Standard Edition*, 281–302. London: Hogarth Press, 1905b.

————. *The Psychopathology of Everyday Life. Standard Edition*. London: Hogarth Press, 1901.

————. The Question of Lay Analysis. Vol. 20 of *Standard Edition*, 177–258. London: Hogarth Press, 1926.

————. Some Early Unpublished Letters of Freud. *International Journal of Psycho-Analysis* 50 (1969): 419–27.

————. *Zur Auffassung der Aphasien. Eine Kritische Studie*. Leipzig: Franz Deuticke, 1891.

Jones, Ernest. *The Life and Work of Sigmund Freud*. New York: Basic Books, 1953.

Kardiner, Abram. *My Analysis with Freud: Reminiscences*. New York: W. W. Norton, 1977.

Lacan, Jacques. *De la psychose paranoïaque dans ses rapports avec la personalité suivi de Premiers écrits sur la paranoïa*. Paris: Editions du Seuil, 1975.

————. Fonction et champ de la parole et du langage en psychanalyse. *La Psychanalyse* 1 (1956): 81–166.

Lain Entralgo, Pedro. *La curación por la palabra en la antigüedad clásica*. 1958. Madrid: Revista de Occidente, 1970.

Litowitz, Bonnie E. From Dyad to Dialogue: Language and the Early Relationship in American Psychoanalytic Theory. *Journal of the American Psychoanalytic Association* 59 (2011): 483–507.

Rizzuto, Ana-María. *The Birth of the Living God: A Psychoanalytic Study*. Chicago: University of Chicago Press, 1979.

————. First Person Personal Pronouns and Their Psychic Referents. *International Journal of Psycho-Analysis* 74 (1993b): 535–46.

————. Freud, God, the Devil, and the Theory of Object Representation. *International Review of Psychoanalysis* 3 (1976): 165–80.

————. Freud's Speech Apparatus and Spontaneous Speech. *International Journal of Psycho-Analysis* 74 (1993a): 113–27.

————. Freud's Theoretical and Technical Models in *Studies on Hysteria*. *International Review of Psycho-Analysis* 19 (1992): 169–78.

————. A Hypothesis about Freud's Motive for Writing the Monograph *On Aphasia*. *International Review of Psychoanalysis* 16 (1989): 111–17.

————. Metaphors of a Bodily Mind. *Journal of the American Psychoanalytic Association* 49 (2001): 535–68.

————. The Origins of Freud's Concept of Object Representation ('*Objektvorstellung*') in His Monograph *On Aphasia*: Its Theoretical and Technical Importance. *International Journal of Psycho-Analysis* 71 (1990b): 241–48.

————. A Proto-Dictionary of Psychoanalysis. *International Journal of Psycho-Analysis* 71 (1990a): 261–70.

————. Psychoanalysis: The Transformation of the Subject by the Spoken Word. *Psychoanalytic Quarterly* 72 (2003): 287–323.

————. Speech Events, Language Development, and the Clinical Situation. *International Journal of Psycho-Analysis* 83 (2002): 1325–43.

————. Transference, Language, and Affect in the Treatment of Bulimarexia. *International Journal of Psychoanalysis* 69 (1988): 369–87.

Sapir, Edward. *Language: An Introduction to the Study of Speech*. New York: Harcourt, Brace, 1921.

2

BREUER, FREUD, THE TALKING LADIES, AND THE MONOGRAPH ON APHASIA

The patient's need to talk and the writing of *On Aphasia*

The year was 1883. Freud describes in *An Autobiographical Study* how his colleague Dr. Josef Breuer told him about a case he had treated between 1880 and 1882 "in a peculiar manner" that "had allowed him to penetrate deeply into the causation and significance of hysterical symptoms" (Freud 1925a, 19). Breuer mentioned that the patient, Fräulein Anna O., could be relieved of many symptoms ". . . if she was induced to express in words the *affective fantasy* by which she was at the moment dominated. Through this discovery, Breuer arrived at a new method of treatment" (p. 20, my italics). Freud asked himself whether such procedure could be generalized: "The state of things which he had discovered seemed to me to be of so *fundamental* a nature that I could not believe it could fail to be present in any case of hysteria if it had been proved to occur in a single one." So deep was Freud's conviction that he "worked at nothing else" (p. 21, my italics). *The power of the spoken word had taken over Freud's professional career.* As late as 1924 Freud insisted: "The cathartic method was the immediate precursor of psychoanalysis; and, in spite of every extension of experience and of every modification of theory, is still contained within it as its nucleus" (Freud 1924, 194). Freud commented in Breuer's obituary that the analysts already in practice at the time could "form no conception of how novel such a procedure must have seemed forty-five years ago. It must have called for . . . a considerable degree of freedom of thought and certainty of judgement" (Freud 1925b, 279). Freud added: "It seems that Breuer's researches were wholly original" (p. 280).

Freud established to his satisfaction that Breuer's "findings were invariably confirmed in every case of hysteria that was accessible to such treatment" (Freud 1925a, 21). What was so original in his approach? Previously, hysterics had been treated with physical procedures, rest cures, medications, massages – and, following Charcot, Bernheim, Pierre Janet, and others – hypnosis in order to remove their symptoms under a physician's guidance. Breuer introduced three innovations: he *listened* to Fräulein Anna O.'s communications, insisting that she tell him everything. He was *truly interested* in her private world and created, not without her insistence, *a continuous treatment* to allow her to develop her convoluted stories. No one up to that moment had listened to a patient with such "immense care and patience" (Freud 1925b, 279). It was the beginning of *a totally new mode of listening to spoken words* and to the *person* who spoke them.

Breuer described the treatment of Anna O. with Freud in the joint publication *Studies on Hysteria* (Breuer and Freud 1893–1895). He presented his twenty-one-year-old patient as "markedly intelligent, with an astonishingly quick grasp of things and penetrating intuition" (p. 21). "This girl . . . led an extremely monotonous existence in her puritanically-minded family. She embellished her life . . . by indulging in systematic day-dreaming, which she described as her 'private theater'" (p. 22). The illness began in July 1880 when her father "of whom she was passionately fond, fell ill of a peripleuritic abscess which failed to clear up and to which he succumbed in April, 1881. During the first month of the illness Anna O. devoted her whole energy to nursing her father" (pp. 22–23). Anna O's treatment "came to its final close in June, 1882" (p. 33). From July 1880 to June 1882, Fräulein Anna O. developed an impressive array of successive and concomitant symptoms, including disturbances of vision, paralyses of different limbs, somnambulism, insomnia, a nervous cough, headaches, hallucinations, inability to speak as well as marked disturbances in speech patterns, even mutism, inability to recognize people, and difficulties in eating and drinking.

Breuer did not fail to notice Anna O.'s great psychological asset: ". . . even when she was in a very bad condition – a clear-sighted and calm observer sat, as she put it, in a corner of her brain and looked on at all the mad business" (p. 46). (This is the first hint of Freud's later concept of an observing ego.) The patient complained "of having two selves, a real one and an evil one which forced her to behave badly" (p. 24). Once when she became mute Breuer made a discovery:

> Now for the first time the psychical mechanism of the disorder became clear. As I knew, she had felt very much offended over something and had determined not to speak about it. When I guessed this and obliged her to talk about it, the inhibition, which had made any other kind of utterance impossible as well, disappeared.
>
> *(p. 25)*

After the death of her father Anna O. developed terrifying hallucinations. Breuer discovered that if he placed her in a deep hypnosis and then "she was able to narrate the hallucinations she had in the course of the day, she would wake up clear in mind, calm and cheerful" (p. 27). Another interesting phenomenon followed:

> If for any reason she was unable to tell me the story during her evening hypnosis she failed to calm down afterwards, and on the following day she had

to tell me the *two* stories in order for this to happen. . . . The effect of the products of her imagination as <u>psychical stimuli</u> and the easing and removal of her state of stimulation when she gave utterance to them in her hypnosis – remained constant throughout the whole eighteen months during which she was under observation.

(p. 29, my underlining)

Breuer had discovered the *power of psychical stimulation* present in the stories while she called her treatment a 'talking cure' because "she knew that after she had given utterance to her hallucinations she would lose all her obstinacy . . ." (p. 30). Another discovery followed: Anna O. freed herself of her inability to drink "as a result of an accidental and *spontaneous* utterance," (p. 34, my italics) describing with disgust how she had seen the little dog of her English lady-companion drinking out of a glass. She expressed her intense anger and then "asked for something to drink . . . the disturbance vanished, never to return" (pp. 34–35). "Spontaneous speech" had entered the psychoanalytic vocabulary.

Breuer theorized that Anna O. had split her personality into a normal part and an insane part, which he called a "secondary state"; the products of the latter acted as "a stimulus 'in the unconscious'" (p. 45).[1] He concluded:

> I have already described the astonishing fact that from beginning to end of the illness all the *stimuli arising from the secondary state,* together with their consequences, were permanently removed by being given *verbal utterance* in hypnosis . . . this was not an invention of mine. . . . It took me completely by surprise, and not until the symptoms had been got rid of in this way in a whole series of instances did I develop a therapeutic technique out of it.
>
> *(p. 46, my italics)*

What have we learned from Breuer's presentation? First, that the pathogenic stimuli for the symptoms were painful and traumatic memories, fantasies, hallucinations that were 'unconscious' to Anna O. in her normal state. Second, that when she verbalized and consciously described those pathogenic stimuli, her private experiences, to Breuer her symptoms disappeared. Third, that she talked about these matters only with Breuer, her dedicated doctor.

Freud presented Breuer's case in 1909 as part of the *Five Lectures on Psycho-Analysis* at Clark University in Massachusetts. He said emphatically about Breuer: "Never before had anyone removed a hysterical symptom by such a method or had thus gained so deep an insight into its causation" (Freud 1910, 13). Freud described how the symptoms originated in emotional experiences, 'psychical traumas' and that they were ". . . 'determined' by the *scenes* of whose recollection they represented residues" . . . and not "capricious or enigmatic products of the neurosis" (p. 14, my italics). He went on to explain that when "subsequently she reproduced these scenes in her doctor's presence the affect which had been inhibited at the time emerged with peculiar violence, as though it had been saved for a long time"

(p. 18). Freud noted that the *scenes* had remained unconscious up to that moment but that their retrieval exemplified the power of unconscious states over conscious ones (p. 19). What Breuer had presented as Anna O.'s traumatic memories, fantasies, and hallucinations Freud described as *scenes*.

The word *scene* has not been attended to in the psychoanalytic literature although Freud uses it frequently in his work: it is not listed in the General Subject Index of the *Standard Edition*, except as part of the later concept of primal scene. The word will acquire further meaning in later chapters of this book.

Freud learns to talk to Frau Emmy von N.

Freud became fascinated by what he was learning from Frau Emmy, a woman in her forties he said he saw for the first time on May 1, 1889. He noted that her "symptoms and personality interested me so greatly that I devoted a large part of my time to her . . . She was a hysteric. . . . This was my first attempt at handling that [Breuer's] therapeutic method" (Breuer and Freud 1893–1895, 48).

Freud published the case following his daily notes and comments. Frau Emmy von N. also had a multitude of symptoms, including disturbances in her speech and numerous memories of frightening childhood events. Freud would hypnotize her and ask her to talk. He was also using customary medical techniques such as bath and massages, as he says at the start of the treatment on May 2: "I shall massage her whole body twice a day." In the morning of that day she told some "gruesome stories about animals" (p. 51) and a dreadful story about a boy in the newspapers. She was very frightened. Freud "dispersed these animal hallucinations" (ibid.) using hypnosis, that is, he ordered her not to think about them. That evening Freud applied Breuer's technique for the first time. "I requested her, under hypnosis, to talk . . . She spoke softly . . . Her expression altered according to the subject of her remarks, and grew calm as soon as *my suggestion* had put an end to the impression made upon her by what she was saying" (p. 52, my italics). It is interesting to note that Freud's intervention was intended to remove *the affect* evoked in the patient by her own words.

A *conviction* emerged in Freud that during hypnosis the patient knew about the events of the previous hypnosis while being ignorant of them in her waking life, a first hint of unconscious processes. He also noticed that his influence was affecting her: during the massage she was able *to talk on her own*, remember some events, and "unburden herself without being asked to" (p. 56). Freud rejoiced at the progress: "It is as though she had adopted my procedure and was making use of our *conversation*, apparently unconstrained and guided by chance, as a supplement to her hypnosis" (ibid., my italics). Strachey comments in a footnote that this is the earliest appearance of *free association*. I suggest that it is also the first hint of transferential phenomena: Frau Emmy was giving Freud what he wanted.

When he asked her *why* she was so frightened and *when* she had been frightened she immediately gave him a long account of four events that appear to Freud as revealing an already existing list in her mind. He commented: "Though these four instances were so widely separated in time, she told me them in a single sentence and in such rapid succession that they might have been *a single episode in four acts*" (p. 57, my italics). Frau Emmy had offered Freud a significant lesson: her mind spontaneously classified together similar experiences that had occurred at different times. It was an early hint about the workings of the unconscious. When he asked *how* she *saw* them she replied that "she saw these *scenes* with all the vividness of reality" (p. 53, my italics) and in colors. Once more, Freud acted as the physician in command: "My therapy consisted in wiping away [*wegzuwischen*] these pictures, so that she is no longer able to see them before her" (ibid.). Obviously, the technique aimed at removing the scenes from her *conscious* awareness. This situation repeated itself many times: Frau Emmy told a story, was very frightened, and Freud used hypnotic commands to *correct* her ideas, to help her repress them, or to diminish the *affective* strength of the memories.

Frau Emmy was very involved in the stories she was telling to Freud. He frequently interrupted her to make some points and observations. Finally, he came up with a realization about the effect of his questioning: "I now saw that I had gained nothing by this interruption and that *I cannot evade listening to her stories* in every detail to the very end" (p. 61, my italics). In spite of this realization, Freud could not stop himself from asking her questions and giving her commands. One day he asked her where her stammer came from and she responded with "violent and angry words." He stopped the hypnosis for that day when he realized that he too was under surveillance: "She kept a critical eye upon my work in her hypnotic consciousness" (p. 62). That night she slept badly, and when Freud asked the next day about her gastric pains, Frau Emmy gave him another critical lesson, saying "in a definitely grumbling tone that I was not to keep on asking her where this and that came from, but to let her tell me *what she had to say*" (p. 63, my italics). Shortly afterward she "began of her own accord to talk about the things that had most affected her" (p. 64) and Freud observed: "What she tells me before the hypnosis becomes more and more significant" (ibid.). Freud's comments about being hard on herself and some moral reflections met with mistrust indicating that she obeyed his commands "because you said so." At one point, he noticed that there were some "false connections" in her narrative. Another discovery followed the repetition of a story: "This taught me that an *incomplete story* [*Erzählung*] under hypnosis produces no therapeutic effect . . . and I gradually came to be able to read from patients' faces whether they might not be concealing an essential part of their confessions" (p. 79, my italics). There was, however, no means of imposing meaning: she clung to her symptoms and "would only abandon them in response to psychical analysis or personal conviction" (p. 99). Freud's "cathartic method" did not allow him to establish a truly confidential mode of conversing with Frau Emmy, however; she kept her erotic life sequestered from the authoritarian physician. When she told him that "since her husband's death, she had lived in complete mental solitude" (p. 102), she was misleading him. Ola Andersson, a Swedish analyst, who traced the historical identity of Frau Emmy found that she had been "a prominent person in the field of philanthropy and was highly respected even outside the community in which she lived" (Andersson 1979, 5), "immensely wealthy and, living in an aristocratic style" (p. 11). He discovered that her neighbors and her daughters knew that "she nearly always seems to have had lovers and erotic relationships, sometimes with doctors whom she consulted at the spas, or who lived in her house as her personal doctors" (ibid.).

After seven weeks of treatment she told Freud that "she had not felt so well since her husband's death" and he "allowed her to return to her home" (Breuer and Freud 1893–1895, 77).

What have we learned reading about doctor and patient in this case? We saw that Freud also had two sides to himself: one was the typical physician of the day who gave orders, lessons, massages, made recommendations to the staff, and used his hands to soothe the patient's physical and psychical suffering. He was capable of having an ordinary chat with Frau Emmy but, as a hypnotist, his orders were *imperious commands.* On the other side, however, there was the Breuer-like physician who wanted to understand the psychical life of his patient by asking pointed questions about *causal connections,* about why, when, how things happened in Frau Emmy's mind and the connections between present real-life events and her *past.* This other Freud examined her spoken language listening for clues that would give meaning to her words and experiences. Such a manner of listening and talking illustrates how *radically new* Freud's use of verbal exchanges with his patients was, both as a medical practice and also as a form of discourse between people: to use words to grasp *intrapsychic* meanings unknown to the patient.

Frau Emmy taught Freud that analysis was the way to go as he said to her daughter in a 1918 letter: "It was precisely in connection with this case . . . that I . . . received the incentive to create psychoanalytical therapy" (Andersson 1979, 14).

Another patient, Frau Cäcilie M., demonstrated that she could feel verbal remarks as real events, such as a 'stab in the heart' or 'a slap in the face.' She was cured of her facial neuralgia when she revived in analysis what she felt like "a bitter insult" by her husband: "She put her hand to her cheek, gave a loud cry of pain and said: 'It was like a slap in the face'" (Breuer and Freud 1893–1895, 178). Freud commented: "The hysteric is not taking liberty with words, but is simply reviving once more the *sensations* to which the verbal expression owes its justification" (p. 181, my italics). Frau Cäcilie also confirmed Freud's obligation to listen to her entire story while giving him graphic illustrations of the *somatic* sources of her words.

The three ladies had functional speech disturbances: Anna O. and Frau Emmy even became mute for a time, while Frau Cäcilie converted verbal insults into somatic symptoms. Freud was facing a great paradox: the 'talking cure' was the treatment of choice for those whose illness seemed caused by the inability to put some experiences into words, *a psychical aphasia.* How was Freud to explain not only his patients' speech pathology, but also, the ill effect of their silence and the curative power of words spoken to Breuer and to him? He had learned that hypnosis was useless. How could he conceptualize the patient's compelling need to tell and complete their stories to get well? Where did such a need come from, from what impulses or stimuli? I have suggested that one of Freud's motives to write *On Aphasia* came from his need to understand the speech phenomena he observed in Anna O., Emmy von N., and Frau Cäcilie (Rizzuto 1989).

Writing *On Aphasia*

In a footnote to the monograph Freud describes his explicit motive to write about speech centers as coming "from papers published by Exner jointly with my late friend Josef Paneth in Pflüger's Archiv" (Freud 1891, 66). He had presented some of these ideas as early as 1886. Aphasia was a critical concern for the neurologists of the time. In his autobiography, Freud declares: "An invitation which I received in the same year to contribute to an encyclopaedia of medicine led me to investigate the theory of aphasia. . . . The fruit of this enquiry was a small *critical and speculative* book, *Zur Auffassung der Aphasien*" (Freud 1925a, 18). Freud had also attended Charcot's lectures on aphasia in the autumn of 1885 in Paris and had translated them upon his return to Vienna. I believe that one must add to Freud's motives to write *On Aphasia* his wish to articulate the speech phenomena he observed in Anna O., Emmy von N., and Frau Cäcilie: their need to say what they had to say, the improvement of their symptoms after feeling once again the vivid memories hidden in their minds and communicating them in words addressed to their doctors.

Freud wrote *On Aphasia* in the spring of 1891. He announced to Fliess on May 2 of that year: "In a few weeks, I shall afford myself the pleasure of sending you a small book on aphasia *for which I myself have a great deal of warm feeling.* . . . The paper . . . is more suggestive than conclusive" (Freud 1985, 28, my italics). The tense of the verb indicates that the manuscript was already completed when Freud wrote the letter. I believe that he might have written it while he was seeing Frau Emmy on her home estate. He must have had much free time between his morning and evening sessions with her while he was trying to grasp the mental processes, the stimuli that led her to want to say what she had to say and to say it spontaneously, not as a response to his questions.

Freud said that Frau Emmy consulted him for the first time on May 1, 1889, and then he saw her a second time. Henri F. Ellenberger found unpublished documents, however, that suggest Freud visited Frau Emmy on her estate around March or April of 1891 (Ellenberger 1977). The chronology between the time of that visit and the letter to Fliess about the "small book" strongly suggests that he might have written it while he was there and had her very much in mind.

Freud dedicated the book to Josef Breuer "in friendship and respect" but his friend's response was unexpected. On July 13, 1891, Freud wrote to his sister-in-law, Minna Bernays: "Breuer's reception of it was such a strange one; he hardly thanked me for it, was very embarrassed, made only derogatory comments on it, couldn't recollect any of its good points, and in the end tried to soften the blow by saying that it was very well written" (Freud 1960, 228). The monograph fared poorly in other ways as well: 850 copies were printed, only 257 were sold, and in

1900, the remaining copies were pulped. Erwin Stengel translated it into English in 1953 and International Universities Press of New York published it. The translation, however, does not do justice to the original since the English terminology selected is imprecise in comparison to the original German.

Freud's other publications placed him among the top neurologists of the time. Nonetheless his well-earned reputation did little to gain acceptance for the monograph *On Aphasia*, and his disappointment was profound. He wrote to Wilhelm Fliess on May 21, 1894:

> I am pretty much alone here in the elucidation of the neuroses. They look upon me as pretty much of a monomaniac, while I have the distinct feeling that I have touched upon *one of the great secrets of nature*. There is something odd about the incongruity between one's own and other people's estimation of one's intellectual work. Look at this book on the diplegias, . . . It has been tremendously successful. . . . And of *the really good things*, such as the *Aphasia* . . . I can expect nothing better than a respectable failure. It confounds one and makes one somewhat bitter.
>
> *(Freud 1985, 74, my italics)*

Frau Emmy von N. had convinced Freud – as Anna O. had convinced Breuer – that she *had to talk* in her own way, *spontaneously* without Freud's interruptions because some stories in her mind called for free expression. The monograph addresses two subjects among others that were not a significant concern for the scholars of aphasia at the time, namely, the sources of the *stimulus* to speak and of *spontaneous speech*. Freud, the keen observer and neurologist, had noticed that in the process of recovery from neurologically caused motor aphasia there is a transition from repetition of words to spontaneous speech. "I dare say" – he asserts in the monograph – "that the attention of the observers has not turned to this point" (p. 32).

Neurologists in Freud's day were intent on creating models of a speech apparatus capable of explaining the pathology of aphasia caused by neurological damage. They were committed to the reflex arch model as the physiological unit for the speech function and localized its components in the anatomical regions of the brain. Detailed anatomical studies, especially postmortem evidence, permitted comparison between clinical symptoms and the locus of the lesion in the brain. Brain topography, including localization of functions, was the intellectual task for neurologists of the time. There was little or no room in those models for the *psychological* aspect of the speech function. Freud must have found this narrow conceptualization to be an obstacle to account for the many functional, not anatomical, speech disturbances presented by the ladies who insisted on speaking spontaneously, even though at times they had functional transient or persistent impediments of speech similar to those presented by neurologically impaired aphasics. Freud commented on Wernicke's understanding of the process of speech "as a cerebral reflex" (Freud 1891, 2): "If one takes into consideration the further connections of the speech centres which are indispensable for the possibility of spontaneous speech, then one must provide a more complicated depiction (*Darstellung*) of the central speech apparatus" (E. p. 5; G. p. 6, my translation).

Freud had to construct a model that would permit him to explain both anatomical and functional aphasias as well as normal speech functions. He analyzed the available data systematically to disqualify the theories of his eminent contemporaries: Wernicke, Lichtheim, Watteville, Heubner, Magnan, Hammond, Bastian, Grashey, Meynert, Gireaudau, and Charcot. He "demolished" their contributions with carefully documented neurological arguments, contending that their models were based on postmortem brain examinations and a topographic conceptualization of brain functions. Freud said instead: "It became our task to attain another way of representing (*Vorstellung*) the construction of the speech apparatus, and to indicate in what ways topical and *functional* factors become effective in its disturbances" (E. p. 102; G. p. 104, my translation, my italics). His "speech apparatus" is the first of the many theoretical constructs upon which Freud would build his progressive understanding of how the mind is structured and how it functions. It is also a direct antecedent of the "psychic apparatus." Several analysts have recognized its value: Ludwig Binswanger considered it essential for the understanding of psychoanalysis (Binswanger 1936). Bernfeld described it as the "first 'Freudian' book" (Bernfeld 1944) while Forrester concluded that "Freud's work on aphasia . . . is the *sine qua non* of the birth of psychoanalytic theory as we can now distinguish it from other contemporary theories of neurosis: a theory of the power of words in the formation of symptoms" (Forrester 1980, 14). Stengel pointed out that it was the first of Freud's "studies dealing with mental activities" (Stengel 1953, x) and that "it brought him [Freud] into direct contact with the evolutionary theories emanating from England, a decisive event in the development of psychoanalysis" (Stengel 1954, 89). Roland Kuhn asserts in the *Préface* to the first French translation of the monograph that it offers "precious instructions," not found in other of Freud's writings, to guide analysts into further understanding of his entire work (Kuhn 1983, 36). After having studied the monograph in depth, I fully agree with these authors that it presents foundational antecedents for understanding the developments of psychoanalytic theory. My paper *A Proto-Dictionary of Psychoanalysis* (Rizzuto 1990a) examines the early appearance of analytic terms: association, divided attention, cathexis, complex, connection, physiological correlate, impulse to speak, memory-image, primary, representation, self-observation, spontaneous speech, and transference. The obvious continuity of Freud's later theorizing was ignored for years because Freud himself refused in 1939 to have the monograph "included in the first volume of the complete German edition of his works on the ground that it belonged to his neurological and not his psycho-analytic works" (Kris 1954, 19).

Freud adopted Hughlings Jackson's (1880)'s idea of "functional retrogression" to explain aspects of the aphasic phenomena. Jackson connected functional levels to stages of development, which explained why what was learned last is lost first, as happens with foreign languages. The concept also facilitates the understanding of the significance of "words in use since the beginning of speech development" (Freud 1891, 87). I can see in this phrase the first allusions to the *genetic* point of view.

In his theorizing Freud used something rarely present in neurological papers: he paid attention to observations of both speech in everyday life and also of psychological speech-related events, such as self-observation and introspection about inner speech. His systematic analysis of cases and neurological reasoning led him to major conclusions:

1 The organization of the speech apparatus is based on *associations* and its functioning results from the use of such associations; its pathology stems from anatomical lesions or functional factors that interrupt the associations (Freud 1891, 89).

2 The will to speak or its volitional stimulation originates in the "object association, or more exactly from the activities of the rest of the cortex" (p. 90). This is a remarkable assertion which Freud repeats in many ways throughout the text of the monograph: every "'volitional' excitation of the speech centres . . . involves the region of the auditory representations and results in its *stimulation* by object associations" (E. p. 84; G. p. 86, my translation, my italics); "all stimuli to spontaneous speech arise from object associations" (E. p. 79). These object associations appeared as a concept connected not only to the isolated representation in the mind of an object in the world, but also to the recollections, events, scenes that spurred the lady patients to say what they had to say. By connecting the speech apparatus with "the rest of the cortex," Freud was making clear that the apparatus has no localizable anatomical centers but is instead constituted by the overall associative functions of the mind. He demonstrated that the speech apparatus is located exclusively in the cerebral cortex and that subcortical organs and functions are not involved in the speech function.

3 The associative power of the mind is absolutely ubiquitous; *to perceive is to associate*: "We cannot have a perception without immediately associating it; however sharply we may separate the two concepts, in reality they belong to one single process which, starting from one point, spreads over the whole cortex" (E. p. 57).

4 All the elements that the speech apparatus utilizes for the construction of object-representations come from *bodily sensory experiences*. Freud explicitly describes their progressive *transformations* at different gray nuclei: "We must then accept the thought that a fibre on its way to the cerebral cortex altered its functional meaning (*Bedeutung*) after each emergence from a gray substance" (E. p. 52; G. p. 54, my translation) and it does so "at the service of representing the body in a manner *suited to the function* [of language]" (E. p. 53; G. p. 55, my translation, my italics). As a consequence, the speech apparatus is indebted to all the body sensory capabilities to form the elements it needs for the construction of its representations and associations.

Freud questioned "in what manner" the body "is reproduced (*abgebildet*) in the cerebral cortex" (E. p. 50). Meynert and his followers postulated "exact representation of the body in the cerebral cortex" (E. p. 48). That meant that the whole body was "projected" on to the cortex "point by point" like visual representations onto the retina (E. p. 47). Freud's associative understanding of the formation of words and object-representations is quite different. For him "only in the spinal cord, and in analogous grey areas, do the prerequisites for a complete projection of the body periphery exist" (E. p. 50). Freud explicitly describes the fiber's progressive *transformations* of meaning at different gray nuclei. They modify the projection by adding connections coming from other regions of the body. Freud's conceptualization added to all perceptions – be they of object-representations or the components of word-representations – a *synaptic modification* at the gray nuclei and their *associative transformation* in the individual's mind. These processes convert the objects perceived and the words heard into *idiosyncratic personal objects and words* with all their particular connotations. Freud did not make this extrapolation explicitly but it is an obvious implication of his theorizing.

The structure of the apparatus

The main *function* of the speech apparatus consists in forming the *psychic* word to be used in listening and speaking. Freud created the following diagram to illustrate the components of the word.

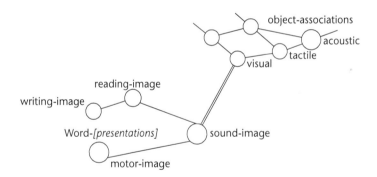

PSYCHOLOGICAL DIAGRAM OF A WORD-PRESENTATION

The word-presentation is shown as a closed complex of presentations, whereas the object-presentation is shown as an open one. The word-presentation is not linked to the object-presentation by *all* its constituent elements, but only by its sound-image. Among the object-associations, it is the visual ones which stand for the object, in the same kind of way as the sound-image stands for the word. The connections linking the sound-image of the word with object-associations other than the visual ones are not indicated.

The Unconscious, Appendix C, SE, 14, p. 214, James Strachey's translation from the German; Freud, 1891, p. 77.

Freud's model of the psychological word includes two linked components organized to serve the speech function. One presents the complex of word-representations and the other the complex of object-representations. They connect to each other – prevalently though not exclusively – by linking the *sound image* of a spoken word to the *visual component* of object-representations. Freud cited a clinical example, an aphasic woman who was able to speak only when her doctor *touched* her to check her pulse, indicating that such tactile stimulation could activate her representations and her capacity to speak (Freud 1891, 79).

The term *representation* requires clarification. Stengel's translation of *On Aphasia* used the term *concept* or *idea* for the German *Vorstellung*. When Strachey translated pages 74 to 81 of the German edition of *On Aphasia* to include them as "Appendix C" to Freud's *The Unconscious* (Freud 1915), he used 'object-presentation' and the complementary 'word-presentation.' I prefer representation as the translation of *Vorstellung*, not only because it is frequently used but because it points to the representational mind as Freud conceived of it. As I have described, Freud, following John Stuart Mill,

> make(s) a clear distinction between a 'thing' (*Ding*), a material object, existing in the real world, and its representation, the 'appearance' of an object in the mind. This *Objektvorstellung* – object representation – is constructed in the process of perceiving and belongs entirely to the *psychic* realm . . . For Kant, whose ideas Freud adopted, an *Objekt* is a human construction made out of sensations originating in an existing thing in factual reality. An *object* representation is therefore a *psychic representation* that resembles a 'thing' that is there in the world.
>
> *(Rizzuto 1990b)*

It is time to examine the structure of the word formed by the speech apparatus and I will do so using Strachey's translation. Let us start with the four components of the word-presentation: (1) the sound image; (2) the motor speech image; (3) the visual letter image, and (4) the motor writing image. Freud suggested that the complexities of speech perceptual activities add associations to all these processes. With respect to the motoric *sound emission* of a spoken word Freud listed two components: (a) "associating a [heard] 'sound-image of a word' with a 'sense of the *innervation* of a word'" (p. 210). "Innervation" appeared as a "sort of sensation connected directly with the discharge of nervous impulses from the motor areas of the brain to the muscles" (footnote to page 210); today, 122 years later, we might wonder about the role of mirror neurons in this process of 'innervation'; (b) "After we have spoken, we are also in possession of a 'motor speech-presentation' (centripetal sensations from the organs of speech); so that, in a motor respect, the 'word' is doubly determined for us" (p. 210). In learning to speak from others we try to "make the sound-image produced by ourselves as like as possible to the one which gave rise to our speech-innervation. We learn in this way to 'repeat' – to 'say after' another person" (p. 211). Comparable processes are involved in learning to spell, read, and write. Freud concluded that the spoken and written word correspond to "a complicated associative process into which the elements of visual, acoustic and kinaesthetic origin enumerated above enter together" (p. 213), thus forming a complex, as shown in the diagram.

Freud continues: "A word, however, acquires its *meaning* by being linked to an 'object-presentation', at all events if we restrict ourselves to a consideration of substantives" (p. 213). Freud considered the word as "the functional unit of speech" (1891, E. p. 73). The limitation of speech to nouns as its unit appears like a contradiction to me. Speech, in particular associative speech, cannot do without verbs and all other word classes. By limiting himself to nouns Freud disregarded Jackson's repeated assertion that the unit of speech is the preposition and that "To speak is to propositionize" (Jackson 1880, 209). A proposition needs all the parts of speech to be meaningful and intelligible. The referent of words to distinct object-presentations in *On Aphasia* points to a surprising concretization of a psychic function that Freud embedded in an interconnected system of associations. It is far removed from the convoluted *scenes* that Breuer and Freud helped the ladies to put into words. Perhaps Freud the neurologist was limiting himself to nouns as a way of explaining the varieties of disconnections between word and object-presentations in the two types of aphasia he proposed: those "verbal aphasias, in which the associations between the separate elements of word-presentation are disturbed" by an anatomical affection and "*asymbolic aphasia*, in which the association between the word-presentation and the object-presentation is disturbed" by functional factors (Strachey 1957, 214). Freud also proposed the category of "agnostic aphasia," due to widespread anatomical destruction of cortical areas where representations are registered.

Now let us turn to the other component of the word formed by the speech apparatus: "The object-presentation itself is once again a complex of associations made up of the greatest variety of visual, acoustic, tactile, kinaesthetic and other presentations" (Strachey, p. 213). This description, as I read it, points to *multisensory scenic perceptions* of objects and their surroundings rather than to an object represented singly. Freud's conviction that perceiving in any sensory modality involves associating led him to assert that object-presentations remain open and can add new features. This is in contrast to word-presentations that are "closed, even though capable of expansion" (Strachey, p. 214).

A question remains. Speech is the volitional act of a living person. How did Freud conceive of a voluntary activity when the speech apparatus is formed by "self-sufficient systems of representation" (Forrester 1980, 29)? Freud does not explain it but repeats in the monograph that "all stimuli to spontaneous speech arise from object associations" (Freud 1891, 79). He made it more specific: "Every 'volitional' excitation of the speech centres, however, involves the area of the auditory images [representations] and results in its *stimulation* by object associations" (E. p. 84, my italics).

I ask: how could Freud speak of volition when neither empirical studies nor neurological research has the tools to explore the will or to speak of its source? Nonetheless, for Freud the question seemed essential. Freud's conclusion was not the result of a neurological demonstration. The assertion must be classified as psychological. Quite plausibly it originated in Freud's carefully constructed functional conceptual model of a neurologically founded imaginary speech apparatus, one created to explain not only physical pathological causes of speech disturbances that are neurological and non-volitional, but also the broader range of functional speech and psychic disorders exhibited by Anna O., Frau Emmy von N., and Frau Cäcilie. The conclusion explains why the women *had to* speak spontaneously to describe the *scenes* that made them ill: such scenes remained affectively alive in their unconscious minds. It also explains why they became mute when other scenes were dystonic to them. The entire model of the speech apparatus identifies the object associations complex, the recorded scenes, as the primary movers of the act of speech. That said, the model fails to explain why telling them to Breuer or Freud helped the women to improve their symptoms. The speech apparatus was a *one-person* functional unit and could not include the need for a listener, even though it was obvious that the patients insisted that their doctors listen to what they had to say, and in spite of the fact that in everyday life there is no speech without a listener and no aphasic if there is not a person who *wants* to talk to another and fails in the attempt.

How does Freud conceive of the relation between the speech apparatus and the rest of the neural and anatomical organization of an individual's central nervous system? What is most peculiar about the speech apparatus is that it has no anatomical structures of its own. It is a virtual apparatus that borrows existing anatomical structures to carry out its functions. It shares its afferent pathways with the organs that bring all sensory information to the cortex including sensory input originating in muscles involved in speech functions. The same holds true for its efferent pathways. Freud says explicitly that it "has no afferent or efferent pathways of its own, except for a fibre tract [to the motor centre] the lesion of which causes dysarthria," a neurological condition (Freud 1891, 72). The executive organs of the phonetic apparatus – the mouth, tongue, larynx, and all the muscles for speaking – are not part of the apparatus itself, but serve many functions. This applies equally to the cortical regions that are the anatomical foundation for the speech function. While the sensory information arriving in the respective cortical areas have efferent pathways to connect to the body periphery, the speech area of the cortex has no "projection fibres" of its own: "The [cortical] field of speech associations . . . does without (*entbehrt*) these direct relations to the periphery of the body. It certainly has no sensory and most probably no special motor 'projection fibres'," (E. p. 69; G. p. 68, my translation). The speech apparatus is mostly an *associative apparatus* that benefits from a particular process that Freud *attributes* to the fibers coming from the body periphery. He had mentioned that such fibers change their functional significance (*Bedeutung*) each time they emerge from a gray nucleus. Then he says that the fibers have undergone transformational processes, in order to represent the body "*in a manner suited to the function* [of language]." This is an astonishing statement. As I read it, it implies that significant aspects of *the perceptive/associative function of the nervous system are organized to suit the speech function.* Contemporary research seems to support Freud's daring proposition. Neuroscientist and evolutionary anthropologist Terrence W. Deacon concludes: "It is simply not possible to understand human anatomy, human neurobiology, or human psychology without recognizing that they have all been shaped by something that could be best described as an idea: the idea of symbolic reference" (Deacon 1997, 409–10). I daresay that 'symbolic reference' has much in common with Freud's representational word as described in *On Aphasia*.

In discussing those fibers Freud makes a striking comparison: "They contain the periphery of the body as . . . a poem contains the alphabet, i.e., in a reordering

(*Umordung*) of the individual topographic elements, in manifold connections (*Verknüpfung*) serving other purposes, whereby several [topographic elements] are represented (*vertreten*) several times, others not at all" (E. p. 53; G. p. 55, my translation). I ask: in what way does a poem encompass the alphabet? I have responded:

> Besides the three factors mentioned by Freud, re-ordering, manifold connections, and serving other purposes, a poem utilizes the alphabet for rhyme, metrics, musicality and, more than anything else, for transformation of meaning through imagery and sound and their multiple echoes. Freud's metaphor brings to the fore the richness of transformational meanings he envisions in the fibers' function: to organize representations which then will be suitable for the cortical function of human speech. The metaphor hints indirectly at the presence of an affective component.
>
> *(Rizzuto 1990b, 244)*

This manner of understanding the connections between the body and speech suggests that *speaking always implies presenting in words the experiences of a sentient bodily mind.*

Freud's conception of the representational pathways implies the notion of psychic *determinism*. The mind may form many associations but cannot invent the original representational pathways: it has to use what is already there. Freud's notion also encompasses, to my way of thinking, the earliest theoretical antecedent of the psychoanalytic technique of *free association*: "Most of the factors listed here result from the general properties of an apparatus arranged (*eingerichtet*) for associations" (E. p. 89; G. p. 91, my translation). Its nature is that of a "mechanism of association" (*seine Natur als Associationsmechanismus*) (E. p. 104; G. p. 106, my translation).

How do we bring to awareness an unconscious representation? Freud affirmed that "whenever the same cortical state is stimulated the psychical (*das Psychische*) emerges anew as a remembered image (*Erinnerungsbild*)" (E. p. 56; G. p. 58, my translation). The expression 'remembered image' points to the conscious subjective nature of the representation, clearly indicated by Freud when he referred in the same passage to 'our consciousness' (*unser Bewusstsein*) (ibid.).

The function of the apparatus being what it is, to associate, Freud's thesis is just what we have come to expect: "all aphasias are based (*beruhen*) on the interruption of associations" (E. p. 67; G. p. 69, my translation). The interruptions are exclusively intracortical. In cases of anatomical lesions an interruption is established between one neural component of the word associations and another. In the case of psychopathology, we have what Freud called *asymbolic aphasia*, that is a functional interruption in the connection between the object associations and the word associations required to express what has been stimulated in the former. The treatment of choice thus calls for a technique capable of re-establishing the missing connection. *It is this connection that makes conscious the representation and gives meaning to the spoken words.* Hence, word associations that stimulate the object associations prompt the patients' communications to the doctor and facilitate the healing of hysterical asymbolic aphasia.

It is time for now to leave the topic of speaking and examine what *On Aphasia* has to say about listening to the words of another person. Freud makes some interesting suggestions possibly based on self-observation:

> Probably, we are not to consider the understanding of words [coming] from peripheral stimulation [another person] as a simple conduction (*Fortleitung*) from the acoustic elements to those of the object associations; it seems, rather, that in listening to speech with understanding, the verbal associative activity is stimulated at the same time, in such a way that we *repeat internally*, to some extent, what we heard and at the same time we support (*stützen*) our understanding with our feelings of the innervations [kinaesthetic sensations] of speech.
>
> *(E. pp. 91–92; G. p. 93, my translation, my italics)*

Is this an early and surprising antecedent of today's mirror neurons? Two fascinating conclusions seem obvious to me: if we repeat a word we have heard in order to grasp it, then we somehow transform it into *our own word*, linked to all our existing private associations. Therefore we automatically color the word heard with our own manner of understanding and *feeling* it. Something similar happens to the object associations that prompted our interlocutor to speak. When the word heard from another person links to our own object associations, the latter will have something in common with those of the person who spoke to us, but will also have the *idiosyncratic connections* of our own personal associative network. This description of the process of hearing and understanding opens up the vast field of analytic listening, in which the analyst *hears, senses, envisions* derivatives of the object associations that prompted the patient to speak a given sentence and narrative. The analyst's own object associations to the words heard from the analysand may elicit in her echoes and imagery beyond the intended meaning of the patient's words. In this conception the mystery of hearing unconscious components in the patient's verbalization finds a meaningful description. I conclude that Freud's understanding of speaking and listening is a direct antecedent of his later technique of free association as foundational for accessing unconscious mentation. The invitation to free-associate consists in giving to the analysand's object associations the freedom to appear in his or her mind, and then to put them into words to help the analytic process unfold. After all, in Freud's understanding, *what makes the patient ill is the stimulation of those object associations that are not put into words but transformed into symptoms*. In his work with Frau Emmy, Freud was always asking what she was *seeing* in her mind. He used this same technique for several years with other patients. At this point it is important to recall Freud's statement that the visual component of the object-representations – his patients' mental scenes – were the link to finding words to express them. The deleterious effect of unexpressed representations may come from any point in development because, in Freud's understanding, they are inseparable from sensations, perceptions and their associations. I have drawn some conclusions about the representational process in an earlier publication:

(1) The representational process begins at the time sensations are biologically feasible and the cortex is developed enough to register information. (2) The ever expanding network of associations makes it theoretically possible that nothing that has been experienced is ever representationally lost, and might be capable of becoming psychically available, even if in derivative form. (3) When the time comes for the formation of word representations the developing child has accumulated a vast array of object representations, some of which may be able to connect with words, and some may not. (4) The process of formation of representational object complexes is so primary and directly linked to all types of sensations, and so independent of the formation of word representations, that one can easily see in it the foundations of a direct and primary mode of representing oneself and the world to oneself which does not need words to integrate some psychic meaning. Freud returned to many of these ideas in *The Interpretation of Dreams*, especially in Chapter VII. (5) Finally, the existence of such enormous number of virtual representations, some of which may theoretically never be retrieved again, points in the direction of unconscious processes, continuing their associative chaining outside the realm of awareness.

(Rizzuto 1993, 119)

The spoken word capable of linking with such representations is the critical instrument to make subjective experience consciously available, to objectify ourselves, to grasp what we are feeling, and, most important, to share it with others. Without words we have no direct access to the inner world of another person. Words reveal the internal reality that makes us unique as a species. To be human is to be a speaking being. The talking cure opened the door, closed up to that moment, of the secret mental life of human beings and there is only one key to that door: the patient's words.

Conclusions

I concur with Forrester that "Freud's work on aphasia . . . is the *sine qua non* of the birth of psychoanalytic theory . . . : a theory of the power of words in the formation of symptoms" (Forrester 1980, 14). The meaning of the psychoanalytic terms introduced in the monograph evolved with newer discoveries but their original source in *On Aphasia* colors their later meaning and links them to the Freudian conception of the talking cure. As mentioned above, the monograph also offers a solid foundation for psychoanalytic technique and possibly even for the elaboration of a theory of technique based on the complex functions carried out when people exchange words.

Note

1 Strachey points out in a footnote that "This seems to be the first published occurrence of the term 'das Unbewusste'" ('the unconscious') in what was to be its psycho-analytic sense (p. 45, n. 1).

References

Andersson, Ola. A Supplement to Freud's Case History of 'Frau Emmy v. N.' in *Studies on Hysteria* 1895. *Scandinavian Psychoanalytic Review* 2 (1979): 5–16.

Bernfeld, Siegfried. Freud's Earliest Theories and the School of Helmholtz. *Psychoanalytic Quarterly* 13 (1944): 341–62.

Binswanger, Ludwig. Freud und die Verfassung der Klinischen Psychiatrie. *Schweizen Archives Neurologie und Psychiatrie* 37 (1936): 177–99.

Breuer, Josef, and Sigmund Freud. *Studies on Hysteria*. Vol. 2 of *Standard Edition*. London: Hogarth Press, 1893–1895.

Deacon, Terrence W. *The Symbolic Species: The Co-Evolution of Language and the Brain*. New York: W. W. Norton, 1997.

Ellenberger, Henri F. L'histoire d'"Emmy von N'. *L'Evolution Psychiatrique* 42 (1977): 519–40.

Forrester, John. *Language and the Origins of Psychoanalysis*. New York: Columbia University Press, 1980.

Freud, Ernest L., ed. *Letters of Sigmund Freud*. New York: Basic Books, 1960.

Freud, Sigmund. *On Aphasia: A Critical Study*. Trans. Erwin Stengel. 1953. New York: International Universities Press, 1891.

———. Five Lectures on Psycho-Analysis. Vol. 11 of *Standard Edition*, 3–56. London: Hogarth Press, 1910.

———. The Unconscious. Vol. 14 of *Standard Edition*, 159–215. London: Hogarth Press, 1915.

———. A Short Account of Psychoanalysis. Vol. 19 of *Standard Edition*, 191–212. London: Hogarth Press, 1924.

———. An Autobiographical Study. Vol. 20 of *Standard Edition*, 1–74. London: Hogarth Press, 1925a.

———. Josef Breuer. Vol. 19 of *Standard Edition*, 277–80. London: Hogarth Press, 1925b.

———. *The Complete Letters of Sigmund Freud to Wilhelm Fliess 1887–1904*. Trans. and ed. Jeffrey Moussaieff Masson. Cambridge, MA: Belknap Press of Harvard University Press, 1985.

Jackson, Hughlings H. On Affections of Speech from Diseases of the Brain. *Brain* 2. Reprinted in Vol. 38 (1915) (1880): 130–86.

Kris, Ernest. Introduction. In *Sigmund Freud: The Origins of Psychoanalysis. Letters to Wilhelm Fliess* (pp. 3–47). New York: Basic Books, 1954.

Kuhn, Roland. Préface. In *Freud, S. Contributions à la conception des aphasies. Une étude critique* (pp. 5–45). Paris: Presses Universitaires de France, 1983.

Rizzuto, Ana-María. Freud's Speech Apparatus and Spontaneous Speech. *International Journal of Psycho-Analysis* 74 (1993): 113–27.

———. A Hypothesis about Freud's Motive for Writing the Monograph *On Aphasia*. *International Review of Psychoanalysis* 16 (1989): 111–17.

———. The Origins of Freud's Concept of Object Representation ("*Objektvorstellung*") in His Monograph *On Aphasia*: Its Theoretical and Technical Importance. *International Journal of Psycho-Analysis* 71 (1990b): 241–48.

———. A Proto-Dictionary of Psychoanalysis. *International Journal of Psycho-Analysis* 71 (1990a): 261–70.

Stengel, Erwin. Introduction. In *On Aphasia. A Critical Study*, by Sigmund Freud. New York: International Universities Press, 1953.

———. A Re-Evaluation of Freud's Book *On Aphasia*: Its Significance for Psychoanalysis. *International Journal of Psychoanalysis* 35 (1954): 85–89.

Strachey, James. Appendix C to Freud's *The Unconscious*. Vol. 14 of *Standard Edition*, 209–15. London: Hogarth Press, 1957.

3

HYSTERIA AS ASYMBOLIC APHASIA

'Psychical treatment' denotes . . . treatment taking its start in the mind, treatment (whether of mental or physical disorders) by measures which operate in the first instance and immediately upon the human mind.

Foremost among such measures is the use of words; and words are the essential tool of mental treatment.

Sigmund Freud, *Psychical (or Mental) Treatment*
(Freud 1905, 283)

The impact of *On Aphasia* as a guide in creating a therapeutic model for hysteria

Freud's *first* paper about psychical treatment, which he defines as starting in the mind and using words as its essential tool, dates from 1890[1] (Freud 1905) and thus preceded *On Aphasia* by a year. Breuer's treatment of Anna O. and Freud's of Frau Emmy had already confirmed the assertion quoted above. In *On Aphasia* Freud described *asymbolic aphasia*, a functional disturbance that results from the *intrapsychic* disruption in linking representations to words that can articulate our experiences. In *Studies on Hysteria* (Breuer and Freud 1893–1895) he presented three other cases besides that of Frau Emmy of such a disruption in which he tacitly used the model from *On Aphasia*. I would now like to make his use of the model from the monograph explicit. The patients Miss Lucy R., Katharina, and Frl. Elisabeth von R. had no damage to their nervous tissues, but only a psychical dissociation in their minds between the representations of their experiences and the words they needed to restore the integrity of their own mental processes as he had suggested: "It is the psychotherapist's business to put these together once more into the organization which he presumes to have existed" (p. 291). Full *psychic words* had to be found to link both and help them gain access to the personal meaning of lived moments from the past. This model is present even today in the background of our clinical work (Rizzuto 1993).

How did Freud conceptualize the processes involved in the formation of hysterical symptoms and the technique that would lead to their resolution? The patients presented in *Studies on Hysteria* – all of them female – had multiple and complex symptoms. He understood the difficulty of his enterprise and described his task as throwing light "from different directions on a highly complicated topic which has never yet been represented" (Breuer and Freud 1893–1895, 291). Freud also discovered that in hysterics there is an "intimate connection between the story of the patient's suffering and the symptoms of his illness" (p. 161). His model of hysterical psychopathology and psychotherapy had to demonstrate how hysterical symptoms are formed and what kinds of therapeutic intervention contribute to their resolution. In all cases the proof of a theory and its therapeutic technique rested on its curative effect.

Breuer and Freud said that the patient's experiential process as it "originally took place must be repeated as vividly as possible; it must be brought back to its *status nascendi* and then given verbal utterance" (p. 6). What does *status nascendi* mean in this context? I read this passage in hindsight as referring to the mental revival on the patient's part of *scenes* in which she found herself involved and that she had registered in her memory. The monograph offered a theoretical foundation for the possibility of such a revival. After the moment of a particular perception has passed – he asserted in the monograph – the representational process has left behind a *physiological correlate*, a modification of the nervous system, which is available for later retrieval as a memory. The conscious return of the representation emerges whenever the previously established path of associations is stimulated: ". . . the psychical (*das Psychische*) emerges anew as a remembered image (*Erinnerungsbild*)" (Freud 1891, E. p. 56, my translation, G. p. 58). We know by now that for Freud perceiving is the same as associating because "they belong to one single process" (E. p. 57; G. p. 58). The expression 'remembered image' also clearly suggests the conscious nature of the representation that is retrieved, what he calls "our consciousness" (*unser Bewusstsein*) (E. p. 56; G. p. 58). The aphasia model lacked a critical component, however: the apparatus as such had no room for feelings while for the work with hysterics the presence of the original affect was indispensable. Yet it seems clear that associations as intrapsychic processes cannot fail to bring with them affective elements of the *perceiving individual's* psychic life. In working with his patients Freud took for granted the affective color of perceptions and their associative links. In fact, it was the patient's personal *interpretations* of those internal perceptions that transformed Freud's case presentations into short stories.

We must recall that in the aphasia model, Freud had insisted: "All stimulations to speak spontaneously come from the region of the object associations" (E. p. 78; G. p. 81). This statement means that all conscious, voluntary speech originates in previously registered representational processes. The phrasing suggests that the speech apparatus is a closed system that can provide its own stimulation. In the same monograph, however, Freud gives an example of the *will* to speak mentioning the case of the man who made "the most desperate effort to express himself," but remained aphasic until a piece of bone was removed from his brain whereupon he recovered his normal speech function (Freud 1891, 27). Here we can observe the ever-present tension in Freud between the theoretician who created a model of the speech *apparatus* and the careful observer of *human beings*. The wish to speak belongs to the sentient person, who is in charge of stimulating the speech apparatus and getting its gears going to produce spoken words. The individual *wants* to say them, or – to put it even more clearly – feels he wants to say them. Freud took for granted his patients' willingness to speak with him but had no theory to explain it. A willing action is always psychologically motivated and involves some affect.

The aphasia model, regardless of its shortcomings, could not be discarded because it described so clearly and accurately that *all* any one of us has to talk about are "object-representations" – *scenes* – that remain ready to spring into conscious psychic life. Freud based the model for hysteria on three pillars: the preexisting model of the speech apparatus, clinical data from the psychical processes he observed in his patients, and new concepts he was creating to help connect the first two. Although he never explicitly acknowledged using the model of *On Aphasia* to build his model of hysterical pathology and his analytic technique to treat it, I conclude that he conceived of hysteria as a functional aphasia – *asymbolic aphasia* – in which sectors of the patient's representations are severed from their connection to words and to other representations (Rizzuto 1989; 1992). The hysteric has rejected some representations and they become a pathogenic organization, the cause of the psychic and somatic symptoms. To treat his patients Freud had to help them connect the visual components of the object associations with the acoustic component of words suitable for describing what had been split off. The model remained exclusively *intrapsychic*: the linking of representations and words had to occur in the patient's mind with the analyst's help. Freud did not pay much attention to the fact that they were speaking to him and that the person of the doctor was crucial, even though Breuer had documented its importance for Anna O.: "She would never begin to talk until she had satisfied herself of my identity by carefully feeling my hands" (Breuer and Freud 1893–1895, 30).

Freud describes the intrapsychic process of symptom formation in the case of Miss Lucy, the second case he presents in *Studies on Hysteria:*

> The actual traumatic moment, then, is the one at which the incompatibility [*Wiederspruch*, contradiction] forces itself upon the ego [*sich dem Ich aufdrängt*][2] and at which the latter decides on the repudiation [*Verweisung*] of the incompatible idea [*Vorstellung*]. That idea is not annihilated by a repudiation of this kind, but merely repressed into the unconscious [*ins Unbewußte gedrängt*].[3] When this process occurs for the first time there comes into being a nucleus and centre of crystallization for the formation of a psychical group divorced from the ego [*Ich*] – a group around which everything which would imply an acceptance of the incompatible idea subsequently collects. The splitting

[*Spaltung*] of consciousness in these cases of acquired hysteria is accordingly a deliberate and intentional one [*eine gewollte, absichtliche*]. At least it is often *introduced* by an act of volition [*Willkürakt*]; for the actual outcome is something different from what the subject intended. What he wanted was to do away with an idea [*Vorstellung*], as though it had never appeared, but all he succeeds in doing is to isolate it psychically.

(Breuer and Freud 1893–1895, 123, italics in original)

Freud's description portrays a patient that cannot accept a representation as pertaining to herself, her ego [*Ich*]. The process of isolating this representation involves the defensive attempt to interrupt the normal perceptual pathways in their automatic and instantaneous associative functioning. The perceptual and associative pathways continue to function normally, however, and cannot fail to leave behind a *physiological correlate* that remains stored in the mind. The process of isolation cannot alter neural functioning or associative processes: it only eliminates conscious awareness by avoiding integrating the representation into the person's self-recognition. The therapeutic effort aims at activating that latent correlate to bring back to conscious memory the event – object-representation – thus registered.

The associative processes, however, do not permit a complete isolation of what has been repressed: "Its external strata pass over in every direction into portions of the normal ego; and, indeed, they belong to the latter just as much as to the pathogenic organization" (p. 290). To put it in terms of the model of *On Aphasia*, one can say that the obligatory nature of the associative process prevails over a person's "deliberate and intentional" efforts to cancel out the unwelcome representation.

Freud introduces a new term and concept to the model: "The repressed idea [*Vorstellung*] would persist as a memory trace that is weak (has little intensity), while the affect that is torn from it would be used for a somatic innervation. (That is, the excitation [*Erregung*] is 'converted'). . . . it is precisely through its repression that the idea becomes the cause of morbid symptoms – that is to say, becomes pathogenic" (p. 285). The traumatic pathogenic potential of distressing affects is also conditioned in Breuer's and Freud's opinion by "*the susceptibility of the person affected*" (p. 6, my italics). The notion that affect is *torn* from the representation is confusing, for up to this point we have not heard that representations *have* affect that can be defensively torn from them. I feel obliged to ask: does the affect *belong* to the representation or, alternatively, is the affect the subjective feeling of the person confronted with an intolerable scene, representation, or thought? In fact, Freud never resolved the difficulty of how to integrate representation and affect in his theory even though their connection is crucial for understanding hysteria and psychopathology. I reflect that the underlying model of *On Aphasia*, as an apparatus, had no room to integrate the "susceptible person," or the clinical observation of the person's intentional splitting of consciousness as the cause of the symptoms.

Freud does not specify what is incompatible in certain representations to the point of making them traumatic, an equivalent to excessive stimulation. In their *Preliminary Communication*, Breuer and Freud had concluded: "Any experience which calls up distressing affects – such as those of fright, anxiety, shame or physical pain – may operate as a trauma of this kind" (Breuer and Freud 1893–1895, 6). Frequently, the trauma stems from a *private perception* of oneself in a particular situation. Freud reflects that the incompatible idea "must originally have been in communication with the main stream of thought. Otherwise the conflict which led to their exclusion could not have taken place. It is at these moments that conversion takes place, of which the results are the splitting of consciousness and the hysterical symptom" (p. 167). The motive for splitting it from consciousness is to avoid the pain it would cause the patient if the idea were not repressed. Nonetheless, the *physiological concomitant* of the experience and the associations elicited by it are still there with the potential to bring it back to consciousness: "The pathogenic idea which has ostensibly been forgotten is always lying ready 'close at hand' [*in der Nähe*, 'in the vicinity'] and can be reached by associations that are easily accessible. It is merely a question of getting some obstacle out of the way" (p. 271).

Freud's analytic technique for overcoming repression

Freud believed that the spoken word had the power to revive the original traumatic moment and bring it to conscious awareness, the goal being for the patient to integrate it into her ego [*Ich*], that is, her understanding of herself. In the "*Preliminary Communication*" Breuer and Freud observed: "An injury that has been repaid, even if only in words, is recollected quite differently from one that has had to be accepted"; they remind the reader that everyday German describes "an injury that has been suffered in silence" as a *Kränkung*, a humiliation, but in its most literal sense 'something that makes a person sick' (p. 8). On the other hand, speech can revive the repressed moment. Strachey renders the statement in question as "language serves as a substitute for action; by its help, an affect can be 'abreacted' almost as effectively" (p. 8). His translation strikes me as misleading, however. The original German says: "in der Sprache findet der Mensch ein Surrogat für die Tat, mit dessen Hilfe der Affekt nahezu ebenso 'abreagiert' werden kann" (p. 87). I would translate it as: "human beings find in speech a substitute for the deed; by its help, an affect can be abreacted almost as effectively." I believe that something essential is lost when *Tat* is translated as action and *Sprache* as language in a broad sense. As for the meaning of "*Tat*," Farrell explains in his *Dictionary of German Synonyms*:

> It refers to the completed act or action, the result, which is seen plastically and as a whole. Whether it is brief or lengthy, morally good or bad, is irrelevant. Its outstanding characteristic is that *it is vivid, dramatic*, refers to something of imposing proportions, and is *personal* in that one thinks of the doer as an individual.
>
> *(Farrell 1977, 4, my italics)*

This conception of speech as a substitute for the deed facilitates the understanding of Freud's selection of the spoken word, with its essential *visual* component in the object-representations, as the optimal instrument to bring the pathogenic moment back to its original vividness. Then the revived experience may enter normal associative processes leading to expression of the painful affect and its integration into the person's conscious awareness.

The aim of the treatment is to gain access to the patient's private reality, the pathogenic core experiences that lie isolated in the repressed unconscious. Freud's *On Aphasia* already expressed his confident conviction that the determinism of the associative process involving pre-established pathways and non-erasable physiological correlates would bring the sought-after pathogenic experience to life. The question is how to activate such determinism. What part of the model would be most effective? Breuer and Freud offer an early interesting example. They present the case of a little girl who had epileptic seizures. When she had one of her customary attacks under hypnosis she was asked to describe what she was *seeing*. She responded: "'The dog! the dog's coming!'; and in fact it turned out that she had had the first of her attacks after being chased by a savage dog" (p. 14). With this knowledge available the treatment succeeded.

I now want to ask, what processes were involved in treating the patient? The authors mention that in cases like this "there is an underlying memory of the psychical trauma or series of traumas, which usually comes to our notice in a hallucinatory phase" (p. 14). The process seemed to have three steps: (1) the physician *verbally instructed* the girl to describe in words what she was *seeing* in her mind not what she was feeling (or any other instruction). The assumption is present that she *was* seeing something and, furthermore, that she would see precisely the scene that caused her symptoms; (2) this supposes that the particular scene, one among many others in her mind, was the one that was ready to be stimulated to produce what Freud had called in the monograph "*das Psychische*"; (3) the next assumption suggests that – as in fact happened in this case – the activated representation would stimulate the right word to name it, and as a result she would say to her doctor a truly *psychic word* that made the symptom unnecessary. While this process was certainly *internal* to her psyche, a question remains. What stimulated her representation of being chased by a dog at that moment although she had been unable to summon it up before? The aphasia model is totally intrapsychic, it involves only one person. I suggest that the doctor's order to see and give words to her vision acted as *the* stimulant that activated her previously unnamed representation. In other words, the spoken words of her doctor ordering her to report what she was seeing *facilitated* the stimulation of the representation. Although neither Breuer nor Freud comment on this aspect of the technique, that she spoke in response to being spoken to, they do say that "if one succeeds in getting into *rapport* with the patient during the attack . . . one finds that . . . there is an underlying memory of the psychical trauma" (p. 14). I understand the word "rapport" as the condition for *speaking* to occur between people, and that the doctor's spoken request is, in turn, the condition for the activation of memories the patient had been unable to deal with but that were waiting to achieve mental integration.

The results are clear: the experience is now conscious; the words to describe it are full psychical words; the stimulus has been processed; and the affect has been registered subjectively. When all this has been accomplished, the symptom will vanish because consciousness has recovered its associative integrity. Given this analysis, I would assert that the key to the psychotherapeutic procedure to treat hysteria can now be identified as already present in *On Aphasia*: "*It brings to an end the operative force of the idea which was not abreacted in the first instance, by allowing its strangulated affect to find a way out through speech; and it subjects it to associative correction by introducing it into normal consciousness*" (Breuer and Freud 1893–1895, 17). The patient now able to *feel* has spoken a meaningful psychic word and has undone her *asymbolic aphasia*.

The revival of the original experience may bring about great psychical pain and new forms of resistance. Once all the impediments to full recollection of the traumatic experience have been overcome and access to the original affect regained, however, the patient becomes capable of accepting its meaning for her.

Evolving clinical procedures

Each of the three cases Freud presents in *Studies on Hysteria* opened new horizons for him and prompted him to use new technical approaches and to elaborate theoretical explanations.

Freud first presents Miss Lucy R. as an English governess for the children of a Viennese widower, the owner of a factory in the suburbs of the city. She was thirty years old at the time and was referred to Freud for a suppurative rhinitis accompanied by subjective and inexplicable olfactory sensations of burnt pudding. She also complained of depression, fatigue, loss of appetite, and headaches. She did not see Freud on a regular schedule but "from time to time" (p. 106) in his office. Freud's *physical* examination uncovered only some general anesthesia and rhinitis.

Miss Lucy failed to respond to Freud's hypnotic induction and he became tired of hearing "But, doctor, I'm *not* asleep!" (p. 108). Hence he opted to take her as she was and follow his colleague Bernheim's opinion that memories "are only *apparently* forgotten in the waking state and can be revived by a mild word of command and a pressure with the hand intended to indicate a different state of consciousness" (p. 109). He opted for a new technique based on Bernheim's ideas:

> I decided to start from the assumption that my patients knew everything that was of any pathogenic significance and that it was only a question of *obliging* them to communicate it. Thus when I reached a point at which, after asking a patient some question such as: 'How long have you had this symptom?' or: 'What was its origin?', I was met with the answer: 'I really don't know', I proceeded as follows. I placed my hand on the patient's forehead or took her head between my hands and said: 'You will think of it under the pressure of my hand. At the moment at which I relax my pressure *you will*

> see something in front of you or something will come into your head [Einfall]. Catch
> hold of it. It will be what we are looking for. – Well, *what have you seen* or
> what has occurred to you [*eingefallen*]?'
>
> (p. 110, my italics)

Once more Freud was searching for the *visual components* of representations as
the link to help the patient put her experiences into words, while he was using his
own order for the patient to *see something* as the stimulus to revive the pathogenic
original scene.

Freud had asked Miss Lucy about the smell and she responded that it was that
of burnt pudding; she reported a clear memory of it from two days before her
birthday. She was cooking some pudding with the children, when the postman
delivered a letter from her mother. The children took it from her hand and said
they would give it to her on her birthday. She then smelled that the puddings
were burning. Freud was interested in the *scene* and asked: "Do you see this scene
clearly before your eyes?" Her answer was unequivocal: "As large as life, just as I
experienced it" (p. 114). The story unfolded without much effort on Freud's part.
She was very fond of the children but there was a conflict: other members of the
household staff had reported to the children's grandfather that she was putting
herself above her station. She had offered her resignation to her employer, but he
had asked her to reconsider, so she stayed on. She also disclosed that she had promised the children's dying mother – a distant relative of hers – to take her place and
care for the children.

Freud reflected on the impact of conflicting affects in forming the burned
pudding olfactory hallucinations and asked a critical question: "Why did she not
always call to mind the scene itself, instead of the associated sensation which she
singled out as a symbol of the recollection?" (p. 116). He had come to suspect that
Miss Lucy had "*intentionally repressed [verdrängt] from consciousness*" an incompatible
idea (p. 116). Freud concluded: "The basis for repression itself can only be a feeling
of unpleasure, the incompatibility between the single idea that is to be repressed
[*der einen verdrängenden Idee*] and the dominant mass of ideas constituting the ego
[*Vorstellungsmasse des Ich*]. The repressed idea [*verdrängte Vorstellung*] takes its *revenge*,
however, by becoming pathogenic" (p. 116, my italics). He *thought* about what
Miss Lucy's repressed idea could be and boldly said to her: "I believe that really you
are in love with your employer" (p. 117). Her laconic answer was that she was but
did not want to know about it. Freud asked: "Why didn't you tell me? . . . were
you ashamed of loving a man?" (ibid.). She responded that it was because she was
poor and he was a rich member of a good family; people would laugh at her if
they knew.

This therapeutic moment is very illuminating: Miss Lucy reports the scenes
related to her symptoms while Freud, in turn, is concocting potential scenarios
in his mind that could give meaning to her experience. Her words activated *his
own associative processes* and brought to his conscious awareness scenes of a woman
in love. The governess' symptoms did not disappear completely and since she

remained depressed they continued the search. At that point of his presentation Freud uses the pronoun "we" as an indicator of their collaboration in the looking for the sources of her troubles: "*We* therefore looked about for anything else that might have to do with the scene of the burnt pudding; *we* went into the subject of the domestic friction, the grandfather's behaviour, and so on, and as *we* did so the burnt smell faded more and more" (p. 118, my italics).

The treatment was interrupted over the Christmas holidays. The smell of burnt pudding had disappeared but another sensation of cigar-smoking had taken its place. Freud was disappointed for he realized that the preceding treatment had dealt only with the symptom. Some of the old Freud returned: "I did not hesitate to set about the task of *getting rid* of this new mnemic symbol by analysis" (p. 119, my italics). Miss Lucy did not know where the new smell came from. Freud went back to *commanding* his patient to remember the scenes that he needed to make sense of the symptom. He described her as "a 'visual' type" (p. 119) and expected vivid recollections from her: "*I* then *insisted* that she should try to remember under the pressure of my hand" on her head (p. 119, my italics). Under Freud's urging "a picture gradually emerged," but not without hesitation. Freud *persisted*: "'Go on *looking* at the *picture*; it will develop and become more specialized'" (ibid., my italics). Freud was acting as if he were certain that she would find something and kept on repeating the phrase. We can see in this new technique a modulated form of his imperious commands to Frau Emmy. His injunctions to Miss Lucy have a more personal touch because they require her *conscious* collaboration in the search for the source of the symptom. The story emerged of episodes in which visitors had kissed the children and her employer had been furious with her. He had also shouted at the man who kissed them: "Don't kiss the children!" Miss Lucy described her feelings at the moment: "'I feel a stab at my heart; and as the gentlemen are already smoking, the cigar-smoke sticks in my memory'" (p. 120). Freud returned to a more personal way of talking to Miss Lucy by asking her whether she was embarrassed or concerned about her employer's vehemence. Freud's questions at this point in his technique leave the *historical scene* for a moment to pay attention to the *subjective* experience of Miss Lucy. After the last episode, the children's father had been so angry with the governess that he told her that if somebody else kissed the children again she would be dismissed. Freud commented: "This had happened at a time when she still thought he loved her . . . The scene had crushed her hopes" (p. 120). Miss Lucy became convinced that he could never have warm feelings for her. The session at which this came up was their penultimate meeting. She returned in two days, "transfigured": "She was smiling and carried her head high" (p. 121). Freud asked whether there was a romance going on or not. Miss Lucy replied: "Nothing has happened. It is just that *you don't know me*" (p. 121, my italics). Yes, she was still in love with the director but had decided not to be unhappy about it, reasoning that "After all, I can have thoughts and feelings to myself" (ibid.). An accidental encounter four months later at a summer resort confirmed that Miss Lucy was well and that "her recovery had been maintained" (ibid.).

Miss Lucy had helped Freud to understand that the traumatic drama had occurred in the interior of her mind, in her conflict with herself. She also conveyed to him that he did not know her well enough; she could live with contradictory wishes without making herself ill. Freud had understandably been searching for mental mechanisms to explain Miss Lucy's illness and recovery. She made it clear that it was also, and primarily, due to her attitude, to her *owning and accepting* her conflicting feelings about *herself* that made the difference. She was right: Freud had correctly ascertained the *processes* she carried out in her mind but had failed to see Miss Lucy's mettle and her capacity to face her conflicts as a self.

Again let us ask what we have learned from this brief and charming case. Miss Lucy provided Freud with the opportunity to give up the cathartic method and hypnosis. He learned that he could help her to remember the traumatic moments related to her symptoms while she was in a normal state of consciousness. When he encountered a difficult moment he reverted to the method of pressing Miss Lucy's forehead *to force* her to remember under the weight of his medical authority. Nonetheless they found moments of collaboration in analytic dialogue, signaled by the pronoun "we" in the report. They ended the treatment with a delightful *conversation* in which a curious Freud inquired about her excellent disposition and her erotic involvement as well as the perspectives for her further employment. Miss Lucy demonstrated with her cheerful answer that she [her *Ich*] could live at peace with components of her mental life that she had previously considered contradictory. She could love her employer in the privacy of her heart *and* continue to work for him.

The case highlights the importance Freud attached to Miss Lucy's therapeutic need to *see* the pictures in her mind to the smallest details and to describe them in words, so that he could find the key to the type of experiences she had undergone. As he listened he was organizing what he heard, in order to form *a meaningful plot* in his mind that would explain the symptoms. Freud needed to complete *his picture* of her problems and offered his first 'construction': she was in love with her employer.

Freud and Miss Lucy R. found significant actual and mental scenes that permitted them to elucidate the *historical* source of her sensations of burnt pudding and cigar smoke. The factual events led Freud to unveil a truly psychoanalytic explanation of her suffering: external circumstances become traumatic only when they elicit the formation of incompatible internal representations. Miss Lucy R. recovered under Freud's new technique of "compelling the psychical group that had been split off to unite once more with the ego-consciousness [*Ichbewusstsein*]" (p. 124). She achieved this by linking internal representations with the words that described them to Freud. One observation remains: from this moment on it is as though Freud considered the "ego" [*Ich*] to be a very extended object-presentation that, if it is to keep its integrity and be free of pathology, cannot reject the obligatory associations of its perceptions in matters significant to the person (*Ich*). Freud seems to confirm this notion by using the expression cited above: "the dominant mass of ideas constituting the ego [*Vorstellungsmasse des Ich*]."

Miss Lucy's asymbolic aphasia had been overcome: she could see herself as in love with her employer and articulate the feelings of disappointment and shame; she had succeeded in naming and accepting the "stab in the heart" of her crushed hopes for his love. She no longer had a need to smell the odors associated to the perceived moments of suffering *because* she could express her experiences in words to Freud and to herself, and integrate them into her representational reality.

The new method yielded a significant gain for Freud, namely, giving him "insight into the *motives* which often determine the 'forgetting' of memories" (p. 111, my italics), Miss Lucy did not want to think her thoughts, that is, she *intentionally repressed* her conflicting thoughts. In the terminology of *On Aphasia* it means that interference had occurred with the associative process that links a perception to previously acquired information, and as a result the object-presentation is not integrated into the person's mind. Nonetheless, the perception has taken place and repression from consciousness cannot erase it entirely. The representations of what was perceived remain along with related associations, since the association process is involuntary and cannot be completely inhibited. Freud connects remembering to "the theory of aphasia, namely that recognizing something is a lighter task for memory than thinking of it spontaneously" (p. 112).

Freud's handling of Miss Lucy's case makes it abundantly clear that he uses the terms *representation* and *scene* almost interchangeably. 'Representation' appears in his theorizing; while 'scene' occurs in connection with the patient's external experiences or internal recollection of them. He uses the term 'picture' [*Bild*] when requiring that Miss Lucy look at what is present in her mind. I find his insistence on her observing or reviewing the internal scenes to be clinical confirmation of his axiom in *On Aphasia* that all stimulation to speak comes from object-representations. If the governess is able to fully activate the internal scene/representation she will find the right words to convey what she sees to Freud. In fact, in his understanding of the matter there is no other way for a person to speak her mind.

Finally, a brief comment: Miss Lucy appeared "transfigured" in her last hour. Could it be that having found integration of the complex sources of her contradictory scenes and representations had a twofold effect, not only removing her symptoms but also returning more psychic life to the *bodily* sources of her mental processes?

Katharina

Freud introduced the developmental point of view in presenting Katharina's case by suggesting that ignorance of sexual matters in a young person postpones the formation of the psychic traumatic moment until the person understands the meaning of a memory that had been kept stored in the mind.

He encountered her on a trip to the eastern Alps in August 1893. He climbed to the top of a mountain and was absorbed in thought when a "sulky-looking" eighteen-year-old girl asked to talk to him as a doctor because her "nerves were bad" (p. 125). He accepted her request and reported "the *conversation* that followed *between us* just as it is impressed on my memory" (p. 125, my italics). He reasoned: "I could not venture to transplant hypnosis to these altitudes, but perhaps I might succeed with *a simple talk*" (p. 127, my italics).

Katharina complained of being "out of breath" (p. 125). He listened and posed questions seeking the thread that linked as yet unknown events to her symptoms. She reported that the symptom had occurred for the first time two years earlier. Freud then responded, "I'll tell you how *I* think you got your attacks. At that time, two years ago, you must have seen or heard something that very much embarrassed you, and that you'd much rather not have seen" (p. 127). Katharina agreed and told him she had gone into a room and found her uncle in bed with her cousin. Freud gently invited Katharina to tell him the whole story: "Won't you tell me all about it?" (p. 127). The "me" of the sentence points to himself as a special kind of listener and Katharina replied: "You can say *anything* to a doctor, I suppose" (p. 127). Freud's next moves to explore her private reality: "'Fräulein Katharina, if you could remember now what was happening in you at that time, when you had your first attack, what you thought about it – it would help you'" (p. 128). She reported that there was a frightening face that she saw repeatedly but she realized it could not be her uncle's face.

Katharina then added that a few days later she had fallen ill. Freud, connecting sickness and disgust in his mind, guided her further: "So I said: 'If you were sick three days later, I believe that means that when you looked into the room you felt disgusted'" (p. 129). Katharina agreed but asserted she did not know what the disgust could be about. Freud comments: "*I* had no idea either. But I told her to go on and tell me whatever occurred to her [*was ihr einfiele*], in the confident expectation [*Erwartung*] that she would think [*das einfallen*] of precisely what I needed to explain the case" (p. 129). Once more Freud *assumed* that the pathogenic scenes or representation would be the first to be *activated* by his request. Katharina recalled three situations with her uncle: one in which she found him in her bed, another when he was drunk and she had to defend herself from him, and finally an occasion when she had to stop him from coming into her room one night. Freud said to her that she thought he was doing to her cousin what he wanted to do with her: "That was what you were disgusted at, because you remembered the feeling when you woke up in the night and felt his body" (p. 131). Freud's focus of attention is her inner world, her thought processes, her bodily sensations, her frightened understanding when she saw her uncle having intercourse with her cousin.

Katharina's sharing her previously untold story to Freud changed her: now her face was lively and her eyes bright. Her putting the frightening scenes into words, undoing her asymbolic aphasia changed her bodily appearance just as happened with Miss Lucy, as though by giving words to painful somatic sensations and perceptions she had not only integrated her experience but also revived the body that was the source of her representations.

Katharina helped Freud confirm that in a certain sense patients *do* know what troubles them. It is a matter of helping them to piece together their memories, thoughts, and feelings until they take on a particular form and are put into words, something that even *a simple conversation* can accomplish. He also learned that talking with the intention of understanding the internal world of the patient was good enough. His words addressed her *intrapsychic* reality that she had been unable to articulate on her own.

Fräulein Elisabeth von R.

The patient in this case was a young lady suffering from leg pains and difficulties in walking who started her treatment in the autumn of 1892. Her younger married sister had recently died. While her sister was alive Elisabeth von R. had wished that she too could find a man who would make her as happy as her brother-in-law made her sister. It was Freud's first full-length analysis and he explained the technique he had used as follows:

> I arrived at a procedure which I later developed into a regular method and employed deliberately. This procedure was one of clearing away the patho-genic psychical material layer by layer, and we liked to compare it with the technique of excavating a buried city. I would begin by getting the patient to tell me what was known to her and I would carefully note the points at which some train of thought remained obscure or some link in the causal chain seemed to be missing. And afterwards I would penetrate into deeper layers of her memories at these points by carrying out an investigation under hypnosis or by the use of some similar technique. The whole work was, of course, based on the expectation that it would be possible to establish a com-pletely adequate set of determinants for the events concerned.
>
> (p. 139)

Strachey's translation, cited above, strikes me as misleading in an important respect. The German text reads: "*Die Voraussetzung der ganzen Arbeit war natürlich die Erwartung, daß eine vollkommen zureichende Determinierung zu erweisen sei*" (p. 201), which I translate as: "The premise for the whole work was, *naturally*, the expecta-tion that a perfectly sufficient *determination* could be demonstrated" (my italics). 'Determinants' refers to concrete events while, in my understanding, Freud is talking about a *process of determination* that never fails, because as he had said in *On Aphasia,* the memories are registered as latent physiological correlates and asso-ciations documenting the events that have the potential to be reactivated as *das Psychische* (the psychical).

This procedure was intended to follow that associative process to discover the psychically traumatic moment that had given rise to her symptoms. When he was unable to hypnotize her, Freud resorted, as he had done with Miss Lucy, to press-ing her forehead and instructing her to report to him "faithfully *whatever appeared before her inner eye or passed through her memory* at the moment of the pressure" (p. 145, my italics). In the chapter on "Psychotherapy of Hysteria" Freud explains that: "The procedure by pressure is no more than a trick for temporarily taking unawares an ego which is eager for defence" (p. 278). His intention was to create a state of divided attention – an expression he had used in *On Aphasia* – so as to distract the patient's ego. What emerged was an impression of intense conflict between her erotic feelings for a young man and the worsening in the past of her sick father's condition. Freud concluded that she had repressed the tension-laden idea and removed it from the associative chain while the pain in her legs was linked to the suppressed affect. He described as *scenes* many of the moments that contributed to the formation of her symptoms. When she said that nothing had occurred to her he did not accept her response and returned to applying pressure to her forehead. He wanted "pictures and ideas" (*Bilder und Einfälle*) (p. 153). His persistence produced good results: "Sometimes, indeed, her behaviour fulfilled my highest expectations, and during such periods it was surprising with what promptitude the different *scenes* relating to a given theme emerged in a strictly chronological order. It was as though she were reading a lengthy book of *pictures*, whose pages were being turned over before her eyes" (ibid., my italics). Freud's satisfaction was obvious: "I derived from this analysis a literally unqualified reliance on my technique" (p. 154). In the terminology of *On Aphasia* one can say that the technique was bringing out those very complex object-presentations – scenes – that had been prevented from combining with many other associations in Elisabeth von R's mind as part of the natural associative process. Now they could be expressed in words and she could accept the emotional meaning of some of her repressed experiences, feelings, and thoughts.

Freud wanted to know about the *scenes* that were the source of her symptoms. Encouraged by the results he reported:

> I resolved, therefore, to adopt the hypothesis that the procedure never failed: that on every occasion under the pressure of my hand some idea [*Einfall*] occurred to Elisabeth or some picture [*Bild*] came before her eyes, but that she was not always prepared to communicate it to me, and tried to suppress once more what had been conjured up. I could think of two motives for this concealment. Either she was applying criticism to the idea, which she had no right to do, on the ground of its not being important enough or of its being an irrelevant reply to the question she had been asked; or she hesitated to produce it because – she found it too disagreeable to tell. I therefore proceeded as though I was completely *convinced* of the trustworthiness of my technique.
>
> (pp. 153–54, my italics)

He was also convinced that the *scenes* would lead him to understand the formation of her symptoms. Fräulein Elisabeth was no easy patient. She resisted and refused to talk about what was in her mind. Her painful legs "joined in the conversation" by hurting at particular moments. He confirmed what he had learned with Frau Emmy: only the complete story, the entire representational process, was therapeutic. The pain became a clue for Freud. It "would reach its climax when she was in the act of telling me the essential and decisive part of what she had to communicate, and with the last word of this it would disappear" (p. 148). If the pain did not go away, Freud knew that "she had not told me everything, and insisted on her continuing her story till the pain had been talked away" (ibid.). It became clear to him that *her leg pains were in fact Fräulein Elisabeth's manner of speaking* what she could put into words only at Freud's insistence that she say everything to him. In spite of all his efforts Freud's treatment offered only meager results. Freud was determined to find the incriminating evidence and persisted in his search for actual traumatic memories. He resorted to a *detective's* technique, bringing the accused to the *scene* of the crime: he did not hesitate to send her "to visit her sister's grave," or to go "to a party at which she might once more come across the friend of her youth" (p. 149). Nothing came of it.

The treatment was carried out at the patient's home. One day circumstances gave a critical clue: when Fräulein Elisabeth heard the steps and the voice of her widowed brother-in-law, she "got up and asked that we might break off for the day" and it was at that moment that "her facial expression and gait betrayed the sudden emergence of severe pains" (p. 155). Freud, *the detective*, took notice. His exploration led to the day when Fräulein Elisabeth and her brother-in-law had taken a long walk together that awoke in her a strong desire to have a husband like him. A few days later, she returned to the place and replayed her wish to herself. That afternoon the pains returned never to go away. Then, with Freud's help, she recovered the key memory that would solve the mystery. It proved to be the moment when she found herself looking at her dead sister in her bed and a "thought had shot through Elisabeth's mind, and now forced itself irresistibly upon her once more, like a flash of lightning in the dark: 'Now he is free again and I can be his wife'" (p. 156). Finally this powerfully repressed wish had come to light and been shared with Freud. Very strong defenses had been overcome. Fräulein Elisabeth cried intensely yet Freud did not spare her his conclusion: "So for a long time you had been in love with your brother-in-law" (p. 157). She immediately experienced intense pain and made one last desperate effort to reject the explanation: "it was not true, I had talked her into it . . . It was easy to prove to her that what she herself had told me admitted of no other interpretation" (p. 157). Finally, and after much suffering, she accepted his interpretation as correct.

In discussing the case Freud wrote a sentence that has become well known and received much comment: "It still strikes me myself as strange that the case histories I write should read like short stories" (p. 160). He came to understand that real-life scenes created "an intimate connection between the story of the patient's sufferings and the symptoms of his illness" (p. 161). Moral conflict was at the center of Fräulein Elisabeth's suffering: "The *motive* was that of defence, the refusal on the part of the patient's whole ego [*Ich*] to come to terms with this ideational group [*Vorstellunggruppe*]. The *mechanism* was that of conversion: i.e. in place of the mental pains which she avoided, physical pains made their appearance" (p. 166, my italics). In Freud's view at this point in his theorizing, the psychic trauma occurred at the moment in which there had been a transient communication between the incompatible idea – I am in love with my brother-in law – and "the main stream of her thoughts" (p. 167). The conversion did not take place at that moment, however, but when the memory of it re-emerged. Freud attributed the physical symptoms – that is, the conversion – to the displacement of affect from the psychic realm to the somatic. In my view a question remains: where do we locate the affect when the *motive* is the inability to tolerate *seeing oneself* in love with a person one should not love? When one cannot conceive of oneself as capable of loving such a person? Is it true that the affect can be separated from the representation? The fact is that Elisabeth von R. improved when she became able to accept that *she* was capable of being in love with her sister's husband and to acknowledge that *she* had actually rejoiced after her sister's death because she thought her brother-in-law was now free to marry her. Now she could *see herself* in the *scene* of loving him and even marrying him without having to repress it, even if this recognition simultaneously caused her joy and great moral repugnance and shame. Is the symptom the result of converting the quota of affect or the result of converting the mode of presenting oneself to oneself and others in a particular cultural context? Is it a manner of saying, "I am sick: my legs hurt terribly," instead of "I hurt terribly because I cannot have the man I want most." This is the great conundrum of the representational mind: do we feel what we feel *because* we perceive and represent ourselves in lived *scenes* all the time?

Fräulein Elisabeth showed Freud what psychical resistance can do. The term *resistance* originated in the patient's efforts not to do what the analyst has insisted must be done: to remember, to visualize the event, to feel, and to communicate it all. Freud described what intense effort it cost *him* to overcome the patient's resistance to doing such psychic work. Her first line of resistance was not to remember lived moments of her life; her second line dismissed the importance of what had come to her mind and she kept it to herself. Freud had to repeat his injunctions to get her to remember and to communicate her memories to him. Once he even threatened her, saying that she would never get well if she did not talk about her private life. Freud proposed that the resistances arise from "the subject's will" (p. 271), from her determination to avoid seeing, feeling, and describing what was there in her mind "close at hand" (ibid.). Theoretically he says that they are there "in proper order. It is only a question of removing the resistances that bar the way to the organized material" because in the past "they have been completed at some time and are stored up in the memory" (p. 287).

Let us now consider this case in the terminology of *On Aphasia*: once the object-representation, that is, scene, event, or experience, has been formed, it is there, ready to be found through its innumerable multisensory associations and to evoke visual components capable of linking it to words. In the therapeutic process fragments or pieces of the original representation will appear in the patient's mind. Freud concludes: "It is the psychotherapist's business to put these together once more into the organization which he presumes to have existed" (p. 291); in other words, to restore the integrity of the psychical representation.

In summary, object-representations and their equivalents in Freud's clinical vocabulary – events, scenes, experiences, precipitating traumas – are never presented in *Studies on Hysteria* as a *replica* of a perceived reality; they have been expanded and subjectively organized due to the automatic associative process of the perceiving subject. The individual's perceptions are never immaculate and remain private, unknowable to others, unless they can be put into the language of the person's community and spoken to another person. The therapist's attempts to revive them in analysis aim at counteracting *the traumatic power still alive in the disowned representations or scenes* from the immediate or remote past. The analyst must insist that the patient remember them and help the analysand by following the inexorable lead given by the patient's associations.

It remains unclear how Freud conceived of the *mechanism* of expressing affects in words and the *location* of the affect in relation to a particular representation. As Forrester points out, the model in *On Aphasia* included only the semantic dimension of words (Forrester 1980, 37); in *Studies on Hysteria* talking serves the purpose of discharging disturbing strangulated affects, a hybrid concept that added *clinical observations* to an affectless theoretical apparatus. But be that as it may, the analysis has the power to cure the *asymbolic aphasia* of the hysteric who had deprived the representation of her pathogenic scenes of their link to verbal and affective expression. Freud's *technical* proposal was unavoidable: "Words are the essential tool of mental treatment." It seems obvious to us today, but it was a most daring proposition to the medical world of the end of the nineteenth century.

I hope to have shown clearly that Freud's understanding of the psychopathology of hysteria and his theory of its treatment were directly linked to the model he had constructed in *On Aphasia* for the disturbance of the speech function he called *asymbolic aphasia*.

Next I will examine Freud's understanding of the function of words in *The Interpretation of Dreams*.

Notes

1 This paper was first published in 1890 under the German title *Psychische Behandlung (Seelenbehandlung)* in *Die Gesundheit*, edited by R. Kossmann and J. Weiss, 1st ed., 1, 368–84 (Stuttgart: Union Deutsche Verlagsgesellschaft). Strachey mistakenly believed that it was published in a later edition of *Die Gesundheit*.

2 The expression *dem Ich* is peculiar. *Ich* – I – is a pronoun and Freud is using it as a noun. The concept of the ego was to come much later in Freud's theorizing. Here, I suggest that we understand it as a hybrid notion, a complex that combines the person who represses the representations and the group of internal processes that carry it out.

3 The term *unconscious* had already been used by Breuer in reporting the case of Anna O. Here the term has acquired its essential meaning of the psychoanalytic term.

References

Breuer, Josef, and Sigmund Freud. *Studies on Hysteria*. Vol. 2 of *Standard Edition*. London: Hogarth Press, 1893–1895.

Farrell, Ralph B. *Dictionary of German Synonyms.* Cambridge: Cambridge University Press, 1977.

Forrester, John. *Language and the Origins of Psychoanalysis.* New York: Columbia University Press, 1980.

Freud, Sigmund. *On Aphasia: A Critical Study.* Trans. Erwin Stengel. 1953. New York: International Universities Press, 1891.

———. Psychical (or Mental) Treatment. Vol. 7 of *Standard Edition.* 1890, 281–302. London: Hogarth Press, 1905.

Rizzuto, Ana-María. Freud's Speech Apparatus and Spontaneous Speech. *International Journal of Psycho-Analysis* 74 (1993): 113–27.

———. Freud's Theoretical and Technical Models in *Studies on Hysteria. International Review of Psycho-Analysis* 19 (1992): 169–78.

———. A Hypothesis about Freud's Motive for Writing the Monograph *On Aphasia. International Review of Psychoanalysis* 16 (1989): 111–17.

4
THE FUNCTION OF THE SPOKEN WORD IN *THE INTERPRETATION OF DREAMS*

In *The Interpretation of Dreams* (Freud 1900) Freud created an extremely complex web of concepts to understand the meaning of dreams. Any attempt to focus on one particular aspect of his theories will necessarily fail to do justice to his carefully orchestrated conception of the elements forming the dream structure. Nonetheless, one can legitimately examine his explicit and implicit understanding of the function of words and imagery in dreaming and ponder what light the model of the speech apparatus and its functioning casts on the interpretation of dreams and the organization of the mental apparatus. This chapter also includes an examination of Freud's later writings on dreams because they form a continuum in his expanding understanding of patients' *intrapsychic* reality. Freud considered that "the interpretation of dreams is like a window through which we can get a glimpse of the interior of that [mental] apparatus" (p. 219). He welcomed such a window for he was convinced that this interior was unconscious: "Everything conscious has an unconscious preliminary stage. . . . The unconscious is the true psychical reality; *in its innermost nature it is as much unknown to us as the reality of the external world, and it is as incompletely presented by the data of consciousness as is the external world by the communications of our sense organs*" (p. 613, my underlining).

Upon examining several of his foundational texts we will come to see the persistence of several concepts first presented in *On Aphasia*. We will discover that when the dream interpretation is completed we witness the undoing of a variety of *asymbolic aphasia*, the expression in words of thoughts and scenes that belong together but have been kept apart by censorship and the masterful efforts of the dream-work. We will notice that the notion of object-representation as the element that must be linked to words to achieve meaning is progressively – and without explanation – replaced by thoughts and scenes in Freud's theorizing. The latter appear as the dominant form for retrieving both the memories used in forming the dream structure *and* selecting words that sustain the imagery. We will learn about Freud's conviction that imagery is regressive and that he anchored this concept in contemporaneous philologists research on 'primitive' languages. We will also encounter the ever-present tension between the *purposive* psychic life of the individual and Freud's conception of a self-sufficient mental apparatus and its predecessor, the speech apparatus. There is also another element present beside the apparatus, namely: the affect that is invariably present in the dreamer's experience.

An analysand's words are the only tool available for opening the dream's window and allow the therapist to *see* (a visual term) the workings of the unconscious mind. The word 'glimpse' is apt for, as Freud shows, most of what is to be uncovered pertains to imagery, scenes, and memories of events in the individual's life. The analyst learns about the dream only when the patient narrates it to her as a visual and sensory description of the situations – scenes – in which the patient found himself in the dream. As we know from *On Aphasia* words have no *personal meaning* unless they find apt representation in the analysand's mind. Freud, however, masterfully demonstrates how far removed from the true personal reality of the dreamer are the words that portray his imagery and experiences in the *manifest dream* he reports to the analyst.

Freud's complex model for reaching the *personal meaning* of a dream (when simplified to its essential elements) has the same structure as the aphasia model. In the latter, meaning comes from the proper articulation of word and representation; in the interpretation of dreams the meaning becomes manifest when the repressed dream-thoughts finally come to light and are articulated in words. The word in both cases – in speech and in dreaming – allows access to the internal perceptions and representations, but cannot encompass all the staggering complexity of the mind's representational processes. This conclusion did not deter Freud from attempting to understand the unconscious processes involved in forming the dream imagery and scenes and in the elaboration of the thoughts and feelings that condition the emergence of a particular manifest dream. In the end, he created a comprehensive theory about the functions, motives, and dynamic processes, a model, that contributes to the understanding of our dreaming life. In this chapter I will limit my discussion to Freud's view of the links between all the mental processes that converge in the formation of the dream imagery and the words that permit access to them.

The structure of dreams

For Freud "dreams are nothing other than a particular *form* of thinking, made possible by the conditions of the state of sleep. It is the *dream-work* which creates that form, and it alone is the essence of dreaming – the explanation of its peculiar nature" (footnote added to p. 506 of *The Interpretation of Dreams* in 1925, italics in the original). Dreams are concerned with the life of the dreamer and form a continuum with it, in particular with his recent experiences (pp. 7, 589). In waking and in dreaming states alike, psychic life is guided by *purposes*. Freud says emphatically: "No influence that we can bring to bear upon our mental processes can ever enable us to think without purposive ideas; nor am I aware of any states of psychical confusion which can do so" (p. 528). Dreaming determines its own processes by following purposes that are not consciously known to the dreamer, but which are nonetheless his own. The essence of dream interpretation consists in making those hidden purposes accessible to conscious awareness. In other words, although dreaming is of one cloth with the psychic life of the individual, the actual *manifest* dream imagery and the words that describe it appear more frequently than not as silly, surprising, incomprehensible, or amusing to the dreamer. The *purpose* of his dream escapes his conscious awareness. Psychoanalysis aims at making that purpose available to the dreamer by articulating it in words.

Freud described four components of the dream structure: (1) the manifest experience and imagery, a virtual reality, that the dreamer perceives internally and describes verbally to the analyst; (2) the dream-thoughts that have contributed to the formation of the manifest dream and that emerge in verbal form upon the analyst's request that the patient describe what occurs to him in relation to individual elements of the manifest content; (3) the dream wish and the latent content as the motivational sources of the dream; and (4) the dream-work, which is the core of dreaming. The dream-work's *unconscious processes* transform memories, somatic stimuli, the day's residues, dream-thoughts, dream-wishes and their latent content, to give them an internal perceptual form in the manifest dream's imagery that is acceptable to the dreamer's censorship.

The dream-work is a transformative process applied to the dream elements to disguise unacceptable wishes. It employs condensation, displacement, conditions of representability, and, finally, secondary revision to give the deceptive manifest content a certain intelligibility (p. 499) and to form a relatively meaningful scenario in the manifest dream content.

The manifest content is what the dreamer knows *consciously* upon awakening about his experience during sleep. The more or less vivid imagery can be described in words to oneself or to another as the internal perceptions and feelings the dreamer recalls. The prevalent form of these images is visual, but the dream may also include verbal and auditory experiences as well as sensations of touch, smell, taste, bodily movements, and visceral feelings. The vividness and dramatization of events in the *manifest content* are decoys to distract the dreamer from his true concerns.

What is this manifest content? First, "it is of it alone that we have immediate knowledge" (Freud 1915–1916, 181). Second, "whatever the dreamer *tells us* must count as his dream, without regard to what he [the patient] must have forgotten or altered in recalling it" (ibid., p. 85, my italics). The patient's *words* report the *dream scene* ['I was riding a big motorcycle on a highway'] that includes visual, sensory, and feeling components. If we were to follow Freud's conception in *On Aphasia*, I should say that the reporting words of the patient have been linked to the entire dream *scene* – a sort of representational complex – that he has seen in the internal *perception* of his manifest dream. At one level we must say that such an assumption *is* correct, but at another level, there is a critical difference. In *On Aphasia*, the word *did* link to the visual representation of a mental object, whose *psychic* value and reality were not challenged: the mental representation of an apple would be named by the word "apple." That is not the case with the manifest dream. Other processes are involved that challenge its validity as a genuine psychical representation. An apple in a dream *is* and *is not* an apple: it functions as a *decoy* in the form of an apple, a *distortion* effected by the displacement and condensation that the *dream-work* has imposed on the actual thought processes of the dreamer. Yet, the dream itself is genuine and must have an anchor in the person's actual (if unconscious) purposes and motives. Freud *adds* to the representational process the affective experience of the dreamer: "*affects* [*Affektentwicklung*] in dreams cannot be judged in the same way as the remainder of their content" (1900, p. 74). He illustrates the point with an example from Stricker (1879, p. 51): "'If, for instance, one is afraid of robbers in a dream, the robbers, it is true, are imaginary – but the fear is real'" (1900, p. 74). In the example, affect means the *feeling* experienced by the dreamer.

Freud clearly separates affect from representational material in the manifest dream content: "It will be noticed that the affect [*Empfindung*] felt in the dream belongs to its latent and not to its manifest content, and that the dream's *affective* content [*Affektinhalt*] has remained untouched by the distortion which has overtaken its *ideational* [representational] content [*Vorstellungsinhalt*]" (1900, pp. 248–49). Here affect [*Empfindung*] refers to the person's feelings. The word "affect" [*Affektinhalt*], therefore, carries two meanings in this context: (1) the person's feeling in the dream; and (2) the various affects linked to the elements that constitute its *latent content.* Freud concludes: "Thus it appears that affects in dreams are fed from a confluence of several sources and are over-determined in their reference to the material of the dream-thoughts. *During the dream-work, sources of affect [Affektquellen] which are capable of producing the same affect [Affekt] come together in generating it*" (1900, p. 480). Freud does not explain *what* the sources are but describes the process in which they play a role: "These sources have succeeded in setting up an associative link with the real releasing cause, and the desired path from the release of their own affect [*Affektentbindung*] has been opened by the other source of affect, which is unobjectionable and legitimate" (p. 479). In my reading of it, this conclusion implies that the mind has found a way of *comparing* the affects of the sources. How could that happen when Freud asserts that there are no unconscious affects?

Many years later in his paper *The Unconscious* (Freud 1915b) Freud attempted to clarify the issue: "Unconscious ideas continue to exist after repression as actual structures in the system Ucs., whereas all that corresponds in that system to unconscious affects [*unbewußten Affekt*] is a potential beginning which is prevented from developing" (p. 178). Much earlier he had given his only explicit description of the process: "In mental functions something is to be distinguished – a quota of affect or sum of excitation [*Affektbetrag, Erregungssumme*] – which possesses all the characteristics of a quantity (though we have no means of measuring it), which is capable of increase, diminution, displacement and discharge, and which is spread over the memory-traces of ideas [*Vorstellungen*] somewhat as an electric charge is spread over the surface of a body" (Freud 1894, 60).

We encounter here a critical problem in Freud's theorizing originating in the speech apparatus model and carried over to the mental apparatus: there is no person in charge of such apparatuses, no subject to experience the feelings. Affect is a quantitative, quasi-electrical process of discharge overshadowing meaningful representations. Freud acknowledged: "We do not regard our knowledge about affects [*Affekte*] as very assured either; it is a first attempt at finding our bearings in this obscure region" (Freud 1916–1917, 396).

The issue is indeed obscure. If the sources connect to give rise to similar *potential affects* as Freud says, how does the mind determine *which* affects should be linked to each other? Would it not make more sense to assume that the mind registers experiences as complete memories of a lived affective moment, *personal scenes*, which, as Freud stated in *On Aphasia* using the term *object-representation*, remain latent until they return to full experiential life when the same state of the cortex is activated? Contemporary experiments seem to support this point (Heilbrunn 1979): reports that Penfield provided direct evidence of the phenomenon. Penfield stimulated the exposed human temporal cortex with electrodes during brain surgery and the patients reported that specific visual and acoustic memories came to mind with the corresponding feelings, ranging from pleasure to fear. The electrical stimulation could elicit these memories at will by stimulating the same or closely adjacent points of the right or left temporal cortex (Penfield 1958).

I am therefore proposing that if experiences are registered as memory processes of scenes that include a *person's* involvement in an event and feelings related to it, then the unconscious mind does have the possibility of comparing different events and combining the feelings into genuine affect in a dream, as Freud asserted. The so-called process of discharge can be conceptualized as the person feeling the full impact of a particular experience, be it in the present, in a dream, or in analysis, as it occurred when Fräulein Elisabeth finally acknowledged her wish to marry her widowed brother-in-law. Reflecting on the *Burning child* dream, Freud comments: "Here we have the most general and the most striking psychological characteristic of the process of dreaming: a thought, and as a rule a thought of something that is wished, is objectified in the dream, is *represented as a scene*, or, as it seems to us, is *experienced*" (Freud 1900, 534, my italics). And I would like to add, experience involves feelings. The dream-work, keeping up with the requirement of repression to suppress the development of distressing affect (Freud 1915b, 178), distorts the representations but without succeeding in its aim in the end. There is no need to disagree with Freud's statement here. What needs to be questioned is the means the mind employs to protect *the person* from feeling an unacceptable affect. Is it true that the mind separates affect from representations as memories? And if it does this, how does the mind recognize that the affect *belongs* to a particular memory? I suggest that it is not the memory or the representation that classifies the affects but rather the feeling person who *remembers himself* in situations in which he experienced the same affect and then activates the memory of events and scenes from the past.

Freud had already added affect to the *On Aphasia* model, specifically the connection between recollected representations and memories to words, when describing the clinical data he and Breuer observed in treating hysterics: if the words did not allow for the *discharge* of affect, the *symptoms* remained unchanged. I would prefer to say in my revised terminology that if the patient did not fully remember and express to her doctor what she had felt in the original experience, she could not change. To my way of thinking the so-called discharge represents the now revived psycho-physiological expression, *das Psychische* of *On Aphasia*, of the impact of the original experience upon the patient's psyche.

Freud uses the same term he had used in *On Aphasia* to describe the manifest dream, namely "complex": "In the case of the psychical complex [*psychischen Komplex*] which has come under the influence of the censorship imposed by resistance, the *affects* [*Affekte*] are the constituent which is least influenced and which alone can give us a pointer as to how we should fill in the missing thoughts." The German original says *"zur richtigen Ergänzung,"* meaning the correct completion of the representational complex after undoing the censorship (Freud 1900, 461). The completion means, I believe, reaching the original repressed thought that motivated the person's dream. When this is achieved the meaningful scene/representation becomes linked to the words that name it in analysis, making it possible to revive the feelings originally experienced and undo the defensive asymbolic aphasia. There are several steps to follow to arrive at this repressed thought by undoing the dream-work's many deceptive maneuvers. Freud presents the case of the young woman who dreamed she saw her sister's only surviving child lying in a coffin and felt no pain nor was she aware of a wish for him to die. Her associations disclosed that when her sister's first child had died, a man she was in love with had come to offer his condolences. The dream suggested that he could return if the other child also died. Freud commented: ". . . the emotional behavior in the dream was appropriate to the real content which lay in the background [latent dream-thoughts and wishes] and not to what was pushed into the foreground [manifest dream of the dead child]." Because "the dream-situation anticipated the meeting she had so long desired, it offered no basis for any painful feelings" (Freud 1901, 675).

Freud came to understand that "dreams insist with greater energy upon their right to be included among our real mental experiences in respect to their affective [*Affekinhalt*] than in respect to their ideational content" (Freud 1900, 460). Now, he had to find an explanation for the primacy of the affect over the representation. His solution consisted in removing the affect as an obligatory component of a representational complex. He said: "A necessary premise to all of this is that the release of affect [*Affekentbindung*] and the ideational content [*Vorstellungsinhalt*] do not constitute the indissoluble organic unity as we are in the habit of treating them, but that these two separate entities may be merely *soldered* together and can thus be detached from each other by analysis. Dream-interpretation shows that this is in fact the case" (pp. 461–62). All the dream-work can do is to transform the representations of "the dream-thoughts into the fulfillment of a wish, while the distressing affect [*Affekt*] persists unaltered" (Freud 1915–1916, 215).

The censorship is responsible for the separation: "the censorship exercises its office and brings about the distortion of dreams . . . it does so *in order to prevent the generation of anxiety or other forms of distressing affect* [*Affekts*, as feelings]" (Freud 1900, 267). There is a problem with this formulation, however, because what is prevented from emerging is not the affect as something *soldered* to the representational complex, but rather the affect [feeling] that may emerge if *the person becomes aware of the dream-thoughts* and their implications.

As late as 1933 in *New Introductory Lectures* Freud asserted: "The different ideas [*Vorstellungen*] in the dream-thoughts are, indeed, not all of equal value; they are cathected with quotas of affect [*mit . . . Affektbeträgen besetzt*] of varying magnitude" (Freud 1933, 20). He continues: "In the dream-work these ideas are separated from the affects [*Affekten*] *attaching* to them. The affects are dealt with independently; they may be displaced on to something else, they may be retained, they may undergo alterations, or they may not appear in the dream at all" (ibid., my italics). Here Freud is talking about affect not as a feeling, but as something that *exists on its own*. Finally, if we return to the motives of the censorship, the ideas must be distorted to avoid the *generation* of painful affect [feelings]. He returns to his conception in *On Aphasia* regarding the *innervation* of representations: "as a motor or secretory function, *the key to whose innervation lies in the ideas* [*Vorstellungen*] *in the Ucs.* Owing to the domination established by the *Pcs.* these ideas are, as it were, throttled, and *inhibited from sending out impulses* which would generate affect [*Affekt*, feelings in the person]" (Freud 1900, 582, my italics). In the monograph the representations would stimulate the person's production of pertinent speech, but in here Freud seems to say that if that happens an affective experience would follow.

I am once again struck by the ever-present tension in Freud's work between mental *mechanisms* and *purposes, will, and subjective experiences.* Speaking is the intentional action of a person; feeling is also an experience of the total person, yet Freud seemed to locate the 'innervation' of affect in ideas [*Vorstellungen*] that are in themselves unconscious. The confusion stems from the models proposed in *On Aphasia* where stimulated representations lead to speech and in *The Project* (Freud 1950 [1895]) where affect is presented as a quantity. Laplanche and Pontalis reflect: "It is hard to see how the term affect could remain intelligible without some reference to self-consciousness" (Laplanche and Pontalis 1973, 14). I may sum up this discussion by saying that the representational processes of the mind offer to a self-conscious subject the opportunity to respond to what they mean to him with a corresponding affect [feeling], and that such affect would remain potential – as Freud stated – as long as the thoughts remain unconscious. This conclusion seems compatible with Freud's assertion that the preconscious [of the person] inhibits the ideas from sending out impulses which could generate affect if we keep in mind that it is not impulses that generate the affect [feeling] but the subject's awareness and interpretation of the *meaning* they have for him. The young woman mentioned above did not want to acknowledge her wish to see the man she loved again, so she unconsciously created a dream scenario where he would appear.

The wish to see the man constitutes what Freud described as the latent content of the dream. It emerges after the entirety of the dream-thoughts have been examined and interpreted during the analysis; they converge to show the person's central concerns: "It is from these dream-thoughts and not from a dream's manifest content that we disentangle its meaning" (Freud 1900, 277). They encompass every element of the person's life that has contributed to the elaboration of the dream-thoughts to create the dream scenes: memories from childhood and later life; bodily experiences and impressions; a multitude of events from the past or the present; thoughts about things seen, read, or imagined; in brief, anything that forms part of our everyday mental processes. All of these components center around scenes consciously or unconsciously desired by the individual.

Freud's constant use of the terms "scene" and "event" or their equivalents to refer to the dream imagery, the patient's memories and imaginings, convinces me that Freud had the actual person in mind when writing about dreams but his concern about creating a scientific model for speech and the mind as *apparatuses* capable of producing the observed phenomena through the functioning of their gears interfered with his including the living person in his models. The mental apparatus worked like a well-oiled machine without the formal inclusion of the dreamer's agency as the central organizer. Meissner (1999)[1] suggests the concept of self-as-agent to address this problem.

As theoretical constructs the speech apparatus and the mental apparatus offer the basic tenet of Freud's understanding of what is needed in clinical work, namely, to give meaning to unconscious processes. Regardless of whether they are representational complexes or a dream, they need to have their visual component(s) linked to words spoken to the analyst so that their meaning emerges.

Dream-work and the manifest content of dreams

Freud conceived of dreaming as a "particular *form* of thinking" during sleep. The construction of a dream calls for two separate functions: "the production of the dream-thoughts, and their transformation into the [manifest] content of the dream" (Freud 1900, 506). The task of the "dream-work is under some kind of necessity to combine all the sources which have acted as stimuli for the dream into a *single unit* in the dream itself" (ibid., 179, my italics). The core issue of the dream-work concerns the process of transforming thoughts into the specific visual, sensory, experiential scenes of the manifest dream.

Freud did not clarify what he meant when he introduced the term "dream-thoughts." Later in Chapter VII he described thought as the process that starts with the early experience of satisfaction and continues in an effort to attain a re-cathexis of that memory by carrying out particular actions. Freud introduced two types of thought available to the mind: (1) the primary process whose aim consists in obtaining a replication of the experience of satisfaction in a 'perceptual identity' [*Wahrnehmungsidentität*]; and (2) the secondary process which seeks to establish a 'thought identity' [*Denkidentität*]. He added: "Thinking must concern itself with the connecting path between ideas [*Vorstellungen*], without being led astray by the intensities [*Intensitäten*] of those ideas" (1900, p. 602). Does the term "intensities" here mean a subjective feeling or quota of affect? Freud is talking about rational logic-based thinking, yet the phrasing implies that the 'intensities' *belong* to and can *lead* the idea. The primary process, however, in its search for satisfaction connects the representations [*Vorstellungen*] freely and issues substitutions at will but the dream-work has to process them to produce a dream that avoids unpleasure, fulfills the dreamer's wish, and is acceptable to the censorship. This is the essence of dream-work. To make the nature of such work clear Freud resorted to a metaphor about language:

> The dream-thoughts and the dream-content are presented to us like two versions of the same subject-matter in *two different languages*. Or, more properly, the dream-content [manifest] seems like a *transcript* [*Übertragung*] of the dream-thoughts into another mode of expression, whose *characters and syntactic laws* it is our business to discover by comparing the original and the *translation* [*Übersetzung*]. The dream-thoughts are immediately comprehensible, as soon as we have learnt them [from the patient's words]. The dream-content, on the other hand, is expressed as it were in a *pictographic script*, the characters of which have to be *transposed individually* into the language of the dream-thoughts. If we attempted to read these characters according to their pictorial value instead of their *symbolic function*, we should clearly be led into error.
>
> *(Freud 1900, 277, my italics)*

In this passage Freud established a drastic separation between imagery and thoughts, thoughts which were only accessible to the analyst through what came to the patient's mind [*Einfälle*] and was expressed in spoken associations. There is no reference to the conception of the spoken word in *On Aphasia*, in which the visual component of the thing-representation and the word-representation must be joined together for the word to acquire meaning. It is true that thought might not require words, but it is equally true that the analyst has no access to either the dream imagery or the dream-thoughts unless the patient describes them in words. According to Freud, the dream imagery and the scenes it presents are a deceptive portrayal of the thoughts, another language that calls for translation. Freud opted to apply to imagery the laws that apply to ordinary language. He was determined to decipher the "characters and syntactic laws" of the pictorial language and then find a way of "comparing the original and the translation." We have here the essence of Freud's theorizing about the emergence of the dream imagery and scenarios. He used the contemporaneous theories about languages, philology, and ancient scripts as models to understand the two components of the dream "language," the pictorial manifest dream and the dream-thoughts with their complex symbolic and dynamic meanings. The *translation* from one language into the other was critical for Freud because he wanted to rebut the notion that dreams were nonsensical as they seem to be in the manifest dream (Freud 1900, 278), and also to affirm that they can be "used in analysis like any other communication" (Freud 1933, 9).

The dream-work has transformed meaningful dream-thoughts into the non-sensical *pictographic* dream content. Freud was determined to undo the separation inflicted by the defenses upon the desires and the conflicting thoughts by joining them together again during the analytic process. *It was another way of undoing a different variety of asymbolic aphasia by given words and feelings to what the analysand wanted and did not want to articulate to himself in conscious words and feelings – his unconscious wishes.* The dream wishes "exist in the unconscious" (Freud 1900, 308) and "are always on the alert" (ibid., p. 553). In Freud's appraisal "*a conscious wish can only become a dream-instigator if it succeeds in awakening an unconscious wish* <u>with the same tenor</u> *and in obtaining reinforcement from it*" (ibid., my underlining). In a footnote on the same page Freud returns to concepts he had presented in *On Aphasia* (without mentioning it), which can now be linked to the manner of functioning of the primary process: "They [unconscious wishes] share this character of *indestructibility* with all other mental acts which are truly unconscious, i.e. which belong to the system *Ucs* only. These are the *paths which have been laid down once and for all which never fall* into disuse and which, whenever an unconscious excitation re-cathects them, are always ready to conduct the excitatory process to discharge" (footnote, p. 553, my italics). He had described in the monograph the indestructibility of registered perceptions and the facilitation paths they leave behind.

Laplanche and Pontalis reflect about the primary process: "With the notion of perceptual identity, we leave the economic realm and direct our attention to the equivalences which are set up between ideas" [*Vorstellungen*] (Laplanche and Pontalis 1973, 305). In fact, the experience of satisfaction gives a *new meaning* to the term 'object' as a representation. In the *Project for a Scientific Psychology* and in Chapter VII of *The Interpretation of Dreams*, Freud links such experience to the infant's need for *a person* who offers relief. Such a person becomes the satisfying object linked to the registration of the experience of satisfaction. Here Freud has given a different meaning to the word 'object' as a perception and a representation: it no longer means anything that can be represented but the encounter with the person who offered satisfaction. What is the form that the person-object takes as a representation in the mind? Once more, Freud seems to isolate the object as a part of the total experience. The representation will be formed as any other object is, but as I have suggested (Rizzuto 2003), it involves the total experience including the experiencing child's self – inchoate as it is at that period – in relation to the helping object. To put it briefly and in Freud's own words, the representation must include the *total scene* of the *experience* of satisfaction, not just the object of satisfaction. The perceptual identity therefore seeks the reproduction of an experiential scene. The dream-work ensures that an unacceptable "object of satisfaction" does not appear explicitly.

The concept of regression in relation to thoughts, words, and imagery

Freud believed that in normal thinking remembering brings back memory traces and images, but we never consciously achieve the "revival of the *perceptual* images" (Freud 1900, 543). Dreams, however, achieve a regression that reaches *primitive* forms of representation (p. 548). Later, in *A Metapsychological Supplement to the Theory of Dreams*, he explains how this happens: "In this process thoughts are transformed into images, mainly of a visual sort; that is to say, word-presentations are taken back to thing-presentations which correspond to them, as if, in general, the process were dominated by considerations of *representability*" (Freud 1917a, 228, my underlining). In my reading, 'taken back' must mean *before* the already formed thing-presentation found a word-presentation to create a meaningful word. This brings up the notion of "functional retrogression" of the speech apparatus "to earlier states of its functional development" Freud 1953 [1891], 87, a notion in *On Aphasia* that Freud adopted from British neurologist Hughlings Jackson. In the present context it means a regression to *earlier* sensory representations, in particular to their visual component. Freud also calls them *primitive* in the formal sense of regression to primary modes of expression (Freud 1900, 548). He says explicitly in the *Introductory Lectures on Psycho-Analysis* that "the regression of the dream-work is not only a formal but also a *material* one. It not only *translates* our thoughts into a *primitive* form of expression; but it also revives the characteristics of our *primitive* mental life" (Freud 1915–1916, 211, my italics). In the same work, Freud compares his manner of interpreting dreams to the deciphering of cuneiform Babylonian-Assyrian inscriptions, that is., the arrival at an understanding of earlier dead languages by those who investigated them (p. 232). He is saying that primitive early mental representations use thing-representations for thinking. Once more, this conception implies that early in development *isolated things* – object-representations – are direct objects of perception rather than the child's complex perceptual experience of an event. I believe that the persistence of such a conception relates to the fact that Freud attended only to substantives and the external objects of perception in *On Aphasia*. Now this same view reappears in the 'considerations of representability' in *The Interpretation of Dreams*.

I find it impossible to accept that babies have this kind of perceptions – isolated objects – and to call what babies perceive a primitive process. Even early in development babies are fairly competent in forming representations. Freud implied it when he described object-representation as expandable. In his December 6, 1896, letter to Fliess, Freud returns to the ideas about memory traces he had expressed in *On Aphasia*:

> I am working on the assumption that our psychic mechanism has come into being by a process of stratification: the material present in the form of memory traces being subjected from time to time to a *rearrangement* [*Umordnung*] in accordance with fresh circumstances – to a *retranscription* [*Umschrift*], thus what is essentially new about my theory is the thesis that memory is present not once but several times over, that it is laid down in various kinds of indications. I postulated a similar kind of rearrangement some time ago (*Aphasia*) for the paths leading from the periphery [of the body to the cortex].
> *(Freud 1985, 207)*

Freud was referring to the changes in *meaning* which he postulated the sensory information undergoes whenever a nerve passes through a gray nucleus in the nervous system. Rearrangements and retranscriptions are seen as processes taking place in *developmental time*; this means that they must add the modalities of the new mental capacities acquired by the individual at the moment of their occurrence. Such conception creates grave difficulties for the task of achieving unconscious *perceptual identity*, the aim of the primary process. I believe, once more, that Freud's theoretical problem stems from the absence of a self-as-agent who is in charge of desiring and achieving, not the perceptual identity of an *experience* but the unconscious striving to reproduce a similar state of self in the present (Rizzuto 2003). The unconscious components of the agent-self guide the dreamer's search for the satisfaction felt in the past. This reformulation of the experience of satisfaction permits me to reconceive of object-representations not only as expandable but also as harboring the stimuli that in due time may prompt people to speak, as Freud postulated in *On Aphasia*. When the representational complex is expanded and updated it must also include a synchronically integrated representation of the self experienced as satisfied by the caring object that is registered as a significant *unconscious event* or *scene*. Regardless of the level of organization of the subject's self at the time, it is the self's satisfaction felt during the experience that the person might attempt to reproduce in an unconscious search. In other words, perceptual identity creates a state of self-experience *similar* but never identical to the first experience of satisfaction.

Regression and imagery

The dream-work brings permutations and transformations to all the dream's components to form its manifest imagery: wishes seeking fulfillment, earlier mental processes, thoughts from the past, representations and imagery from past experiences or the present, the cathexes [*bezetzen*] of those ideas, transformational processes, and finally, unconscious wishes that claim fulfillment while facing the demands of the censorship.

The dream-work is entirely unconscious and guided by the mode of functioning of the primary process with no access to any high-level function:

> The dream-work is not simply more careless, more irrational, more forgetful and more incomplete than waking thought; it is completely different from it qualitatively and for that reason not immediately comparable with it. It does not think, calculate or judge in any way at all; it restricts itself to giving things a new form. It is exhaustively described by an enumeration of the conditions which it has to satisfy in producing its result. That product, the dream, has above all to evade censorship, and with that end in view the dream-work makes use of a *displacement of psychical intensities* to the point of transvaluation of all psychical values. The thoughts have to be reproduced exclusively or predominately in the material of visual and acoustic memory-traces, and this imposes upon the dream-work *considerations of representability* which it meets by carrying out fresh displacements.
>
> *(1900, p. 507)*

How does the dream-work achieve such change? The general method is all-encompassing: it "makes use, for the purposes of giving visual representation of the dream thoughts, of any methods within its reach, whether waking criticism regards them as legitimate or illegitimate" (ibid., p. 411). It uses condensation, displacement, and considerations of representability, and with some preconscious help, secondary revision to give shape to the dream. The final product, the manifest dream, is nothing but an *illusion* intended to avoid the censorship. Technically, to be able to interpret a manifest dream, the analyst has to insist that it "be broken up once more into fragments" (ibid., p. 449), to access the original wish and thoughts that have been distorted. In fact,

> The dream-work is doing nothing original in making substitutions of this kind . . . it merely follows *the paths which it finds already laid down in the unconscious*; and it gives preference to those transformations of the repressed material which can also become conscious in the form of jokes or allusions and of which the phantasies of neurotic patients are so full.
>
> (ibid., pp. 345–46, my italics)

The paths already there are the facilitation paths Freud described in *On Aphasia*. In dream formation the process involves transforming thoughts into imagery. Freud proposes:

> Of the various subsidiary thoughts attached to the essential dream-thoughts, those will be preferred which admit of *visual representation*; and the dream-work does not shrink from the effort of recasting unadaptable thoughts into a new *verbal form* – even into a less usual one – provided that that process facilitates representation and so relieves the psychological pressure caused by constricted thinking.
>
> (ibid., p. 344, my italics)

I observe that Freud *assumes* that the thoughts to be transformed are connected to words and that the manipulation of the words makes it easier to give visual form to the thought; he thereby returns to the structure of the *meaningful* word in *On Aphasia*. Freud does not say if consciously repressed thoughts have kept their verbal form but clearly states that *thoughts transform words to produce visual imagery*.

Meanwhile, the dream-thoughts undergo their transformations separated from the affects 'attached' to them: "The affects are dealt with independently; they may be displaced onto something else, they may be retained, they may undergo alterations, or they may not appear in the dream at all" (Freud 1933, 20), yet they persist unaltered by the dream work (Freud 1915–1916, 215). Freud asserts that affects are subjected to the process of over-determination, a statement quoted earlier in another context: "*During the dream-work, sources of affect [Affektquellen] which are capable of producing the same affect [Affekt] come together in generating it*" (Freud 1900, 480). Once more the statement implies that the affects *act as organizational agents* on their own initiative, unconsciously gathering similar affective experiences in the formation of the dream. The dreaming person's self who unconsciously organizes the dream and experiences the conscious affect is not part of the equation in the theory, yet it is always there in the *clinical examples*. At one level the dream-work suppresses the affect elicited by unacceptable dream-thoughts and elicits a reversed affect. Freud presents the example of the old gentleman who was afraid of dying and found himself "roaring with laughter" in his dream: "The dream-work succeeded in transforming the gloomy idea [*Idee*] of impotence and death into a comic *scene*, and his sobs into laughter." The next day *he* "was very depressed" (ibid., p. 473, my italics).

Let us look now at some of the illustrations Freud provides to show how words and their transformation function in dream formation. There is something obvious in Freud's understanding of how the dream-work uses words and speech. *It is as though the dream-thoughts have the form of spoken sentences.* The model Freud follows is that of sentence construction in everyday life. This contrasts with his conviction that the dream-work can only use words it borrows from daily life: "For the dream-work cannot actually *create* speeches" (Freud 1900, 418). All it does is to take a piece here and a piece there to form what it needs from consciously worded thoughts or from sentences the person has heard or read (ibid., pp. 419–20). Something similar applies to the manifest dream that has transformed words into images. "A [manifest] dream is a conglomerate which, for purposes of investigation, must be broken up once more into fragments" (ibid., p. 449).

The dream-work's final task is to create the dream's manifest content from multiple and diverse dream-thoughts by finding a common element in them. If it is not readily available "the dream-work sets about *creating* one, so it might be possible for the thoughts to be given a common representation in the dream. The most convenient way of bringing together two <u>dream-thoughts</u> which, to start with, have nothing in common, is <u>to alter the verbal form</u> of one of them, and thus bring it half-way to meet the other, which may be similarly clothed in a new form of words" (Freud 1901, 650, my underlining). What does this assertion imply? Let us look at the example Freud gives from a dream of his own using German words: a noun '*Kosten*', which means economic 'cost' and a verb '*kosten*' which means to try and taste food. The words do not appear in the dream, but in Freud's associations when he found that his latent wish was to get something without paying for it. In the analysis of the dream he realized that the *form* of the thought was useless and changed it to "*<u>I</u> should like some enjoyment without cost*" ['*Kosten*'] (ibid., p. 650, my underlining). In the dream there was a scene where ". . . *spinach was being eaten* . . ." (ibid., p. 636, italics in original). Freud's association to this part of the dream is the maternal scene of encouraging children to taste – '*kosten*' – the spinach before refusing to eat it, as he had done as a child. The identical *sounding* word was the common element. Freud comments: "It may seem strange that the dream-work should make such a free use of verbal ambiguity, but further experience will teach us that the occurrence is quite a common one" (ibid., p. 650). The spinach in the manifest dream had become a *decoy* for the unflattering (repugnant?) thought of wanting enjoyment without cost. He uses this example as an illustration of condensation in dreams.

Freud compares finding of common elements of the dream-work to Francis Galton's construction of family photographs by superimposing single photographs and obtaining a composite picture in which "contradictory details more or less wipe one another out" (ibid., p. 649). Here he is speaking of images superimposed upon one another, but this is different from "verbal ambiguity." It seems to me that Freud is *implicitly* talking about both, images and words. '*Kosten*', the noun in the thought, abstract as it may seem, has as a referent the *scene* of his friend paying for the taxi cab they took together. '*Kosten*' as a verb, on the other hand, refers to another *scene*, in which Freud the child is encouraged by his mother to taste – '*kosten*' – the spinach he disliked. The identical *sound* of the two different words appears in this dream as the bridge to link the two representational components – enjoyment and no cost – in Freud's wish.

In *A Metapsychological Supplement to the Theory of Dreams* Freud states: "It is very noteworthy how little the dream-work keeps to the word-presentations; it is always ready to exchange one word for another till it finds the expression which is most handy for plastic representation." He adds in a footnote that "the dream-work must first replace the text that consists of abstract thoughts by one more concrete" (Freud 1917a, 228). This means that words search for the imagery to give "plastic" form to the dream. We know, however, that in Freud's theory a word is an empty sound unless it is linked to the corresponding multisensory object-representation. On the next page, Freud clarifies that "for a dream all operations with words are no more than a preparation for a *regression* to things" (my italics). What does he mean by "regression to things"? His own answer to this question appears to be: "Regression of *Pcs.* dream-thoughts to mnemic images of things [*Sacherinnerungsbildern*] is clearly the result of the attraction which the *Ucs.* instinctual representatives – e.g. repressed *memories of experiences* [*Erlebniserinnerungen*] – exercise upon the thoughts which have been put into words" (ibid., p. 231, my italics).

We have here a conceptual change: the regression is not to things but to *experiences*, which in my reading take the form of registered *scenes*. The preconscious in dreams permits "a free communication between (*Pcs.*) word-cathexes and (*Ucs.*) thing-cathexes" (ibid., p. 229), which facilitates the creation of "verbal bridges between different groups of material" (ibid.). In brief, there could be verbal *and* pictorial matches searching for imagery fitting the manifest content and capable of avoiding censorship. In fact, I consider that Freud's conception in *On Aphasia* of an ever-expandable object-representation offers a multitude of components readily available for comparison, in particular if one takes into consideration – as I propose – that the experiences that create and expand the representation include some aspect of the subject who does the experiencing. As Freud said in *On Aphasia* there are no pure perceptions or, I say now, pure experiences, because according to him, *to perceive is to associate.* In this respect, the imagery of the *memory* of the childhood *scenes* of tasting spinach, '*kosten*', and the cost, '*Kosten*', that such experience might have had for Freud in the past (as well as the cost of the taxi ride) might be as important as the words that appeared in Freud's associations and contributed to the appearance of spinach in the manifest dream. Words and experiential imagery must converge to create a manifest dream content such as that of spinach being eaten in Freud's dream.

Freud also proposes a *temporal* regression to an earlier stage of psychic development: "Now our thoughts originally arose from sensory images of that kind [mostly of a visual sort]: their first material and their preliminary stages were sense impressions, or, more properly, mnemic images of such impressions. *Only later were words attached to them* and the words in turn linked up into thoughts. The dream-work thus submits thoughts to a *regressive* treatment and undoes their development" (Freud 1915–1916, 180–81, my italics). Freud refers specifically to the attraction of the 'instinctual representatives' from early experiences and the 'mnemic images' of sense impressions prior to language. We must recall that the instinctual representative emerges from the experience of satisfaction that revealed the instinct to the mind (Green 2000). In other words, I am claiming that the *form* in the mind of the instinctual representative and sense impressions *involves registrations of experiential gestalts*. I believe Freud said as much when he conceived of an object-representation in *On Aphasia* as a multisensory complex. The representational process starts at birth and unless we are willing to see an infant as a purely cognitive being, we must acknowledge that psychical representatives ought to register the experience of the *subject* with all type of objects.

The key question that must be asked now is why Freud invokes regression in this context. Is it really necessary to call what occurs regression, that is, a return to an earlier period of development (temporal regression), and to describe earlier representations as more primitive forms (formal regression)? In both dreams and waking life, after all, the imagery of many past moments is always potentially available for recollection and retrieval and the mind calls on it constantly. What is primitive about imagery as a representational means and form, except that in developmental terms it precedes speech? Do we not constantly use sensory imagery to orient ourselves in the external and internal world? Freud's conception seems to me to originate in his comparison of dream language with the findings of philologists of the time about ancient languages. In the *Introductory Lectures on Psycho-Analysis* he stated: "we have long since forgotten from what *concrete image* the word originated and consequently failed to recognize it when it is replaced by the image" (Freud 1915–1916, 121). This assertion does not rest on psychoanalytic theory, rather it is borrowed from the conception of primitive languages and their evolution from pictorial to written form, a view held by many linguists who were contemporaries of Freud. We know today that there are no primitive languages, even if they are pictorial. On the other hand, the *analytic* version of regression is taken from the model developed in the monograph *On Aphasia*:

> The only way in which we can describe what happens in hallucinatory dreams is by saying that the excitation moves in a *backward* direction. Instead of being transmitted towards the *motor* end of the apparatus it moves towards the *sensory* end and finally reaches the perceptual system. If we describe

as 'progressive' the direction taken by psychical processes arising from the unconscious during waking life, then we may speak of dreams as having a 'regressive' character.

(Freud 1900, 542)

The 'progressive' sequence in *On Aphasia* established that the object association produced the stimuli and used its visual component to reach the sound component of the word to activate the motor execution of the spoken word. In *The Interpretation of Dreams* the direction is reversed. There is no motor act; instead the sound component of the word in the mind of the dreamer (*kosten/Kosten*) acts as the stimulus to *activate* the visual image of multisensory object-representations such as a childhood eating scene or a recent taxi ride. To sum up: in normal speech the object associations stimulate the motor articulation of an apt word sound while in dreams the words' sound *in the mind of the dreamer* stimulates the reactivation of previously registered object-representations and scenes.

There is another aspect to the analytic work with dreams that Freud leaves mostly unattended: what happens in the mind of the analyst when she listens to the words describing the dream scene? Freud says very little on the subject, but one of his examples provides important clues. He was listening to a patient's dream that included stairs and reported: "The piece of the dream-content which described how the climb began by being difficult and became easy at the end of the rise *reminded me*, when I heard it, of the masterly introduction to Alphonse Daudet's *Sappho*" (Freud 1900, 285, my italics). We have here a succession of images going through Freud's mind: (1) the images of climbing evoked in his mind while listening to the patient's words describing the dream, (2) Freud's memory of *reading* Daudet's *Sappho*, (3) the images Freud formed in his head when *reading* it, and (4) his recollection of the reading and the images during the analytic session. It turned out that the imagery from Daudet's book fitted quite well with his patient's story. At the very least one must conclude that hearing people's words gives rise to a sort of narrative imagery, conscious or unconscious, in our minds and that in reading most of us create imagery as a matter of course (Esrock 1994).

Freud did call attention to the other side of this phenomenon: "Part of the difficulty of giving an account of dreams is due to our having to *translate* these images [of the manifest dream] into words" (Freud 1915–1916, 90, my italics) because they are "qualitatively different." Today, in hindsight, we could say that imagery [like its antecedent, the complex and expandable object-representation] is inexhaustible in its synchronic multisensory details (either explicit or implied) while a spoken description has to submit to the linearity of temporal sequencing.

Dream-thoughts

Dream analysis follows the fundamental rule of having a patient associate freely to individual elements of the dream. In his self-analysis, Freud systematically wrote down the thoughts, images, memories, experiences that occurred to him about each dream element. The German term *Einfall* literally means "something that falls into the mind." The technique aims at raising the associations to conscious awareness until together they take a certain shape or point in a particular direction. Finally the patient, assisted by the analyst's explorations and interpretations, arrives at the latent dream-thoughts that have prompted the formation of the dream. The task is not as simple as it may seem because the associations are not yet the latent dream-thoughts. In fact, "an association often comes to a stop precisely before the genuine dream-thought" (Freud 1933, 12). Such resistance requires that the analyst "fill in the hints, draw undeniable conclusions, and give explicit utterance to what the patient has only touched on in his associations" (ibid.) because his task is "to re-establish the distressing latent dream-thoughts from these obscure remaining hints" (Freud 1915–1916, 225). Once again the task is to restore personal meaning by linking the repressed painful representation to words that make them conscious and tolerable: another instance of undoing an asymbolic aphasia.

Where the *quality* of the thoughts is concerned, Freud sees dream-thoughts as thoughts "like any other" (Freud 1923, 112), related to recent concerns and interests in waking life (Freud 1915–1916, 238). As for their 'location', "They have their place among thought-processes that have not become conscious – processes from which, after some modification, our conscious thoughts, too, arise" (Freud 1900, 506). This sentence, in my reading of it, goes back to the perceptual-associative processes described in *On Aphasia* that are *not repressed* but have simply been registered without having been articulated into words. This conception seems compatible with Freud's proposal that "the unconscious activity of the imagination has a large share in the construction of dream-thoughts" (Freud 1900, 591–92), implying, I believe, the mind's non-conscious continuation of associative processes.

Freud describes how the dream-thoughts appear:

> These usually emerge as a *complex* of thoughts and memories of the most intricate possible structure, with all the attributes of the trains of thought familiar to us in waking life. They are not infrequently trains of thought starting out from more than one centre, though having points of contact. Each train of thought is invariably accompanied by its contradictory counterpart, linked with it by antithetical associations.
>
> (ibid., pp. 311–12, my italics)

It is important to notice here that frequently the thoughts that come to mind are vivid *scenic recollections* of the patient's actual or thinking life. In analyzing his rich dream 'Non *vixit*' (ibid., pp. 421–25). Freud traces the look with which he annihilated his friend P. in the dream to the "terrible blue eyes" of Professor Brücke, whose reprimand reduced him "to nothing" when Freud had arrived *late* for work. His words in the dream 'Non *vixit*' were extracted from an inscription he had read on the Kaiser Josef memorial in Vienna. Freud connects his feelings in the dream scenes to his simultaneously hostile and affectionate feelings for P. when he was alive; they then remind him of having acted the role of Brutus at the age of fourteen, in a play he performed together with John, his nephew and contemporary, who was an equally ambivalent figure in Freud's affective life. This scene in turn leads him to recollect the time when he was two years old and came to blows with the same nephew. Finally, Freud connects the Latin expression to the verb 'to hit', which is what he had done to John in the early childhood episode. He found that "the exciting cause of the dream" was his concern that his friend Fliess, who had to undergo an operation, could die and he would "arrive *too late*" as Freud had done at Brücke's laboratory (ibid., p. 481). I conclude from reading Freud's associations to his dream that memories of scenes from the past are *a necessary* component for establishing "points of contact" in the dream-thoughts. The mind not only forms rationally organized thoughts, but as mentioned earlier, also is capable of retrieving unconsciously registered *perceptual* elements and combining them into scenes in the dream-thoughts; these are then disguised to create the imagery in the manifest dream. When Freud notes the possibility that symbols and mythic creatures in folklore, legends, and idioms may have been formed unconsciously (ibid., p. 351), he does not mention that such symbolic figures always come in scenic contexts: dragons threatening people, lovely unicorns with romantic maidens, and so on. The dreamer, during the dream, may reflect and have feelings about what is portrayed in the scenes and form intricate dream-thoughts out of them. These seem to be the dream-thoughts that call attention to another aspect of Freud's theorizing.

He frequently gives the impression that dream-thoughts are organized as sentences whose grammatical structure calls for the ingenuity of the dream-work so that linguistic functions can be transformed into the imagery of the manifest dream. He considers that the pictorial non-verbal nature of the manifest dream imposes on the *translation* of the dream-thoughts the same limitations encountered in the "plastic arts of painting and sculpture" (Freud 1900, 312): "What representations do dreams provide for 'if', 'because', 'just as', 'although', 'either-or', and all the conjunctions without which we cannot understand sentences of speech? . . . Dreams have no means at their disposal for representing these logical relations between dream-thoughts. For the most part dreams disregard all these conjunctions, and it is only the substantive content of the dream-thoughts that they take over and manipulate" (ibid.). Again, we have here echoes of *On Aphasia*, where Freud dealt only with substantives. He makes clear that "the restoration of the connections which the dream-work has destroyed is a task which has to be performed by the [verbal] interpretative process" (ibid.). In short, dream-thoughts have to be restored to their original logic and grammar. The dream-work uses pictorial simultaneity in time to convey logical connections; elements close together reveal intimate connections; simultaneity represents a conditional; to represent causal relations the introductory dream presents the dependent clause while the main dream portrays the principal clause. To interpret the dream the analyst must follow these steps in the reverse.

When they are uncovered, dream-thoughts take the form of one or a few well-structured sentences that the dream-work has transformed into visual and sensory scenes. Here is an illustration: in discussing the dream about *Three theater tickets for 1fl.* [florin] *and 50 kr.* [crowns] (Freud 1900, 415), Freud sums up his woman patient's latent thoughts: "'It was *absurd* to marry so early. There was *no need for me to be in such hurry.* I see from Elise L.'s example that I should have got a husband in the end. Indeed, I should have got one *a hundred times* better' (a *treasure*) 'if I had only *waited*' (in antithesis to her sister-in-law's *hurry*). 'My money' (or dowry) 'could have bought *three* men just as good'" (ibid., p. 416). To my way of thinking, such *latent* dream-thoughts are completely unintelligible without the compensatory fantasized scene of buying three better husbands than the one she got in her hurry to marry.

Conclusions

In my review of Freud's work on dreams I was surprised to find the direct continuity between his concepts in *On Aphasia* and many of his key ideas in relation to dream formation and interpretation. The conception of two *apparatuses*, one for speech and one for the dreaming mind, a notion aimed at fitting with the science of the time, interfered with Freud's theorizing and did not permit him to create a theory about the person who was speaking and dreaming, the patient's agent-self. There is a clear dissociation here between Freud, the clinician who never ignored the patient, and Freud the theoretician who wanted a well-functioning apparatus to give scientific credibility to his theories. The subtle and brilliant clinical observations of his patients' maneuvering to fulfil their wishes and comply with their own censor were converted into the parts of the mental apparatus's mechanisms without a subject using them.

In Freud's technique and theory of dream interpretation, even when words are misleading they take precedence over the deceptive imagery of the manifest dream, while in the dream-thoughts imagery cedes its place to the grammatical structure of the sentences behind it. I agree that *translation* of the dream into the dream-thoughts [and the imagery they suggest] is the essence of dream interpretation. Nonetheless, I must insist that words are empty sounds without their personal *intrapsychic* multisensory and visual representational component, so closely related to the unconscious of our true psychic reality. We do not live on words alone but also on the *perceptual scenes* that integrate our encounters with reality, both external and internal, and our memories of ourselves in it. I am saying that it is time for us to look more deeply and systematically at the role imagery and scenes, as part of our thinking processes, play in organizing our mental life. It is also necessary to rescue imagery from its classification as a 'primitive' and inferior mental process and to find a way of articulating its psychic functions. Thinking is more than verbal thoughts – and Freud said as much. I believe – based on Freud's own conceptions – that we think with all our senses and organize their percepts into non-conscious, unconscious, and conscious scenes linked to the stance of the self in relation to itself, others, and its environment. It is true that we consciously connect our perceptions with words and make efforts to organize perceptions into recognizable forms and name them. Nevertheless, the perceptions we register unconsciously and consciously far outnumber our capacity to give language to all of their components, as subliminal perceptions demonstrate so clearly. Yet Freud's analytic method, by rightly insisting on the words that give meaning to unconscious representations (as he said already in *On Aphasia*), opened the window and allowed us to see for the first time in history the unfathomable richness of our representational and imaginative private life, what he called our true psychic reality.

In the following chapters, I will review Freud's understanding of the function of words as it developed in his clinical and theoretical papers subsequent to *The Interpretation of Dreams*.

Note

1 Meissner has articulated the relationship between agency and subjectivity: "This essay explores the nature of subjectivity as an integral aspect of the psychology of the self, understood as a supraordinate theoretical construct synonymous with the human person. Aspects of agency and subjectivity are distinguished: Agency is attributed to the self-as-agent, encompassing all actions of the self (conscious, preconscious, unconscious) while the self-as-subject is the author of all conscious (and by implication preconscious) mental action. Self-as-agent and self-as-subject are the same in all conscious activity, but not in unconscious activity. Unconscious action has no subject, only agency. Unconscious derivatives achieve functional subjectivity insofar as they are incorporated and integrated with conscious experience" (p. 155).

References

Esrock, Ellen J. *The Reader's Eye*. Baltimore: Johns Hopkins University Press, 1994.

Freud, Sigmund. *The Complete Letters of Sigmund Freud to Wilhelm Fliess 1887–1904*. Trans. and ed. Jeffrey Moussaieff Masson. Cambridge, MA: Belknap Press of Harvard University Press, 1985.

———. *The Interpretation of Dreams*. Vols. 4–5 of *Standard Edition*. London: Hogarth Press, 1900.

———. *On Dreams*. Vol. 5 of *Standard Edition*. London: Hogarth Press, 1901.

———. *Introductory Lectures on Psycho-Analysis*. Vol. 15 of *Standard Edition*. London: Hogarth Press, 1915–1916.

———. *Introductory Lectures on Psycho-Analysis*. Vol. 16 of *Standard Edition*. London: Hogarth Press, 1916–1917.

———. *A Metapsychological Supplement to the Theory of Dreams*. Vol. 14 of *Standard Edition*, 217–35. London: Hogarth Press, 1917.

———. *The Neuro-Psychosis of Defense*. Vol. 3 of *Standard Edition*, 41–68. London: Hogarth Press, 1894.

———. *New Introductory Lectures on Psycho-Analysis*. Vol. 22 of *Standard Edition*, 1–182. London: Hogarth Press, 1933.

———. *On Aphasia: A Critical Study*. Trans. Erwin Stengel. 1953. New York: International Universities Press, 1891.

———. *Project for a Scientific Psychology*. Vol. 1 of *Standard Edition*, 283–397. London: Hogarth Press, 1950.

———. *The Psychopathology of Everyday Life*. *Standard Edition*. London: Hogarth Press, 1901.

————. Remarks on the Theory and Practice of Dream Interpretation. Vol. 19 of *Standard Edition*, 109–21. London: Hogarth Press, 1923.

————. Repression. Vol. 14 of *Standard Edition*, 141–58. London: Hogarth Press, 1915a.

————. The Unconscious. Vol. 14 of *Standard Edition*, 159–215. London: Hogarth Press, 1915b.

Green, André. The Intrapsychic and Intersubjective in Psychoanalysis. *Psychoanalytic Quarterly* 69 (2000): 1–40.

Heilbrunn, Gert. Biological Correlates of Psychoanalytic Concepts. *Journal of the American Psychoanalytic Association* 27 (1979): 597–625.

Laplanche, J., and J.-B. Pontalis. *The Language of Psychoanalysis*. New York: W. W. Norton, 1973.

Meissner, William W. The Self-as-Subject in Psychoanalysis: I. The Nature of Subjectivity. *Psychoanalysis and Contemporary Thought* 22 (1999): 155–201.

Penfield, W. The Role of the Temporal Cortex in Recall of Past Experiences and Interpretation of the Present. In Ciba Foundation Symposium, *Neurological Basis of Behavior*, 149–74. Boston: Little Brown, 1958.

Rizzuto, Ana-María. Psychoanalysis: The Transformation of the Subject by the Spoken Word. *Psychoanalytic Quarterly* 72 (2003): 287–323.

5

PLIABLE WORDS, SCENES, AND THE UNCONSCIOUS

Introduction

> Words are a plastic material with which one can do all kinds of things.
> *Jokes and Their Relation to the Unconscious* (Freud 1905b, 34)

Freud established in *The Interpretation of Dreams* a new and more differentiated model for understanding the unconscious working of the mind. A year later he published *The Psychopathology of Everyday Life*, with the subtitle *Forgetting, Slips of the Tongue, Bungled Actions, Superstitions and Errors*. He wanted his contemporaries to recognize the active unconscious mental processes at work in their daily lives, to face the truth about themselves and to discover "that the urge to tell the truth is so much stronger than is usually supposed" (Freud 1901, 221). Such truth stemmed from people's repressed intentions overtaking their conscious wish to say or do something and replacing it by what they had avoided.

The *plasticity* of words allows for surprising and highly unpredictable utterances. Freud explores here for the first time the *dynamic* organization of the words we say and the complex unconscious procedures involved in verbal "errors," parapraxes. He has left the consulting room to observe and theorize about words in daily life.

Words and everyday psychopathology

I want to start my discussion of this topic by citing some general principles that Freud does not define as such, but which color the overall context of what he says. Freud describes one aspect of his own experience as follows:

> There . . . runs through my thoughts a continuous current of 'personal reference', of which I generally have no inkling, but which betrays itself by such

instances of my forgetting names. It is as if I were obliged to compare everything I hear about other people with myself; as if my personal complexes
were put on the alert whenever another person is brought to my notice.
This cannot possibly be an individual peculiarity of my own: it must rather
contain an indication of the way in which we understand 'something other
than ourself' in general. I have reasons for supposing that other people are in
this respect very similar to me.

(pp. 24–25)

Such self-referential hearing of words about others points to an ongoing
descriptively *unconscious function of words* when our sense of ourself is compared
with our sense of the other person. Freud's comparison implies the non-conscious
creation of a *mental scene* to establish similarities and differences between himself
and the other person.

Another principle concerns remembering: "This general principle would assert
that when the reproducing function [of memory] fails or goes astray, the occurrence points, far more frequently than we suspect, to interference by a tendentious factor – that is, by a *purpose* which favours one memory while striving to
work against another" (p. 45). The next idea I have selected is a fact of psychic
life that obtains in speech: "One then observes in astonishment how the *wording*
of an assertion *cancels out its own intention*, and how the slip has exposed an inner
insincerity. The slip of the tongue here becomes a mode of mimetic expression –
often, indeed, for the expression of something one did not wish to say: it becomes
a mode of self-betrayal" (p. 86). When we speak we have a *conscious intention* that
we believe will result in our expressing what we want to say. We are not aware
that *we* also have other *intentions* that we want to keep hidden, even from ourselves, until we *hear ourselves speaking*. This is what Freud wanted to demonstrate
to everyone, the so-called normal people, that they harbor unconscious *intentions*
and that their memories, words, actions, and errors may surprise them by giving
them away. Freud wanted to demonstrate how such intentions function as *motives*
for what people actually say and do, but also to describe the *mechanisms* that bring
about such unintended utterances or actions. The motives always arise from a
conflict between conscious and repressed intentions. The mechanisms are more
complex and diverse and require examination of the particular circumstances in
each instance.

The motives indicate that neurotic cases and the banal errors and slips of the
tongue of non-neurotic people have a common root: "*The phenomena can be traced
back to incompletely suppressed psychical material, which, although pushed away by consciousness, has nevertheless not been robbed of all capacity for expressing itself*" (p. 279).
The words *expressing itself* call attention, once more, to the constant problem of
agency in Freud's theorizing originating in *On Aphasia*. Up to this point Freud has
discussed a person's opposing intentions while speaking; in this citation the agency
belongs to the suppressed material that has the capacity for expressing itself, against
the best intentions of the person. Freud never resolved this theoretical problem,

even when he was aware that his unconscious comparisons with others prompted *him* to forget and make mistakes. He offered one example of a motive for forgetting a name in the instance of a Fräulein I. von K. who wrote about one of her critics: "'The grudge I unconsciously bore against him was expressed by my forgetting his name, which, apart from that, I knew so well'" (p. 26), making explicit her agency in forgetting the name.

In presenting the instance when he forgot the name of the painter Signorelli, Freud offers a masterful examination of the motives and mechanisms involved in his producing incorrect substitutes while talking with a stranger in a train trip to Herzegovina. Freud asked his companion if he had seen the frescoes in the Orvieto cathedral, painted by. . . . He could not remember the name of the artist. Just before they had been talking about the customs of the Turks in Bosnia and Herzegovina. At that point Freud *avoided* two types of thoughts: those about the Turks who prefer death to the loss of potency and the news about one of his patients' suicide, which he learned when he was at a place called Trafoi, in the Tyrol. Freud describes his situation:

> I wanted, therefore, to forget something; I had *repressed* something. What I wanted to forget was not, it is true, the name of the artist at Orvieto but something else – something, however, which contrived to place itself in an associative connection with his name, so that my act of will missed its target and I forgot *the one thing against my will*, while I wanted to forget *the other thing intentionally*. The disinclination to remember was aimed against one content; the inability to remember emerged in another.
>
> *(p. 4)*

He considered his memory lapse a compromise between what he wanted to forget and what he couldn't remember. As he tried to remember the name, Freud came up with those of two other famous painters: Botticelli and Boltraffio but knew at once that these were false recollections. On examining possible motives for the emergence of the wrong names he found that he had derived their *syllables* from different sources: 'Bo' was extracted from *Bo*snia and 'traffio' came from the connection to the place – Trafoi – where he heard about his patient's suicide. 'Bo' stood for repressed thoughts about sexuality and death; 'traffio' was linked to repressed thoughts about death. On the side of forgetting and repressing Signorelli, Freud discovered that he had *unconsciously* translated the component *Signor* – Mister – from the German *Herr* in the speech of a Turkish patient who had declared that his life would have no value without an active sexual function, and had connected it to the particle *Her* in the name *Her*zegovina. That component also referred to the repressed thoughts about death and sexuality. His tentative name Botti*celli* included the second part of the forgotten name Signor*elli*. Freud concluded: "On close enquiry, however, one finds more and more frequently that the two elements which are joined by an *external* association (the repressed element and the new one) possess in addition some connection of *content*; and such a connection is in fact demonstrable in the *Signorelli* example" (p. 6, my italics).

Several questions emerge with regard to words that create false recollections: *Bo/ttic/elli* and *Boltraffio*. How are such words formed? How do they combine parts of other words heard and used in other contexts? Freud gives an interesting answer: "The substitute for it [*Signor*] has been arrived at in a way that suggests that a displacement along the connected names of '*Her*zegovina and *Bo*snia' had taken place, without consideration for the sense or for the acoustic demarcation of the syllables. Thus the names have been treated in this process like the pictograms in a sentence which has had to be converted into a picture-puzzle (or rebus)" (p. 5). A rebus is "a representation of words or syllables by pictures of objects or by symbols whose names resemble the intended words or syllables in sound" (*Merriam-Webster's 11th Collegiate Dictionary*, 2003). Freud drew a diagram – a sort of pictogram – demonstrating the syllabic connections. In establishing these links, he is saying that *acoustic components of the words* are unconsciously *used as pictures* (thing-representations), something that can be transposed unconsciously from word to word. What we have here is the unconscious formation of a false word by the *displacement* of sound syllables, which had to be repressed on account of their unacceptable reference to sex and death. The syllables in the wrong name *Boltraffio* reveal the repressed thoughts in disguise. The syllables in the name *Bo/ttic/elli* mix the repressed sexual thoughts with the potentially remembered correct name *Signor/elli*, which includes the repressed Signor/Her/Herr, and the indifferent *elli*.

This magnificent example poses questions about the function – in Freud's mind – of picturing syllables as sounds that are simultaneously repressed, used as pictures and create false recollections. If I follow Freud's model in *On Aphasia* linking word sounds to visual images of thing-representations to form a meaningful word, some observations become unavoidable. In this case the syllables, 'Bo' and 'Her', in Freud's understanding, stood for sexuality and death, together with the distorted 'traffio' as a substitute for Trafoi. The conclusion follows that the syllables and the words had acted in Freud's mind as *real* words – a sort of unconscious neologism – about death and sexuality. Their appearance in the wrong names suggests the condensation in Botti*celli* of a part – *elli* – of the correct intended word and the repressed referent present in 'Bo'. *Boltraffio*, on the other hand, condenses two types of death, sexual death and actual suicide, in its composite representation.

The examination of this example leads directly to two of Freud's conclusions: (1) that forgetting of names as well as making slips of the tongue are psychical processes profoundly influenced by issues of "close personal importance" and "distressing affects," and (2) that many examples of memory problems and slips of the tongue indicate that the *sounds* of the words or the syllables standing for internally organized representations are of no great importance. What counts is the *repressed content* of the thoughts linked to them. Once more the sound leads to the *intrapsychic* meaning of the misremembered word. He cites a case reported by Ferenczi involving a young widow who could not recall Jung's name, which means 'young' in German. Her thoughts were concerned with her wish to marry again and the difficulty she was having finding a second husband. Freud cites Ferenczi's conclusion: "the ideas screening the missing name were associated entirely with its *content* and that associations with its *sound* were absent" (p. 27, my italics). Freud infers from this and other cases that mental operations behind some memory lapses bear a strong resemblance to the work of condensation in dreams, where "a similarity between the things themselves or between their verbal presentations . . . is taken as an opportunity for creating a third, which is a composite or compromise idea" (pp. 58–59). There is a difference in the case of errors of speech: "The formation of substitutions and contaminations which occurs in slips of the tongue is accordingly *a beginning of the work of condensation* which we find taking a most vigorous share in the construction of dreams" (p. 59, my italics).

Freud became convinced that the contact effect of sounds is not enough to explain disturbances of speech: "I almost invariably discover a disturbing influence in addition which comes from something *outside* the intended utterance; and the disturbing element is either a single thought that has remained unconscious, which manifests itself in the slip of the tongue and which can often be brought to consciousness only by means of searching analysis, or it is a more general psychical motive force which is directed against the entire utterance" (p. 61). Freud offered an example from a publication by Steckel, who said to a well-to-do patient he had been seeing for a while: "'If, as I hope, you will *not* leave your bed soon. . . . ,' thus disclosing to himself his interest in the remuneration, although he said it was 'a wish that is entirely foreign to my waking consciousness and which I would indignantly repudiate'" (p. 68).

Freud also asserted that "words with opposite meanings are, quite generally, very often interchanged; they are already associated in our *linguistic* consciousness" (p. 59, my italics). He was making a reference to the contemporary linguistic notion of primitive antithetical words. An example is the instance when the President of the Lower House of the Austrian Parliament opened a session by saying: "Gentlemen: I take notice that a full quorum of members is present and herewith declare the sitting *closed!*" (p. 59).

In sum: forgetting names and slips of the tongue are not related to the *linguistic* or phonetic organization of words but are rather determined by psychical processes that select words or their components and use them in idiosyncratic ways. These are established by unconscious connections between repressed thoughts and the meaning of the syllables of the word on account of their contiguity in actual life (*Bosnia* and sexual *Turks*) or the similarity of sound between words such as *Trafoi* – a place connected to death – and the ending of the name of an actual painter *Boltraffio*. Freud speaks of "an associative series between the words," which cannot be denied. Nevertheless, it seems to me that the associations also play and tamper with the words and use their syllabic components as sounds with their own idiosyncratic referents. These referents have selected a partial component of a word and link it – as though it were a true word – to thoughts that are repressed. In many other cases, the total word acquires a double representation: *Jung*, the person, and *young*, the sad widow finding it difficult to remarry. Freud has made this connection explicit: "Thus we see how a pair of words that are similar in sound can have the same effect as a single word that has two meanings"

(p. 33). The sound is the *occasion* for the *mechanism* of forming the slip of the tongue or other errors of speech. The associated similarity of sound permits the unconscious to give a repressed meaning to the word. It is the tension between the person's need to reveal the repressed thought and simultaneously to conceal it that creates the error in speaking or remembering, while in slips of the tongue it is the unconscious or suppressed thought that prevails by co-opting the spoken words. Although we have the best intentions of keeping hidden what we do not want to reveal, words that inadvertently come out of our mouths at times offer a good demonstration of Freud's observation "that the urge to tell the [unconscious] truth is so much stronger than is usually supposed" (p. 221).

Freud has demonstrated that the *linguistic* meaning and form of words are pliable, bending easily to the dynamic pressure of repressed personal intentions that prompt us to say what we did not intend. In parapraxes our unconscious intention wins the right of expression. The unconscious employs the "plastic material" of words to use them in every possible way: cut them up, create a neologism, give them duplicitous meaning, use them as things, or have them as part of an image in a rebus. To put it briefly, Freud has demonstrated that in parapraxes the psychic plasticity of words overrides their cultural or linguistic meaning because their task is to reveal *intrapsychic* realities barely related to our conscious intention to say something relevant. Besides, the word's power to reveal our insincerity makes a counterpoint to our measuring ourselves in relation to the words of others. It must be added that the plasticity of words does not limit itself to parapraxes but it is subtly present in our everyday speech.

Jokes: Words for another person's unconscious

Jokes and Their Relation to the Unconscious (Freud 1905b) was published following a comment by Freud's friend Wilhelm Fliess that his "interpretation of dreams often impressed him as being like jokes" (Freud 1925, 65). The book can be read, in a certain sense, as a continuation of *The Interpretation of Dreams*. Freud made few references to it in his later writings and made "no more than a half-a-dozen small additions" (Strachey 1960, 5–6) to the second edition. Jokes use the same "technical methods" as the dream-work: "condensation, displacement, the representation of a thing by its opposite or by something very small, and so on" (Freud 1925, 66). It was not until 1927, after developing the structural theory, that he returned to the subject in his brief paper *Humour* (Freud 1927), where he describes the role of the superego in facilitating experiences of humor. Although the book is not well known among analysts and is rarely studied during analytic training, I find it fascinating because it reveals Freud's ways of conceiving the many functions of words, from the intrapsychic to the social when they take the form of jokes.

The book lists the differences between dreams and jokes: (1) "A dream is a completely *asocial* mental product; it has nothing to communicate." "A joke, on the other hand, is the *most social* of all the mental functions that aim at a yield of pleasure." (2) A dream "remains unintelligible to the subject himself." A joke must be understood at least by two people. (3) "Dreams serve predominantly for the avoidance of unpleasure, jokes for the attainment of pleasure." (4) A dream "must actually avoid being understood," while for a joke "the condition of intelligibility is . . . binding on it" to the point that in the case of tendentious jokes the unconscious processes that form the joke "can be set straight by the third person's understanding." In other words, the unconscious of the listener is *able to decode* the condensation, distortion, and representation by its opposite used to construct the joke. (5) "A dream . . . remains a wish; a joke is developed play." (6) Dreams serve "to fulfill needs by the regressive detour of hallucination. . . . Jokes, on the other hand, seek to gain a small yield of pleasure from the mere activity, untrammelled by needs, of our mental apparatus." (7) A dream requires no one outside the dreamer. A joke *needs at least two people* and "often calls for three persons and its completion requires the participation of someone else in the mental process it starts" (Freud 1905b, 179–80). Overall, then, the similarity between dreams and jokes resides in the *unconscious mental processes* they resort to for their formation. The critical difference rests in their purposes: the dream "arises within the subject as a compromise between the mental forces struggling in him" (ibid., p. 179), whereas jokes *seek out other people* for a moment of playfulness, psychical collaboration, and shared pleasure.

Context is important. A joke requires particular circumstances that offer a significant context if listeners are to understand it. For this reason, jokes, be they social or political, are frequently linked with an immediate context that accounts for the pleasure they evoke and the facilitation of unconscious work.

Freud's central thesis about the function of jokes and their capacity to produce pleasure centers on the *economy* of expenditure. He created the term *joke-work* as analogous to dream-work because jokes essentially take form in an unconscious process over which we have no conscious control. For that reason, jokes do not result from the elaboration of thoughts but *occur* to us (p. 134). This is "a decisive point" in Freud's view, one he arrived at by studying the technique of jokes and comparing them with dreams. He explicitly acknowledges that he has reached his conclusion by inference.

> But let us now consider the case in which a thought, not worthless in itself, arises in the course of a train of thought and is expressed as a joke. In order to enable this thought to be turned into a joke, it is clearly necessary to select from among the possible forms of expression the precise one which brings along with it a yield of *verbal pleasure*. We know from self-observation that this selection is not made by conscious attention; but it will certainly help the selection if the cathexis of the pre-conscious thought is reduced to an unconscious one, for, as we have learnt from the dream-work, the connecting paths which start out from *words* are in the unconscious treated in the same way as connections between *things*. An unconscious cathexis offers far more favourable conditions for selecting the expression. Moreover, we can immediately assume that the possible form of expression that involves a yield

of verbal pleasure exercises the same <u>downward drag</u> on the still unsettled wording of the preconscious thought as did the unconscious purpose in the earlier case. To meet the simpler case of the jest, we may suppose that an <u>intention</u> which is all the time on the look-out to achieve a yield of verbal pleasure grasps the occasion offered in the preconscious for dragging the cathectic process down into the unconscious according to the familiar pattern.

(p. 177, my underlining)

This dense paragraph contains the essence of Freud's theory of how jokes are formed and on the links between thoughts, words, unconscious processes, and cathexis. It deserves careful examination. In *chronological* order it seems that the first step is the *intention* to obtain verbal pleasure. The occasion for such an intention appears when a particular thought appears suitable for a joke in a given *social context*. The mind's task is to select words capable of expressing such a thought in a form that produces verbal pleasure *to others*. It is here that the joke-work begins. Its function is to find a way to link "the still unsettled wording of the preconscious thought" to unconscious processes capable of finding the right connections. To explain this process Freud uses his conception about words and things in the context of the topographical theory. There are unmistakable echoes of *On Aphasia*. The joke-work "drags" the word to the unconscious realm of thing-representations and there rapidly selects the appropriate *things* that in turn would provide the wording for a joke guided by primary processes of similarity, condensation and, at times, displacement. At this point the joke-work confronts a potential problem in the form of critical, inhibitory processes that simultaneously interfere with the use of such things and words. The inhibitions stem from an ego that would not tolerate anything that becomes distressing or cause unpleasure. The cleverness of the joke-work is to find a way to get rid of such inhibitions by finding connections that appear unobjectionable. The pleasure experienced in *hearing* the joke results from the way the teller of it, by using clever words, offers listeners an opportunity to release their own critical feelings or inhibitions without any psychic effort. This implies that the joke's unobjectionable connections bypass the listener's superego.

Freud says explicitly of the effect of a joke: "The pleasure that it produces, whether it is pleasure in play or pleasure in lifting inhibitions, can invariably be traced back to *economy* in psychical expenditure" (p. 138, my italics). He does not explain, however, how using words as things and using primary process lead to finding the correct words for the joke. Neither does he explain how the words for the joke can be found in unconscious processes if they are to appear in the actual joke not as things but as words. It seems that some intermediary processes are missing from the explanation, but Freud left these issues unresolved.

Creating a joke entails playing with words and thoughts. Freud makes here a clear distinction between thought and word: "A thought can in general be expressed in various linguistic forms – in various words, that is – which can represent it with equal aptness" (p 16). The thoughts, in this description, need words to make themselves known, but do not depend on words to exist because they seem to be present in the mind *before* they are expressed verbally. The creator of the joke can select different words to convey these thoughts through unconscious processes because words are "a *plastic material* with which one can do all kinds of things. There are words which, when used in certain connections, have lost their original full meaning, but which regain it in other connections" (p. 34, my italics). It is this *plasticity* that makes verbal jokes possible. Other jokes, such as conceptual jokes have deeper roots and use words in a different manner: "What happens is not that we know a moment beforehand what joke we are going to make, and that all it then needs is to be *clothed in words*. We have an indefinable feeling, rather, which I can best compare with an 'absence', a sudden release of intellectual tension, and then all at once the joke is there – as a rule ready – *clothed in words*" (p. 167, my italics). Freud seems to have discovered this feeling through introspection. The metaphor of words as clothes suggests that the *body* of the joke is *dressed* with words. This "clothing" is the great difference between verbal jokes and conceptual jokes. In the former case we play with the words themselves without involving the thought as such. In conceptual jokes there are allusions to known "conceptual connections" not involving "the resemblance in sound between two *words*, but between whole sentences, characteristic phrases, and so on" (pp. 75–76). Yet in both instances the essence of a joke lies in the "ambiguity of words and the multiplicity of conceptual relations" (p. 172). "Nothing distinguishes jokes more clearly from all other psychical structures than this double-sidedness and this duplicity in speech. From this point of view at least the authorities come closest to an understanding of the nature of jokes when they lay stress on 'sense in nonsense'" (p. 172). These assertions about the ambiguity of words, the multiplicity of conceptual relations, and the double-sidedness of speech bring into focus how far Freud has departed from his model in *On Aphasia* with its one-to-one correspondence between the sound of a word and the visual component of its representation. Furthermore, in the monograph he treated a word as an internal form of organization in an individual mind, a *one-person psychology*, while here he insists that the wording of jokes and their purpose demand the presence of the internal worlds of at least two people, since a joke is necessarily a social event. Jokes, as social play, connect the *intrapsychic reality* of the joker to the *intrapsychic reality* of those who grasp it and laugh.

Freud gives a long list of the ways in which we *play with words*, which he divides into three basic categories: (1) condensation, be it by creating a composite word or a modified word; (2) by multiple use of the same material, using part for whole or vice versa, changing the order of words, altering them slightly, or using the same word in its full or modified meaning; (3) giving the word a double meaning in several forms: using it as a name and as a thing, metaphorically and literally, giving it an actual double meaning, making a double entendre, and using a double meaning with an allusion (p. 41). Nevertheless, regardless of how playful we can be in changing plastic words at the service of our jokes, the source of pleasure, in Freud's manner of thinking, depends on the "economy made by the joke-technique" (p. 43).

Conceptual jokes take shape in the unconscious and use techniques very similar to those in dreams: "displacement, faulty reasoning, absurdity, indirect representation, representation by the opposite – which re-appear one and all in the technique of the dream-work" (p. 88). When we hear the joke and experience the effect it has upon us "we are unable to separate the share taken by the thought content from the share taken by the joke-work" (p. 94). An example is the case of two unscrupulous rich Americans who had their portraits painted by a very reputable artist and exhibited them together on a wall at a party. They asked a well-known art critic to give his opinion. The connoisseur looked at them most attentively and "pointed to the gap between the pictures and said quietly, "'But where's the Saviour'" (p. 74). Everybody understood he was "alluding to Christ hanging between two thieves" (p. 75).

All these technical procedures serve the intention of giving pleasure to the person who *hears* the joke. The techniques used to form the joke have the power to elicit such pleasure in the listener if the person is capable of grasping the joke. Freud makes it clear that not all people are capable of making or understanding jokes or finding pleasure in them.

Freud draws a significant conclusion about the *entitlement* to make jokes: "What these jokes whisper may be said aloud: that the wishes and desires of men have a right to make themselves acceptable alongside of exacting and ruthless morality" (p. 110), thus signaling our rebellion against the demands of morality. The pleasure in hearing a joke depends on the ability to overcome internal inhibitions and criticisms of particular thoughts that the psyche, using a good amount of psychic energy, keeps repressed. The listener experiences pleasure because he hears exactly what is inhibited in him, but now needs no effort to overcome the inhibition. His pleasure stems from the repressive energy that has "become superfluous and has been lifted, and is therefore now ready to be discharged by laughter" (p. 149). "The hearer of the joke laughs . . . this quota [of energy] off" (p. 149) because he has managed to "*evade restrictions and open sources of pleasure that have become inaccessible*" (p. 103). The listener is confronted with the double face of the joke. He may regard the wording as meaningless and that is the end of it, there is no joke. He has another option: to let it go to his unconscious, following the hints present in the wording of the joke, and then he "finds an excellent sense in it" (pp. 214–15). Freud was certain of the connection between jokes and the unconscious. He asserts emphatically: "*we* are prepared to extend it to every species and every developmental stage of jokes" (p. 176).

What have we learned about words in reviewing Freud's understanding of jokes? Words have their meaning for certain. Nonetheless, the joke-maker can split them up, join them again, condense, enlarge, combine them at will; he can also alter their meaning by playing with small components of the word's sound, exchange its referent with another by changing contexts, or making many other combinations. In other terms, the joke uses words in peculiar and idiosyncratic ways to achieve its purpose of establishing connections of meanings where there usually are none. This is what Freud calls the *plasticity* of words, their astonishing capacity to bend their own meaning under the joker's ability to give them other significations. Obviously, this approach deals with the words only in relation to their meaning.

Freud attends only indirectly to the *communicative function* of words in considering how many people are needed to have a joke. Non-tendentious, innocent jokes need only two: one who makes it, and one who laughs at it. There are no jokes for private laughter. If something amusing occurs to us, at best we can smile, but laughter has to come from the listener to the joke. Tendentious jokes call for three people: the one to whom the joke *occurs* in a particular circumstance; a person, group, or institution that is targeted, and the listener, who being taken unawares, bursts out laughing. The third person is induced to become an ally and to join into making the second person the target of aggression or obscenity. Such treatment of the person who is the object of the joke meets with strong criticism in ordinary circumstances. However, without the other's laughter the joke has not reached its goal. This phenomenon presents the joke as *an act of speech that can be completed only in another person's hearing.* I am ready to extrapolate this assertion and say that such a condition applies to *all* spoken communications.

Freud's explanation of the laughter is economic, but is that enough to elucidate the source of it? In talking about smut, Freud says explicitly that we are ashamed of obscenity unless it comes in the shape of a joke. He writes:

> Every exposure of which we are made the spectator (or audience in the case of smut) by a third person is equivalent to the exposed person being made comic. We have seen that it is the task of jokes to take the place of smut and so once more to open access to a lost source of comic pleasure. As opposed to this, witnessing an exposure is not a case of the comic for the witness, because his own effort in doing so does away with the determining condition of comic pleasure: nothing is left but the sexual pleasure in what is seen.
>
> (p. 222)

These comments introduce the idea of *seeing* the exposed person in a particular circumstance. Seeing also concerns smut:

> Smut is like an exposure of the sexually different person to whom it is directed. By the utterance of the obscene words it compels the person who is assailed to *imagine* the part of the body or the procedure in question and shows her that the assailant is himself *imagining* it. It cannot be doubted that the *desire to see* what is sexual exposed is the original motive of smut.
>
> (p. 98, my italics)

I believe that it is legitimate to ask if all jokes do involve a certain manner of *seeing* what constitutes the joke itself – even if that occurs preconsciously. The joke recorded by Daniel Spitzer offers a good possibility for reflection: "Mr. and Mrs. X live in fairly grand style. Some people think that the husband has earned a lot and so has been able to lay by a bit [*sich etwas zurückgelegt*]; others again think that the wife has lain back a bit [*sich etwas zurückgelegt*] and so has been able to earn a lot" [p. 33, German terms in the *Standard Edition*]. The joke involves in Freud's view alteration in the *arrangement* of the verbal material (ibid.), double entendre (p. 40), and allusion (p. 75). Personally, I am unable to hear this joke without *seeing* the comparative *images* of the husband's accumulated money lying quietly at the bank and that of the sexual wife actively making money. Freud cites another joke involving a Jewish convert to Christianity who spoke disparagingly about the character of Jews. He received the reply: "Herr Hofrat . . . your ant*e*semitism was well known to me; your ant*i*semitism is new to me" (p. 33). In reading this, I find myself making an almost instantaneous mental operation of place about before and after in reading 'ant*e*' and an equally fast process of comparison between 'ant*i*' as against and 'in favor of.' I am unable not to split the word and I cannot but imagine the slightly stressed pronunciation of the 'e' and the 'i' in them. I have a similar experience when I read the joke about the play on the words 'taken a bath' between two Galician Jews, who supposedly had an aversion to bathing: "Two Jews met in the neighbourhood of the bath-house. 'Have you taken a bath?' asked one of them. 'What?' asked the other in return, 'is there one missing?'" (p. 49). Freud describes the technique as using the same word 'taken' in two different ways, first as a relatively colorless verb in a fixed expression and then in its specific meaning as a synonym for 'stealing', a conclusion that is incontrovertible. Yet, I am incapable of hearing the joke without *seeing* a man in a bathtub and a second later a man 'carrying' one. The ridiculous *comparison* makes me laugh. We have learned earlier that smut forces a person to *imagine* sexual organs or acts. Maybe, I am, as Charcot and Freud would have said, a 'visuelle.' Nonetheless, I doubt I am the only one. All these later comments bring me to return to an old issue that goes all the way back to *On Aphasia*: is it true that the sound of words calls for some visual or even, on some occasions, a sensory link to internal representations, what Freud called the *psychic* word? He did say that words *need* some unconscious, preconscious, or conscious visual/sensory referent to accomplish their task.

Now, let us consider the role of affects as motivation for jokes. Freud cites Heine's joke about a man without means who "boasts to the poet of his relations with the wealthy Baron Rothschild, and finally says: 'And, as true as God shall grant me all good things, Doctor, I sat beside Salomon Rothschild and he treated me quite as his equal – quite famillionairely'" (p. 16). Freud interprets it as the man saying in his condensed word: "'Rothschild treated me quite as his equal, quite familiarly – that is, so far as a millionaire can.' 'A rich man's condescension' . . . 'always involves something not quite pleasant for whoever experiences it'" (p.17). In exploring the "subjective determinant of jokes" (p. 140). Freud discloses that Heine himself was the poor relative of a millionaire uncle and "how much Heine suffered both in his youth and later from the rejection by his rich relative. It was from the soil of this *subjective emotion* that the 'famillionairely' joke sprang" (p. 142). This is the only place in the book where Freud mentions the role of emotions in motivating the formation of jokes.

In a letter written to Dr. Friedrich S. Krauss, however, Freud includes affect as part of the formation of jokes. Kraus had published a collection of popular sexual and anal jokes and had asked Freud to comment on the scientific value of the collection. In his response, Freud commented on the importance of the anal zone in humor and added a new expression, "complexive jokes":

> In psycho-analysis to-day we describe a congeries of ideas and its associated affect as a "complex" and we are prepared to assert that many of the most admired jokes are "complexive jokes" and that they owe their exhilarating and cheerful effect to the ingenious uncovering of what are as a rule repressed complexes.

> (Freud 1910, 234)

Freud does not explain what he means by the repressed complexes used by jokes. The context suggests that he is talking about sexual and anal complexes and their affect. If that is the case, the words of the joke are linked to such complexes.

To understand the comic, Freud observed that "human beings are in the habit of expressing the attributes of largeness and smallness in the contents of their ideas [*Vorstellungsinhalten*] by means of a varying expenditure in a kind of *ideational mimetics* [*Vorstellungsmimik*]" (Freud 1905b, 192, my italics). We are not aware of what we are doing, although we sense that we are somewhat expressing to ourselves our own ideas. Freud continues: "I believe that these mimetics exist, even if with less liveliness, quite apart from any communication, that they occur as well when the subject is forming an idea of something for his own private benefit and is thinking of something *pictorially*, and that he then expresses 'large' and 'small' in *his own body* just as he does in speech, at all events by a change in the *innervation* of his features and sense organs" (p. 193, my italics). Freud considers the issue to be of great importance and suggests that to the expression of emotions he would like to add "the expression of the ideational content" (ibid.). He noticed that in watching others act and trying to understand them "I behave exactly as though I were putting myself in the place of the person I am observing. But at the same moment, probably, I bear in mind the aim [intention] of this movement, and my earlier experience enables me to estimate the scale of expenditure required for reaching that aim" (p. 194, my clarification). The comic effect appears when we notice that the other person's bodily activity is disproportionate to his aim, such as when we prepare to lift something heavy and it turns out to be very light and our movement is out of proportion with the weight of the object. This description and Freud's ideational mimetics appear to me very close to the recent contemporary concept of "embodied simulation," based on the activity of mirror neurons, as proposed by the neuroscientist Vittorio Gallese (2010).

The sublime follows a similar pattern because it is large in a figurative sense. Freud uses himself as an example:

> When I speak of something sublime I *innervate my speech* in a different way, I make different facial expressions, and I try to bring the whole way in which

I hold myself into harmony with the dignity of what I am having an idea of. I impose a solemn restraint upon myself – not very different from what I should adopt if I were to enter the presence of an exalted personality.

(p. 200, my italics)

Freud concludes that these ideational mimetics of his correspond to an increase in expenditure, that is, they represent an economic phenomenon. This example is of interest to me as a speech act. What Freud describes so well is not so much an economic process but *the body's participation in speaking* during communication and, most important, as an *embodiment of the ideas* themselves. I believe that such embodiment is present whenever we speak and is one of the preconscious factors that listeners use to evaluate the meaning of words in interpersonal exchanges.

Humor is the last issue Freud considers in closing his book on jokes. "Humour is a means of obtaining pleasure in spite of the distressing affects that interfere with it; it acts as a substitute for the generation of these affects, it puts itself in their place" (p. 228), thus acting as a defense. He sees the use of humor as "the highest of these defensive processes" (p. 233), because it does not suppress the affect, but bears it.

Freud's book on jokes is a treasure trove of subtle psychical observations and a significant source for understanding aspects of his conception of the interactions between representations, scenes, spoken words, communication, the embodiment of ideas and words, pleasure, and the unconscious. It is intriguing that he seldom returned to it or used the insights he achieved in it when attempting to understand the dynamic organization of the joking process.

In attending to the *social* significance of jokes, Freud insists that a joke needs the participation of two persons to accomplish the aim of the joker. He persistently connects words, imagery, and representations in the formation of the joke's structure. In my view *all utterances* need two persons using words and imagery/representations/ scenes to complete a moment of spoken communication. The point is well illustrated in a moment of Freud's work with his patient Dora.

Dora's words and Freud's imaginary scenes

For three months in the autumn of 1900 Freud treated a hysterical eighteen-year-old girl[1] who had a nervous cough, and at times completely lost her voice, had low spirits, and a poor relation with her parents. She had written a letter indicating she could no longer endure her life and had fainted after a discussion with her father. The father insisted she had to be seen by Freud, who had treated him successfully for a syphilitic condition a few years earlier. He had met Freud then through his friend Herr K. Dora was a spirited adolescent, bright, articulate, and sensitive, who was enmeshed in a web of sexually dysfunctional adults. She knew that her parents had no sexual relations with each other and that her father had a long-standing sexual relation with Frau K. who avoided her marital duties with her husband Herr K. She also knew that her father was impotent. Dora had been a baby sitter for the K.'s when younger and had become a close friend of Frau K. For his part, Herr K.

was very attentive to Dora, gave her presents, and would take walks with her. At one point he kissed her unexpectedly and later on made a proposal to her while on a walk around a local lake. When confronted by the father, Herr K. "denied in the most emphatic terms" that he had approached Dora. Dora insisted to her father that he break off the relationship with the couple, in particular with Frau K. The father reported to Freud: "Dora . . . cannot be moved from her hatred of the K.'s. . . . Please try and bring her to reason" (p. 26). Dora accepted the treatment and stopped it herself after three months.

Freud finished the manuscript of the case on January 25, 1901, but did not publish it until 1905 (Freud 1905a). I will not discuss the case as a whole but rather explore Freud and Dora's words at a particular moment of the treatment. Freud was focused on the *intrapsychic* events and processes revealed in Dora's associations and the internal narrative in order to uncover Dora's intentions because he was convinced that "illnesses of this kind *are* the result of intention" (p. 45). He said to her that "she had an aim in view which she hoped to gain by her illness. That aim could be none other than to detach her father from Frau K." (p. 42).

Freud was conscious of the *overdetermination* of each symptom (p. 47) and began to suspect other sources for Dora's throat problems. She was constantly preoccupied with her father's and Frau K.'s sexual activity. Knowing that her father was impotent she indicated to Freud that she also knew that there were other ways of achieving sexual satisfaction. Freud explains: "I could then go on to say that in that case she must be thinking of precisely those parts of the body which in her case were in a state of irritation, – the throat and the oral cavity" (p. 47). Dora was not inclined to accept Freud's words yet he insisted: "The conclusion was inevitable that with her spasmodic cough, which, as is usual, was referred for its exciting stimulus to a tickling in her throat, she *pictured* to herself a *scene* of sexual gratification *per os* between the two people whose love-affair occupied her mind so incessantly" (p. 48, my italics). Her imagined *visual scene* was enough to arouse in her the 'somatic compliance' of an itching throat, which in turn, prompted her spasmodic cough. Shortly after they had this exchange, her cough disappeared.

I consider it essential to pay attention to the *process* by which Freud arrived at this significant interpretation. Dora was talking and describing what she knew about her father's impotence and oral sex while her symptomatic cough persisted. Freud, in putting it all together, was transforming those words in his mind into *images* of people having oral sex. He went even further in his imagination: he imagined that Dora imagined her father's penis tickling Frau K.'s throat and using her own throat as a substitute for Frau K.'s. To put it briefly, Freud used Dora's words to create a *scene* that he assumed Dora was seeing frequently in her mind: that of her father and Frau K. having oral sex, his penis in her mouth, and the tickling it would produce in her throat. He *assumed* that Dora coughed because she was *imagining the scene* of their love-making and participating in it with her ticklish cough.

How do we establish a continuity between Freud's earliest conception of the formation of the meaningful word in *On Aphasia* and Freud's transformation of the words he was hearing from Dora into scenes in his mind? Freud heard in Dora's words the fantasies he *constructed* she was harboring in her mind and their effective potential to be converted into an instance of 'somatic compliance', an irritated cough. If we turn to Freud's own vocabulary in the case report, it is clear that he was using contiguity between the associations and the similarity of the *imagined sensations* and put them together. The result was the formation in Freud's mind of the *visual and sensory picture* he believed Dora had formed in her mind, namely, a scene of oral love-making producing a tickling in Frau K.'s throat. Her imagining this scene, he concluded, had led her to having her own ticklish throat and cough. In terms of his older vocabulary, the thing-representation formed in *his* mind by the impact of Dora's words was by no means a 'thing' but a complex *scenic* event which he located within Dora's mind. The scene did not include only visual components but also somatic tickling. In other words Freud managed to create in sensory and somatic imagery in his own mind the type of psychic event and experience that caused Dora's cough. Her words became linked in his mind to a *scenic representation* that he assumed existed in her mind – truly a *virtual reality*. Regretfully, Freud did not pay attention to the theoretical implications of this significant advance in his understanding of the functions of the spoken words exchanged between people.

This was not the first time Freud had constructed scenes as he *imagined* Dora's experience. Earlier, in trying to understand the pressure she felt on her thorax, he wrote: "I have formed in my own mind the following *reconstruction* of the *scene*. I believe that during the man's passionate embrace she felt not merely his kiss upon her lips but also the pressure of his erect member against her body. This perception was revolting to her; it was dismissed from her memory, repressed, and replaced by the innocent sensation of pressure upon her thorax" (pp. 29–30, my italics).

In conclusion: Freud used the power of his imagination to create *scenes* in his mind while listening to Dora's words. He was convinced that they reproduced the scenes she had envisioned in her own mind. In the terms of the old model, those scenes became the 'object-representations' that gave meaning to Dora's spoken words, organized her 'somatic compliance', and allowed Freud to grasp her *intrapsychic* reality. I daresay that in psychoanalytic work such unconscious, preconscious, and finally conscious scenes constitute the staple of the interpretive process. The analytic mode of listening calls for – as jokes do – the collaboration of the active minds of two people. Freud certainly implemented his part in working with Dora, yet he did not realize its theoretical import until *Constructions in Analysis:* "at this point we are reminded that the work of analysis consists of two quite different portions, that it is carried on in two separate localities, that it involves two people, to each of whom a distinct task is assigned. It may for a moment seem strange that such a fundamental fact should not have been pointed out long ago" (Freud 1937, 258).

Without a listener, the words remain empty, incapable of delivering their meaning. We speak *for* others' ears because we need them to hear *us* in our words. Freud seems to have grasped this concept quite clearly in relation to jokes. Yet in his analytic listening his exclusive commitment to the intrapsychic reality kept him in the role of the doctor as the auditor of his patients' unconscious intentions and wishes which they could not express in articulate words but in symptoms and actions.

In describing *ideational mimetics* Freud says that we 'innervate' our bodies with the pictorial "size" of our ideas. I consider that this conception must be related to the 'innervations' described in *On Aphasia* that formed representations from the body's perceptual experiences. Finally, he describes how through posture and gesture the entire body conveys the manner in which we want our words to be heard, thus asserting that the communicative function of the words calls for embodied words.

In the next chapter I attend to the technical implications of the use of words in Freud's psychoanalytic method.

Note

1 His patient was actually two years younger. Freud changed her age as he had changed her real name to Dora.

References

Freud, Sigmund. An Autobiographical Study. Vol. 20 of *Standard Edition*, 1–74. London: Hogarth Press, 1925.

———. Constructions in Analysis. Vol. 23 of *Standard Edition*, 255–69. London: Hogarth Press, 1937.

———. Fragment of an Analysis of a Case of Hysteria. Vol. 7 of *Standard Edition*, 1–122. London: Hogarth Press, 1905a.

———. Humour. Vol. 21 of *Standard Edition*, 159–66. London: Hogarth Press, 1927.

———. *Jokes and Their Relation to the Unconscious*. Vol. 8 of *Standard Edition*. London: Hogarth Press, 1905b.

———. Letter to Dr. Friedrich S. Krauss on Anthropophyteia. Vol. 11 of *Standard Edition*, 233–35. London: Hogarth Press, 1910.

———. *The Psychopathology of Everyday Life*. Standard Edition. London: Hogarth Press, 1901.

Gallese, Vittorio. Embodied Simulation and Its Role in Intersubjectivity. In *The Embodied Self: Dimensions, Coherence and Disorders*, edited by T. Fuchs, H.C. Sattel, and P. Henningsen, 78–92. Stuttgart: Schattauer, 2010.

Strachey, James, ed. Preface to *Jokes and Their Relation to the Unconscious*. Vol. 8 of *Standard Edition*, 3–8. London: Hogarth Press, 1960.

6

FREUD'S TECHNIQUE

Translating repressed scenarios into words

Freud wrote *Psychical (or Mental) Treatment* (Freud 1905d) as mentioned in Chapter 3 for a popular medical book, *Die Gesundheit* (Freud 1890), in 1890, a year before writing *On Aphasia*. James Strachey (Strachey 1953, 281) translated it into English believing it had first appeared in the 1905 second edition of *Die Gesundheit*.

There Freud describes psychical treatment as "taking its start in the mind" and using "measures which operate in the first instance and immediately upon the human mind." He clearly affirms: "words are the essential tool of mental treatment" (p. 283), and proclaims that now "*science* sets about restoring to words a part at least of their former magical power" (ibid., my italics). He does not neglect the importance of emotions and their bodily manifestations to the point of saying that "more confidence can be placed [in them] than in any simultaneous verbal expressions that may be made deliberately" (p. 286). Words then are two-sided: they have the power to heal mental processes, but they also may serve to deceive and hide what the speaker does not want to reveal. Freud's new technique aims at using words to heal pathogenic unconscious processes while progressively undoing the layers of cover-up present in *conscious* words.

While studying with Charcot in 1885, Freud had been greatly impressed by the patients' hypnotic obedience during medical experiments and developed "an ineradicable conviction of the unsuspected power of the mind over the body" (p. 297). He became further convinced that in neurotics "the signs of their illness originate from nothing other than a change in the action of their minds upon their bodies and that the immediate cause of their disorder is to be looked for in their minds" (p. 286, italics in the original). Ideas do not exist solely in the head; they echo in the body: "Even when a person is engaged in quietly thinking in a string of 'ideas' [*Vorstellungen*], there are a constant series of excitations, corresponding to the content of these ideas, which are discharged into the smooth or striated muscles" (p. 288). Contemporary neuroscience has confirmed the existence of this phenomenon. A psychical treatment aims at gaining access to the pathogenic ideas through the use of words to undo their harmful power over mind and body. Freud committed his life to perfecting their therapeutic effect and creating theories to explain it.

Freud's evolving technique and theoretical conceptualizations

Freud's technique evolved in the course of many years from its original nucleus in Breuer's hypnotic procedure to its final form, when it had become "as definite and delicate as that of any other specialized branch of medicine" (Freud 1924, 203). In *The Psychotherapy of Hysteria*, the final section of *Studies on Hysteria* (Breuer and Freud 1893–1895), Freud shows how at the beginning the patient lay down, with eyes closed to facilitate concentration, while he behaved as the active physician of the day who *knew* what was best and remained in full command of the treatment. He wanted his patients to recall the thoughts and circumstances that had caused their symptoms. If the analysands claimed that they did not know what it was, he "assured them that they *did* know it, that it would occur to their minds" (p. 268). He applied gentle pressure with his hands on their foreheads and *insisted* that they remember and describe to him what came to their minds. He theorized that they had put the troublesome thought out of their minds, but remained certain that although "the psychical trace of it was apparently lost to view," it must still "be there" (p. 269). He was implicitly using the notion that mental representations cannot disappear he had presented in *On Aphasia*. His hand kept pressing the patient's forehead while he insisted that the patient "will *see* before him a recollection in the form of a *picture* or will have it in his thoughts in the form of an *idea* [*Einfall*] occurring to him; and I pledge him to *communicate* this *picture* or *idea* [*Einfall*] to me, whatever it may be" (p. 270, my italics). The patient had to tell him everything, suppress nothing, and not allow shame or discomfort to stop him from putting it all into words to undo the automatic work of defensive processes (p. 269). When he released the pressure of his hand he asked, "as though there were no question of a disappointment: 'What did you *see*?' or 'What *occurred* to you [*ist Ihnen eingefallen*]?'" (p. 270, my italics).

Regardless of Freud's effort's *to compel* the patient to recall, they frequently did their best *to resist* remembering, increasing Freud's work to overcome their reluctance. It was like a battle of wills. Then, "a new understanding seemed to open before my eyes when it occurred to me [*mir einfiel*] that this must no doubt be the same psychical force that had played a part in the generating of the hysterical symptom" (p. 268). The concept of *resistance* had entered psychoanalysis. Soon he was "astonished to realize in what a mutilated manner all the ideas and scenes (*Einfälle und Szenen*) emerged which we extracted from the patient by the procedure of pressing" (p. 281). Faced with this new difficulty he insisted that the patient *look again* at the picture, or, alternatively, Freud *guessed* himself what was missing. Such guesses never falsify the patient's memory. The fact is that memories and thoughts arrive piecemeal like fragments of a Chinese puzzle, and "it is the psychotherapist's business to put these together once more into the organization which he presumes to have existed" (p. 291). I read *organization* as an equivalent of an object-representation complex understood as a multisensory perceptual unity that had become distressing to the patient.

Freud made several assumptions in doing his work. First, he assumed that his *order* to remember would bring up the pathogenic memories and scenes to the patient's mind. I reason that he must have equated representations, pictures, memories, and scenes with internal perceptual organizations and attributed to them what he had proposed in *On Aphasia*, that they had the capacity to link their visual components to words and that they had kept their potential to stimulate speech when activated. In fact he was seeking the *visual and scenic components of the patient's memory* and wanted the patients to look carefully at them to see *consciously* what could reawaken the pathogenic past experience. Once he discovered the work of resistance and defense in fragmenting the internal imagery, he took on the task of restoring the representations to their initial organization. I consider this as analogous to restoring a representation to its original *perceptual* but disturbing form. Later, in *On Psychotherapy*, Freud described his technique as similar to Leonardo da Vinci's *per via di levare* (Freud 1905c, 260) in which the sculptor "takes away from the block of stone all that hides the surface of the statute contained in it."

The notion that the stimulus present in the representation is at work is confirmed by Freud's clinical observation: "a recollection never returns a second time once it has been dealt with; an *image* that has been '*talked away*' is not seen again" (Breuer and Freud 1893–1895, 296) (my italics) as if the stimulus had spent itself naturally.

Freud was asking his patients to describe what would never be a subject of conversation in ordinary exchanges: that they communicate through speech their most private thoughts (*Einfälle*), scenes, recollections, pictures – in a word, their intrapsychic reality. The first part of the task takes place completely within the patient, the remembering of the images, scenes, ideas, and stories that prompted their symptoms. The doctor's verbal order *assumes* the existence in the patient of a non-conscious process with the capacity to bring to their internal awareness what is pertinent for the treatment in the same manner that it was for the formation of the illness. The patient's task has now become threefold: first, to conjure up the right mental content from the vast array of his stored experiences and pay *attention* to it; second, to tolerate being aware of it; and, third, to select words to *translate* its elements from their thought or visual modality into a verbal form to communicate them to the therapist. Point three contains a sub-task, namely, to select what to say and what not to say because, even though Freud makes no mention of it here, humans cannot speak generically: we size up the person who has instructed us to speak and select the best words *for him* and the *least harmful for us*. A critical question emerges: what are the laws involved in re-producing, in a verbal mode, *translating*, the internal experience that has emerged in the patient's mind as a thought or scene? Freud says nothing about this but when he observed a time delay in the patient's reporting he became suspicious "that the patient is re-arranging what has occurred to him and is mutilating it in his reproduction of it" (Breuer and Freud 1893–1895, 279) to avoid the emergence of affect that a full report on the picture would elicit in him.

Facing such defensive moves, Freud opted to represent himself as infallible "till at last we are really told something" and the patient acknowledges: "I couldn't believe it could be that. It was only when it came back every time that I made up my mind to say it" (p. 279). He knew what he was doing: "The procedure by pressure is no more than a trick for temporarily taking unawares an ego which is eager for defence" (p. 278). In the monograph *On Aphasia* Freud described the phenomenon of *divided attention* that he is using here as a device. There he reported his observation that while proofreading "what I am reading escapes me" (Freud 1891, 75). He took it for granted that if not in the grip of defenses, the patients could easily and accurately put words to what occurred to them while observing that "as soon as this has been done [i.e., told him about it] the picture vanishes, like a ghost that has been laid" (Breuer and Freud 1893–1895, 280–81). Freud did not reflect about what the *communication* of his private experience to the therapist meant to the patient because he was focused on the one-person psychology of the intrapsychic reality he had described in the monograph.

The restoration of the disowned representation is incomplete if it does not reveal the dynamic motivation, "the logical thread, by whose guidance alone we may hope to penetrate to the interior" (ibid., p. 292). I understand this "logical thread" to be the private *narrative* of events, thoughts, and feelings which the patient has rejected as belonging to his person and replaced with symptoms. The analyst then may offer the patient a *narrative* of the pathogenic predicament, as Freud did with Fräulein Elisabeth von R.: "So for a long time you have been in love with your brother-in-law" (ibid., p. 157). In fact, Freud's technique could not lead to anything else but the narration of the private dramas that had prompted the patient's repression and illness. There is a significant theoretical shift here from the restoration of original representations to the *person* revisiting intolerable private narratives and helping him to tolerate the painful affect they bring up.

What are the analyst's tasks as described in *Studies on Hysteria*? Freud lists several, namely, to describe the treatment to patients, to convince them to accept it, and to offer a certain education that will enable them "to free themselves from their intentional thinking and to adopt an attitude of completely objective observation towards the psychical processes taking place in them" (p. 271). Freud's request involves the patients paying attention to the *perceptual reality* of what comes to their mind during analysis. Once a patient enters treatment, the analyst's task is to listen to his words to find in them the "pathogenic psychical material which has ostensibly been forgotten" (p. 287). Freud listened to the *wording* of the psychical material that the patients had recovered. He also attended to their "facial expression" so as to observe "the tension and signs of emotion with which he tries to disavow the emerging recollection, in obedience to defence" (p. 281). Freud did not want to miss any verbal or bodily clues.

His goal was to identify the pathogenic material through the patient's words. Soon he realized it could not be uncovered directly. He heard communications that at best "pointed the way" to the pathogenic idea by offering "intermediate link(s) in the chain of associations" (p. 271). These statements call for a critical question: if Freud was only *hearing his patients' words*, how did he proceed to go from what they were telling him through intermediary associations to the "pathogenic idea"? How did he manage to conceive of it? The only answer I am capable of giving is that he had to *transform* what he was hearing into *imaginary scenes* or experiences connected to the patients' descriptive words in his own mind. In other words, he had to *translate* the patients' communications into his own manner of conceiving what he *assumed* they had pictured, experienced, or thought. Yet although he had to go from the words he heard to their experiences if he was to gain access to the pathogenic ideas, Freud says nothing about the *process* in his mind. The author of *On Aphasia* took it for granted that he could reproduce adequately enough in his own mind the *mental representation* linked to those words *in his patient's mind*. It had to be something sufficient to explain the clinical picture; if that process did not reach its goal he *created* a guess about what had happened in the patient to make the clinical manifestations intelligible and sustained the dynamic logic of the formation of particular symptoms. If the conjecture reached the target the patient was "obliged to abandon his rejection of it" (p. 281). The reasoning has its antecedent in the notion in *On Aphasia* that the representations, now enlarged to encompass scenes, memories, and thoughts, harbor the *stimulation* to speak and once they have been put into words they arrive at a restful state. He says this explicitly in relation to technique: "Thanks to the abundant causal connections, every pathogenic idea [*Vorstellung*] which has not yet been got rid of operates as a motive for the whole of the products of the neurosis, and it is only with the last word of the analysis that the whole clinical picture vanishes, just as happens with memories that are reproduced individually" (p. 299).

Freud's focus on the intrapsychic reality of his patients soon forced him to notice another phenomenon of a different nature, one that the one-person model of the monograph could not encompass, that is, the doctor participation in the process: "It is almost inevitable that their personal relation to him will force itself, for a time at least, <u>unduly</u> into the foreground. It seems, indeed, as though an influence of this kind on the part of the doctor is a *sine qua non* to a solution of the problem" (266, my underlining). The patient cannot help but notice the person of the doctor and to develop complex feelings from a dread of losing her independence, even becoming sexually dependent on him, for example. Furthermore, "the patient is frightened at finding that she is *transferring* on to the figure of the physician the distressing ideas [*peinliche Vorstellungen*] which arise from the content of the analysis" (302, my italics). This is Freud's first use of the term "transference" as a clinical phenomenon. It has to do with a "*false connection*," a concept he had used to describe the mechanism of obsessions in *The Neuro-Psychosis of Defense* (Freud 1894). What happens is that the *affect* of an idea becomes attached to another idea that is not incompatible with it. I must at once point out that Freud has returned to the intrapsychic realm of representations and has surreptitiously inserted the representation of his own person ["another idea"] in the patient's mind. We know today that when we talk to another person we have to form a certain representation of him or her to establish a conversation. In hindsight we can say that the verbal exchanges and the relationship implied in them during the analysis created the occasion for such false connection.

After examining Freud's use of words during treatment as presented in his chapter on *The Psychotherapy of Hysteria* (Breuer and Freud 1893–1895), I am intrigued by Freud's lack of reflection about the fact that he was using words in *unusual* ways – not as dialogue, but as an arrangement agreed upon under Freud's *double command* that the patient *attend* to his own mental processes, something truly new to the patient, and then communicate what he found to the analyst in words. It was indeed *a new manner of speaking* between two people and also an innovative process of re-awakening previously rejected internal representations and unconscious processes to be used as referents for words.

The Interpretation of Dreams *and imagery in mental life*

Freud's patients brought their dreams to the treatment and he concluded "that a dream can be inserted into the psychical chain that has to be traced backwards in the memory from a pathological idea. It was then only a short step to treating the dream itself as a symptom and to applying to dreams the method of interpretation that had been worked out for symptoms" (Freud 1900, 101). He considered "dreams from the very first as being of a composite character, as being conglomerates of psychical formations" (p. 104), and decided to attend to aspects of the dream one at a time, acquire the associations to that portion of the dream, and continue accumulating further thoughts and associations to uncover the dream's meaning. He observed that as the analysis of a dream goes forward, a change occurs: the mental material no longer retains all the visual and sensory forms but appears as *thought processes* and *recollections* related to the dream imagery and the person's life. "'Interpreting' a dream implies . . . replacing it by something which fits into the chain of our mental acts as a link having a validity and importance equal to the rest" (p. 96). It means assisting the patient to accept as his own the thoughts, feelings, and wishes included in the formation of the dream.

What role do words play in interpreting dreams? We need to revisit Freud's conception of how words are used in dream formation:

> A dream-thought is *unusable* so long as it is expressed in an abstract form; but when once it has been *transformed into pictorial language*, contrasts and identifications of the kind that the dream-work requires . . . can be established more easily than before between the new form of expression and the remainder of the material underlying the dream. . . . We may suppose that a good part of the intermediate work done during the formation of a dream . . . proceeds along the line of *finding appropriate verbal transformations* for the individual thoughts.
>
> (p. 340, my italics)

What is Freud saying here? As I understand this passage, Freud *implies* that thoughts are linked to words. Abstract words are useless, but vivid, concrete words became useful in assisting the dream-thoughts to become pictorial representations. He explicitly asserts: "The dream-work does not shrink from the effort of recasting unadaptable thoughts into a new verbal form – even into a less usual one – provided that that process facilitates representation and so relieves the *psychological pressure* caused by constricted thinking" (p. 344, my italics). He considers the multiple and ambiguous potential of words as "nodal points of numerous ideas" (p. 340) and shows that "dreams, make unashamed use of the advantages thus offered by words for purposes of condensation and disguise" (p. 341). In brief, words do have the potential to offer something essential for the *visual* representation of the dream. We may ask whether Freud still had in mind his understanding of *meaningful* words in *On Aphasia*, where he saw them as a composite of word and object-representation, the latter introducing with its visual component *all* its sensory-perceptual richness. Although he does not mention it explicitly, everything he says about word usage in dreams points to their potential to link a given word-presentation to *multiple* thing-presentations that can be used to create condensations and to facilitate displacements during dream formation.

Experiences from everyday life offer graphic imagery for the dream. Climbing stairs has a rhythmical pattern and prompts shortness of breath, not unlike human copulation. Dreams use climbing stairs as a symbolic representation of intercourse. We must notice that the connection between climbing stairs and intercourse rests not on the verbal form, but on the *representation* [scene] of the acts they describe. In sum, words such as "climbing stairs" have the ability to *awaken experiences* and form concrete and complex imagery in the mind of the listener. Such imagery appears capable of linking *simultaneously* to our body, our imagination, our linguistic competence, our conceptions of the world around us, and, in particular, our manner of relating to ourselves and others. Obviously, we are now far beyond the concrete single object-presentation linking to a single word as described in *On Aphasia*, even though our words must still find a complex "representation" to offer us personal meaning.

In this context, I question what is involved in the process in which the dream-thoughts work at "finding appropriate verbal transformations for the individual thoughts." Is Freud referring to the word-presentation (the linguistic form), to the complex formed by object/thing presentation, or to both? Freud provides neither the question nor the answer. Nevertheless a phenomenon has persistently caught my attention in reading Freud's cases on hysteria and in his analysis of dreams. I have observed that frequently patients' memories and associations – be it to dreams or to other material – are linked directly to *scenes* portraying events and experiences in their lives. The associations may take the form of simply remembering the scene – real or imaginary – with or without the feeling experienced in it, or thoughts in relation to it. In one way or another, the associations bring up scenes of one's own life or of the lives of others that the dreamer has witnessed or imagined. They share with the dream the fact that they portray *the dreamer as their central figure*, as Freud notes: "Every dream deals with the dreamer himself" (pp. 322–23).

Freud's dream about *Irma's Injection*'s offers a clear illustration of these points. The associations he noted to each component of the dream reveals that a compatible, complementary, or contrasting scene or scenes from his life came to his mind and elicited in him complex thoughts, feelings, wishes, and reactions. Freud's analysis of his dream appears also as a short story, filled with intricate episodes and sentient, extremely vivid characters acting their assigned dream roles. A conclusion follows: the mind works unconsciously and consciously by resorting to sensory recollections of *episodic life events* intertwined with the inexhaustible referential richness of the words that name them. Memory and the organization of the mind are not based on isolated object- or thing-representations but on episodic, even if confused or confusing, *scenic representations of oneself* as part of them. They are unconsciously organized and many of them remain so when they are pathogenic owing to the affective experiences they may elicit in us if they became conscious.

Transference as a particular representational event came to the fore dramatically when Freud was treating the adolescent Dora as he reported in *Fragment of an Analysis of a Case of Hysteria* (Freud 1905a). He learned that "transference is an inevitable necessity" and that "there is no means of avoiding it" (p. 116). He sees it as a new mental structure, mostly unconscious: "They are new editions or *facsimiles* of the impulses and phantasies which are aroused and made conscious during the progress of the analysis; . . . they replace some earlier person by the person of the physician. To put it another way: *a whole series of psychological experiences are revived* not as belonging to the past, but as applying to the person of the physician at the present moment" (p. 116, my italics). What at first appeared as an obstacle for the treatment turned out to be "its most powerful ally" (p. 117) because psychoanalysis only brings to light a potential transference that was already there.

I believe that psychoanalysis with its peculiar arrangements, its idiosyncratic use of speech, its insistence that the patient reveal deeply hidden feelings and thoughts in words addressed to the analyst creates a situation in which transference *has to occur*. As I mentioned earlier, it is impossible to talk to someone else without forming an internal conception of that person. Most patients, in fact, form two and oscillate from one to the other. At one level, they perceive the person of the analyst as their actual doctor while at another level they revive experiences from the past linked to their relationship to the analyst.

A few years later Freud uncovered a complementary process in the analyst. In *The Future Prospects of Psycho-Analytic Therapy* he acknowledged that some emotional response "arises in him as a result of the patient's influence on his unconscious feelings" (Freud 1910a, 144) and called it counter-transference. He does not mention that the analyst too forms an internal conception of each patient based on her own prior experiences, both clinical and personal. The analyst must recognize this response and find a way to overcome it, because "no psychoanalyst goes further than his own complexes and internal resistances permit" (p. 145).

In *The Dynamics of Transference*, Freud re-examines the transference as the internally organized *modes of relating* to people under the pressure of libidinal urges that now become focused on the person of the analyst as a love object. Freud describes how each person has formed a "stereotype plate (or several such), which is constantly repeated – constantly reprinted afresh" (Freud 1912a, 100) as his or her precondition to falling in love. If reality does not satisfy someone's need for love, he is bound to approach every new person whom he meets with libidinal "anticipatory ideas" [*Erwartungsvorstellungen*] (ibid.), which are mostly unconscious. During the treatment the doctor may appear as a "reprint" of earlier people: the "father-imago," the "mother-imago," or even the "brother-imago" (p. 101). In *Three Essays on the Theory of Sexuality* Freud described the process of forming such "imagos" in terms of human objects as representations saying that when the child is able to form a total idea of the person [*Gesamtvorstellung der Person*]" (Freud 1905e, 222), it recognizes that the breast belongs to the mother.

As a result of the analysis, Freud says, "the libido (whether wholly or in part) has entered on a regressive course and has *revived* the subject's infantile imagos" (Freud 1912a, 102, my italics). He goes on to say: "It is at this point, on the evidence of our experience, that transference enters on the scene" (p. 103). It is the analysis that makes "the patient's hidden and forgotten erotic impulses immediate and manifest" (p. 108). The transference uses the analysis as the *scenario* of a play about love. It is not a theatrical presentation but rather the patient's re-awakened wish to be loved in a particular manner by a desired object. Ultimately, every conflict that arises during analysis "has to be fought in the sphere of transference" (p. 104) because it is the only avenue open to the patient to remove his libido from the archaic object and become free to find love in real life.

Readers may be asking themselves what all this has to do with verbal exchanges between patient and analyst. The analytic situation is a very peculiar setting. Although patient and analyst relate as adults the patient is lying down and has committed himself to uttering his most private thoughts for the first time in his life, without the benefit of having a 'conversation', a normal back-and-forth exchange. Instead, the patient has to talk until the analyst is ready to intervene. It is hard to imagine a more vulnerable situation for someone to reveal himself. This most unusual 'non-conversation' adds a powerful reinforcement to the patient's libidinal disposition. The representational imagos of early figures resurface loaded with libidinal impulses ready to motivate and activate the patient's verbal exchanges. On the other hand, the analyst's calm, respectful, invitational attitude to the patient is bound to awaken earlier real or wished-for conversations and affective exchanges with the objects from the past to whose imagos the patient's libidinal desires are attached. The new exchanges cannot help but bring those imagos to the analytic scenario and blend them with the person of the analyst. We are back in the representational realm with one key difference: to the unnamed "stimulation" to talk, described in *On Aphasia* as present in object-representations, has now been added the libidinal component of the representation of the parental imagos. Transference finds its prototype in the representational organization of the word as conceived in the monograph: *in talking during analysis we unconsciously summon up our objects in our associations and our remembered scenes with them and in so doing reincarnate them in our experience of the analyst.*

Freud reported in his 1904 paper *Freud's Psycho-Analytic Procedure* the technical changes he had implemented in his practice. He writes in the third person, indicates he has given up hypnosis, and describes the procedure:

> Without exerting any other kind of influence, he invites them to lie down in a comfortable attitude on a sofa, while he himself sits on a chair behind them outside their field of vision. He does not even ask them to close their eyes, and avoids touching them in any way, as well as any other procedure which might be reminiscent of hypnosis. The session thus proceeds like *a conversation between two people equally awake*, but one of whom is spared every muscular exertion and every distracting sensory impression which might divert his attention *from his own mental activity*.
>
> (Freud 1904, 250, my italics)

He wants the patient to "let himself go" and ramble freely, apparently trusting that the unexpressed stimulation of the repressed representation or scene will find a way to give indications of its mental presence and lead to finding "the continuity of a consecutive narrative" (p. 251) that has been interrupted by repression. Freud sees his task as "extracting the pure metal of the repressed thoughts from the ore of the unintentional ideas" (p. 252) through offering interpretations. He acknowledges that "this technique of interpretation or translation [*Deutungs-oder Übersetzungstechnik*] has not yet been published by Freud" (p. 252).

Three of the terms Freud uses here deserve closer inspection: "conversation," "translation," and "pure metal." The word "conversation" is surprising because the patient has agreed to talk freely without consciously focusing on anything while the analyst speaks only to facilitate the uncovering of repressed thoughts. "Pure metal" is a fascinating metaphor, because it points to the great effort of extracting something valuable from the abundant "ore" of associations, an unrefined mass that hides the repressed thoughts. "Translation" implies the existence of two languages. The translation Freud wants can be understood as a parallel construction to the metaphor of "pure metal": one language – the actual words of the patient – is only a *medium* carrying hints to hidden repressed material; the other language, the unconscious pathogenic narrative, is the valuable part, the real thing.

In *The Future Prospects of Psycho-Analytic Therapy* Freud indicates that he has introduced fundamental changes in his technique. The patient is offered more freedom to find access to his unconscious while the doctor "no longer works actively to force the patient to recollect." A critical change has also occurred with respect to the aim of the treatment: "we . . . turned away from the symptoms and devoted ourselves instead to uncovering the 'complexes'" (Freud 1910a, 144), which he describes as the many associations connected to a nucleus of unconscious elements and the feelings linked to them. The analyst's task remains the same, namely, "overcoming the 'resistances'" to facilitate "the complexes coming to light" (ibid.). Freud does not explain the processes in the analyst's mind that facilitate the emergence of such complexes in the patient's mind to make their translation possible.

Over time he discovered other prerequisites for achieving successful translation of repressed material. In *'Wild' Psychoanalysis* he presents two conditions as indispensable for the patient's readiness to hear an interpretation of his complex: he must "himself have reached the neighbourhood of what he has repressed, and he must have formed a sufficient attachment (transference) to the physician for his emotional relationship to him to make a fresh flight [from treatment] impossible" (Freud 1910b, 226). The second condition points indirectly to the patient's need for a sense of safety in working with his analyst. In brief, the analyst must respect both the affective and cognitive levels of his patient's readiness to hear communications about his unconscious complexes. Freud added a third condition in *On Beginning the Treatment (Further Recommendations on the Technique of Psycho-Analysis I)*: "One must be careful not to give a patient the solution of a symptom or the translation of a wish until he is already so close to it that he has only one short step more to make in order to get hold of the explanation for himself" (Freud 1913b, 140). The analysand may be conscious of what is repressed "but his thought lacks the connection with the place where the repressed recollection is in some way or another contained. No change is possible until the conscious thought-process has penetrated to that place and has overcome the resistances of repression there" (p. 142). Only when this happens will the patient be able to change and integrate what he has discovered about himself into his conscious thoughts. Freud elaborates these ideas further in Lecture XXVII of the *Introductory Lectures on Psycho-Analysis* (1916–1917) where he calls *translation [Übersetzung]* the process of making the unconscious conscious. The analyst's task is to give some hints to the patient to facilitate his access to the struggle taking place in his unconscious, so that he can connect it with the pathogenic event and moment: "We must look for it in his memory at the place where it became unconscious owing to a repression. The repression must be got rid of – after which the substitution of the conscious material for the unconscious can proceed smoothly" (Freud 1916–1917, 436). In brief, Freud wants to find the genesis of the defense.

The work of the patient's memory in reviving the pathogenic moment carries the risk of remaining merely a mental exercise: "At this point what turns the scale in his struggle is not his intellectual insight – which is neither strong enough nor free enough for such an achievement – but simply and solely his relation to the doctor" (p. 445). Another sort of translation has taken place, in that an "artificial neurosis" has been established: "It is not incorrect to say that we are no longer concerned with the patient's earlier illness but with a newly created and transformed neurosis which has taken the former's place. We have followed this new edition of the old disorder from its start, we have observed its origin and growth, and we are especially well able to find our way about in it since, as its object, we are situated at its very centre" (p. 444). Now the translation involves not only the effort of the analyst to make the unconscious conscious but the patient's unconscious *transposition* of the libidinal investment in early objects to the person of the analyst. Returning to Freud's theory in *On Aphasia* about the always expanding representations, I would say that the transference offers the possibility of revisiting and re-examining old dialogues, scenes, and experiences with invested early objects by adding the person of the analyst *in vivo* to the old prototypes. In other words affect, which was missing in *On Aphasia*, has now been integrated into the structure of the representational world: "A man is only accessible from the intellectual side too, in so far as he is capable of a libidinal cathexis of objects" (p. 446). The term "object" here has evolved in meaning: it is a representational complex, no longer of things but of a person's internal human objects, expanded now to include the analyst. Speaking with the analyst creates the occasion for becoming libidinally attached to her and transferring onto her the patient's desires. The focus of the talking cure has moved from giving priority to the *content* of the 'conversation' to the libidinal investment aroused by patient and analyst speaking to each other.

The analyst's mode of listening

Freud instructs the patient how to talk to him by using a fascinating metaphor: "So say whatever goes through your mind. Act as though, for instance, you were a traveller sitting next to the window of a railway carriage and describing to some-one inside the carriage the changing views which you see outside" (Freud 1913b, 135). This metaphor insists on the *visual* component of the task when the patient is invited to take a trip through his own mind and describe the *internal landscape he sees*. Bertram Lewin concludes that in Freud's exposition of technique he aligns "free association with a visual analogue" (Lewin 1970, 84). It makes sense because Freud was seeking – in accordance with his aphasia model – unexpressed represen-tational realities in the patient's mind; even though they were repressed they still could find unconscious visual connections with his words.

As for his listening to the patient's internal landscape, Freud believed "that everyone possesses in his own unconscious an *instrument* with which he can inter-pret the *utterances* of the unconscious in other people" (Freud 1913a, 320, my ital-ics). Before I reflect on this assertion we need to attend to Freud's descriptions of his mode of listening.

In *Recommendations to Physicians Practicing Psycho-Analysis* Freud says: "The tech-nique, however, is a very simple one. . . . It consists simply in not directing one's notice to anything in particular and in maintaining the same 'evenly-suspended attention' . . . in the face of all that one hears" (Freud 1912b, 111–12). He aims to avoid any deliberate attention because "the things one hears are for the most part things whose meaning is only recognized later on" (p. 112). Besides, purposeful attention cannot help but select one aspect of what is present in the patient's words. Any selection follows the personal expectations of the analyst and forecloses what does not conform to them in the patient's utterances. The analyst must hear it all, hear *beyond any habit of listening he has already formed*. The technique recommends that "he should simply listen, and not bother about whether he is keeping any-thing in mind" (p. 112). With these recommendations Freud *created a new way of listening* to words and *to the people* who speak them. He believed that the patient's utterances describing the pictures of his inner landscape had the power to disclose to the analyst what is hidden from the analysand himself.

Freud sums up the rule for the doctor: "He should withhold all conscious influences from his capacity to attend, and give himself over completely to his *'unconscious memory'*" (p. 112, my italics) and adds that the analyst "must turn his own unconscious like a receptive organ towards the transmitting unconscious of the patient" (p. 115). We must ask: in what way do the patient's words transmit his unconscious? How do they reach the analyst's unconscious memory? In ordinary conversations the interlocutors follow the subject matter, making constant adjustments to remain in contact with each other and keep what they are talking about in focus. In analytic listening the focus is on the unconscious, that is – in Freud's words – a communication from unconscious to unconscious.

Throughout his work Freud insists that perception, external and internal, is *all* we have to organize our psychic life. Is Freud's *unconscious instrument* the result of allowing subtle subliminal perceptions in the patient's speech to find echoes in the analyst's unconscious memory? And if not, how does the unconscious of one person transmit and listen to that of another? What perceptual system do they use? Reflecting about these questions prompts me to return to *On Aphasia* and Freud's grounding of the entire speech function, as representation and utterance, on bodily sensory perceptions. The patient's voiced utterances have an astonishing sensory richness. Their semantic, prosodic, melodic, affective tone and subtle or overt bodily gestures are bound to be perceived by the hovering attention of the analyst. In the patient's words the analyst hears semantic denotations, connotations, descriptive imagery, metaphors and similes and other figures of speech colored by a steady or fluctuating affective tone of voice in the context of the specific analytic moment. How does the analyst use this information to arrive at an understanding of unconscious processes? How does the analyst's mind work to find in such utterance the complexes and defenses in the patient's unconscious? Freud limits himself to describing what the analyst is to do, seemingly taking for granted the *processes* that assist him in *translating* the patient's words into recognizable unconscious complexes. He is convinced, however, that such manner of working must never be disrupted if the analysis is to achieve its goal.

I must repeat here that in *On Aphasia* Freud clearly established that the entire speech function is based on associative processes and that to perceive is to associate. The patient's perceived words *must* call for associations to them in the analyst's mind. Furthermore, he believed that "in listening to speech with understanding . . . we more or less repeat to ourselves the words heard, thus supporting our understanding with the help of kinaesthetic impressions (*Sprachinnervationsgefühle*) (Freud 1891, 91–92). This is to say that in listening to her patient's voiced words the analyst spontaneously associates them to her own words and internal representations and even activates her own speech muscles subliminally. As I mentioned above, in Freud's view, even thinking activates our muscles. In *Jokes and Their Relation to the Unconscious* he described ideational mimetics. I mentioned this phenomenon in Chapter 5, and his words are worth repeating here: "I believe that these mimetics exist, even if with less liveliness, quite apart from any communication, that they occur as well when the subject is forming an idea of something for his own private benefit and is thinking of something *pictorially*, and that he then expresses 'large' and 'small' in *his own body* just as he does in speech, at all events by a change in the innervation of his features and sense organs" (Freud 1905b, 193, my italics). Freud's description of this type of embodied simulation and "innervation" must be present in the listening analyst's subliminal bodily responses and must contribute to the awakening of representational and affective internal processes in his own non-conscious memory in the form of imagery and thoughts. I believe that this perceptually based organization of the analyst's mind is the instrument that facilitates the *bodily mediated* unconscious communication in analysis.

This interpretation finds support in Freud's metaphor comparing the unconscious to the telephone as an instrument that transmits and receives communications:

> He must turn his own unconscious like a receptive organ towards the transmitting unconscious of the patient. He must adjust himself to the patient as a telephone receiver is adjusted to the transmitting microphone. Just as the receiver converts back into sound waves the electric oscillations in the telephone line which were set up by sound waves, so the doctor's unconscious is able, from the derivatives of the unconscious which are communicated to him, to reconstruct that unconscious, which has determined the patient's free associations.
>
> (Freud 1912b, 115–16)

The patient's sound waves are understood to transmit to the analyst's unconscious some sort of hints about *scenes* and thoughts of experienced frustration and expected satisfaction that find an echo in the analyst's reservoir of associated memories, imagery, and thoughts. Here we must pose the next critical question: how does the analyst convert spoken words into *internal perceptions* of unconscious derivatives? The bodily based imagery and thoughts of the repressed *experiences* must be linked to the patient's transmitting words. In short, if the transmission from unconscious to unconscious is to convey the unacceptable repressed experiences, thoughts, fantasies, and desires, then it has to find a way to give them imagery and thoughts derived from the body with which they are bound to be connected. In a roundabout way, Freud has returned to his conception in *On Aphasia*: meaningful spoken words are connected to representational complexes, and receive from them *unconscious stimulation* to speak when defenses do not interfere. Some support for this idea may be found in another comment in the same paper:

> Those elements of the material which already form a *connected context* will be at the doctor's *conscious* disposal; the rest, as yet unconnected and in chaotic disorder, seems at first to be submerged, but rises readily into recollection as soon as the patient brings up something new to which it can be related and by which it can be continued.
>
> *(Freud 1912b, 112, my italics)*

In other words the analyst must wait until enough material is added to acquire an organized representational form, one that can become conscious in the analyst's mind. Chaos is not perceivable, either consciously or unconsciously. Once the analyst has recognized the unconscious complexes, she needs to find an apt moment when the patient will be receptive to hearing about them. She can then begin the twofold process of overcoming his resistances and achieving his acceptance of them, as he works through both the old neurosis and the new transferential illness.

We must now return to Freud's assertion in his 1904 paper that his interpretive task of translation consists in "extracting the pure metal of the repressed thoughts from the ore of the unintentional ideas" (Freud 1904, 252). He elaborates his conception in *The Question of Lay Analysis: Conversations with an Impartial Person:*

> You would not find it at all such a simple matter to deduce from *what the patient tells you* the *experiences* he has forgotten and the instinctual impulses he has repressed. He says something to you which at first means as little to you as it does to him. You will have to make up your mind to look at the material which he delivers to you in obedience to the rule in a quite special way: as though it were ore, perhaps, from which its content of precious metal has to be extracted by a particular process. You will be prepared, too, to work over many tons of ore which may contain but little of the valuable material you are in search of.
>
> *(Freud 1926b, 219, my italics)*

This means that "the patient's remarks and associations are only distortions of what you are looking for – allusions, as it were, from which you have to guess what is hidden behind them" (ibid.). Finding the precious metal calls for a protracted struggle against the patient's resistances. We are reminded in this paper that *the words in the patient's associations and occurrences are no more than ore*, a mass of material through which the analyst must sift to find the dynamically repressed material and the libidinal attachments to internal objects. Words are deceptive, as such they do not reveal what ails the patient. They have to be heard as *means to an end* that penetrates to the depth of the unconscious representations exerting their influence. I agree with Freud that in analysis words cannot be taken at face value, yet there is a conundrum here: patient and analyst have no other tools available to them except words, not only to find repressed material but also to further the analysis. If all words and associations were ore, merely ore, how could we analyze, help the patient, or facilitate the conviction that our interpretations are correct? Where is the other side of the patient's and analyst's words, the part that *communicates and engages*, that reveals where "he is at"? How do our interpretative words reach the patient emotionally so that he accepts what has been unbearable to him up to now? Or to put it differently, how do we establish with our words a true and healing form of *communication* with him? I believe that Freud is right when he establishes the patient's attachment to the analyst as the essential condition of the treatment, one that prepares us to translate his complexes to him and enables him to accept them as his own. It is this attachment to the actual person of the analyst, even if mixed with transference, that offers the possibility of using words not as 'ore' but as a meaningful and acceptable personal exchange.

At the start the patient has been suffering from a *gap* in his mind resulting from the repression of significant aspects of his representational reality. Once the resistances are removed by the analyst's translation, the elements of the mind find a new unity: the "ego fits into itself the instinctual impulses which before had been split off and held apart from it" and, as a result, a "psycho-synthesis is . . . automatically and inevitably" achieved (Freud 1919, 161), restoring the narrative that organizes the patient's inner life.

Remembering may involve more than recollecting thoughts and imagery. In *Remembering, Repeating and Working-Through (Further Recommendations on the Technique of Psycho-Analysis II)*, Freud describes different ways of remembering. Screen memories represent "not only *some* but *all* of what is essential from childhood" (Freud 1914, 148). They serve defensive functions and are linked to repressed experiences. They may appear in conscious recollection or in the patient's dreams and they must undergo analytic exploration to uncover their significance.

Then there are cases in which "the patient does not *remember* anything of what he has forgotten and repressed, but *acts* it out. He reproduces it not as a memory but as an action; he *repeats* it, without, of course, knowing that he is repeating it" (ibid., p. 150). This represents such a person's way of remembering. Freud concludes, "we must treat his illness, not as an event of the past, but as a present-day force" (p. 151). The patient's illness takes the form of re-enacting scenes from the actual or imagined past under the compelling stimulation of the scenes themselves. Here I must ask: are these scenes cathected as a unit of experience, feeling, memory, and action? What Freud has indicated so far suggests that the response must be in the affirmative. Repeating is "conjuring up a piece of real life" (p. 152), and the treatment has to trace this event back to its original occurrence. The aim is to help the patient achieve "a reconciliation with the repressed material" (p. 152) and to assist him with his compulsion to repeat: "We render the compulsion harmless, and indeed useful, by giving it the right to assert itself in a definite field. We admit it into the transference as a playground in which it is allowed to expand in almost complete freedom and in which it is expected to display to us everything in the way of pathogenic instincts that is hidden in the patient's mind" (p. 154).

I find this assertion technically powerful, emotionally moving, and theoretically fascinating. The playground metaphor opens up the analytic space for the replaying of previously intolerable scenes, feelings, and modes of relating that find in the analyst a willing and all-committed playmate, capable of taking the heat of the "pathogenic instincts" and helping the patients to accept them as their own. Freud puts it this way: "We regularly succeed in giving all the symptoms of the illness a new transference meaning and in replacing his ordinary neurosis by a 'transference-neurosis'" (p. 154). Analysis becomes living theater, at times a drama where the patient provides the successive scenes and the analyst assists him in working through his resistances and defenses until their meaning in the present is revealed, and, most important, their significance in the past. Freud insists that the experience *convinces* the patient that his previously unknown impulses really exist and helps him to effect actual changes in his life.

Once again readers may be asking themselves: what does all this have to do with the use of words? My reply would be: everything. The acting-out behaviors acquire meaning only when they are linked to the patient's associations and his progressive discovery of the connection between the present and the past. Only words may lead patient and analyst together to uncover the *subjective meaning* of the acting out and its connection to people in the past and to the analyst in the present. The patient's words – metabolized during the analytic process – are the only avenue to link "the real life" of the analysis to earlier days.

There is another function of words that Freud discusses in *Remarks on the Theory and Practice of Dream Interpretation* when he attends to "the multiple appearance of the ego in a waking thought, especially when the ego [*das Ich*] divides itself into subject and object, puts one part of itself as an observing and critical agency in contrast to the other, or compares its present nature with its recollected past, which was also ego once [*einmal Ich war*]; for instance, in such sentences as 'When *I* think what *I*'ve done to this man' or 'When *I* think that *I* too was a child once'" (Freud 1923, 120).

Freud's first sentence is of a structural nature and addresses the division between the experiencing subject and the same subject as the object of the critical superego, while the second involves a distinction between the speaking subject in the present and a view of itself in the past. Both comments point to one function of language that is ever present in analysis but that Freud never made fully explicit: the patient's spoken word functions as the instrument to *identify his private reality and to objectify his self-perception, present and past, and make it accessible to himself and the analyst.* Without the articulation into words, his thoughts, dreams, feelings, and wishes could not contribute to his conscious self-awareness and ego integration.

Freud reflects in his paper *Analysis Terminable and Interminable* on the need for meta-psychology: "Without metapsychological speculation and theorizing – I had almost said 'phantasying' – we shall not get another step forward" (Freud 1937a, 225). I am grateful to Freud for saying 'phantasying.' Theorizing is a manner of creating frames of reference in which to locate the material presented by the patient. Scientific understanding cannot emerge without the use of fantasy, as the study of creative and scientific minds has repeatedly demonstrated. This kind of speculation commonly involves visual, spatial, and scenic imagery and Freud's theorizing is no exception: the *super*-ego represents one such spatial conception, and *depth*-psychology is another. It is worth looking at the complex description Freud provides of the patient's predicament while keeping in mind his use of the imagination in theorizing:

> The psychical apparatus is intolerant of unpleasure. . . . But one cannot flee from oneself; flight is no help against internal dangers. And for that reason the defensive mechanisms of the ego are condemned to falsify one's internal

perception and to give one only an imperfect and distorted *picture of one's id*. In its relations to the id, therefore, the *ego is paralysed* by its restrictions or *blinded* by its errors; and the result of this in the sphere of psychical events can only be compared to being out walking in a country one does not know and without having a good pair of legs.

(ibid., p. 237, my italics)

What I wish to point out here is that metapsychology and theory cannot fulfill their organizing task without resorting to imagery, spatial constructs, scenes, similes, and metaphors that, as functions of a linguistic system, cannot fail to form and inform the phenomena we are trying to describe. This applies not only to psychoanalysis but equally well to physics and the other hard sciences. The kind of theory we select *shapes* the phenomenon we observe. Freud's comparative description of the defended ego's situation presents a vivid *scene* of a weak-legged person walking in unknown territory. Even in our most elevated conceptual thinking we cannot escape the imagination's contribution. Freud's words illustrate it: the id, an abstract concept, needs to be *pictured* correctly; the ego, another abstract concept, may suffer from paralysis and blindness. While these are certainly metaphors, they shape how we hear what our patients are saying. Do these words hide other realities, just as the patient's defensive views do? Do the conceptual words *id, ego, superego* create, by their very existence, new 'realities' that add complexity to our understanding of the patient's communications? These questions must remain open for now.

In the last paper Freud published during his lifetime, *Constructions in Analysis*, he reports: "We are reminded that the work of analysis consists of two quite different portions, that it is carried on in two separate localities, that it *involves two people*, to each of whom *a distinct task is assigned*. It may for a moment seem strange that such a *fundamental fact* should not have been pointed out long ago" (Freud 1937b, 258, my italics). It was not pointed out earlier because Freud was so intent on unraveling *intrapsychic* processes that he enlisted his patients to *help him* in that task, leaving not much analytic or psychic time to attend to other aspects of their work. The patient's task is "to remember something that has been experienced by him and repressed" (p. 258); while the analyst, in turn, searches for "a picture [*vollständiges Bild*] of the patient's forgotten years that shall be alike trustworthy and in all essencial respects complete" (p. 258). Her analytic task "is to make out what has been forgotten from the traces which it has left behind or, more correctly, to *construct it*" (pp. 258–59). The analyst's communication of this construction to the patient "constitute the link between the two portions of the work of analysis, between his own part and that of the patient" (p. 259). Freud compares the analyst's work to that of the archeologist who "reconstructs the *mural decorations* and *paintings* from the remains found in the debris" (p. 259, my italics); she draws "inferences from the fragments of memories, from the associations and from the behaviour of the subject of the analysis" (ibid.). Their reconstructions differ in that the archeologist has *actual physical* fragments, whereas the analyst must use her mind to form *virtual* pictures of the patient's experiences from the fragmentary memories he has expressed in words. In fact, I think she has to form *two virtual scene-like representations*, one of the supposedly historical event and a second of the *internal* stance of the patient in relation to it. Freud provided an illustration of how he reconstructed a patient's early history:

> 'Up to your *n*th year you *regarded yourself* as the sole and unlimited possessor of your mother; then came another baby and brought you grave disillusionment. Your mother left you for some time, and even after her reappearance she was never again devoted to you exclusively. Your feelings towards your mother became ambivalent, your father gained a new importance for you,' . . . and so on.
>
> (p. 261, my italics)

The "historical truth" in the patient's narrative reads: "then came another baby," "she was never again devoted to you exclusively." Then, the analyst offers the constructed *psychical* historical truth: "unlimited possessor of your mother," "grave disillusionment," "ambivalent."

In this essay Freud, once more, reveals that construction in analysis uses visual imagery. In constructing the patient's early life and the moments of symptom formation the analyst must form a *complex, sensory virtual representation* of what happened to the patient in actual life and internally. I propose that such representational complex comes to exist through the power the patient's words have to *create imaginary scenarios* in the unconscious/conscious mind of the analyst, that is to say, through a process analogous but by far more complex than Freud's early version of object-presentations in *On Aphasia*.

In the last section of the paper, Freud acknowledges that constructions do not necessarily elicit confirmatory recollections from the patient, but still "we produce in him an assured conviction of the truth of the construction which achieves the same therapeutic result as a recaptured memory" (p. 266). Freud apparently intended to address this issue in "a later enquiry" (p. 266), but in fact left it unresolved. I suggest that if progressive construction of the patient's earlier experience is a joint effort to re-assemble the fragments in order to grasp what the child needed at the time, the patient's conviction arises from an emotionally felt and shared experience of having been understood.

In the posthumously published paper *An Outline of Psycho-Analysis* Freud reflects on the speech function in relation to consciousness, a phenomenon familiar to everyone but which "defies all explanation or description" (Freud 1940, 157). We are conscious not only of what we perceive, but also of our internal processes. Being aware of our private reality "is the work of the function of speech [*Sprachfunktion*], which brings material in the ego into a firm connection with mnemic residues of visual, but more particularly of auditory, perceptions" (p. 162). Yet Freud has not forgotten his basic philosophical stance, namely, that actual and psychical reality will always remain unknowable as such (p. 158). The best an analyst can do is to assist the analysand in becoming conscious of his internal processes and of the events of his past life by inferring those 'unknowable' processes and interpolating them into his conscious awareness, reasoning in this manner: "if it had entered our consciousness, [it] could only have been described in such and such a way" (p. 197). The analyst's construction of the representation and his wording of it to the patient restore his capacity to speak meaningfully about himself, his words are now *psychical* words.

In the last section of the essay, entitled "The Internal World," Freud calls attention to the limitations of our means of expression: "We have no way of conveying knowledge of a complicated set of simultaneous events except by describing them successively; and thus it happens that all our accounts are at fault to begin with owing to one-sided simplification and must wait till they can be supplemented, built on to, and so set right" (p. 205). Freud continues the section talking about the formation of the ego, the superego, and the internal world. For my part I reflect that language as a means to express our internal world remains temporal, directional, and linear, while representational processes are simultaneous. As required by linguistic rules, words must be linear and directional, but once heard in their proper order they are used by the mind in more than one way. They affect the listener *simultaneously* at many levels: emotionally, somatically, and intellectually. They awaken thoughts and imagery, retrieve memories, involve other mental activities, and are invariably, as Freud has convinced us, placed in a vast associative network, both conscious and unconscious, that extends far beyond their actual or even intended meaning. Psychoanalysis would not be possible without this *associative simultaneous multipotential* of all words spoken and heard.

Reflections and conclusions

I was greatly surprised by the paucity of Freud's remarks on the function of words in his technical writings. He called *On Aphasia* "a truly good thing" and explicitly asserted there that a word is a composite of word- and object-representation. How could he have neglected to elaborate on the technical significance of such a composite and the staggering complexity that psychoanalysis added to that early conception over time? I have a hypothesis in mind as a response to this question. It has to do with Freud's absolute determination to make psychoanalysis "the science of unconscious mental processes" as he states in *Psycho-Analysis* (Freud 1926a, 264), an article written for the thirteenth edition of the *Encyclopaedia Britannica*. Freud was intent on being a scientist and being seen as one, too. He was determined to prove the existence and function of unconscious processes in normal people as well as in neurotics. He was single-mindedly focused on discovering and elucidating every aspect of pathogenic, unconsciously repressed processes – their existence, function, and dynamic organization. He wanted to demonstrate that transforming them into consciously accepted processes capable of being integrated into the patient's awareness had an unquestionable therapeutic effect. Freud insisted further that psychoanalytic *interpretation or translation* of unconscious processes into conscious awareness is the only truly effective way to treat neurotic symptoms and to help people suffering from neurosis. It must be acknowledged that he was facing a monumental task at the therapeutic level, and even more so at the theoretical level.

His keen ability to observe facts and connections and his unfailing ingenuity in creating new concepts were placed at the service of creating both a theory about the unconscious and a technique for gaining access to it that would be as comprehensive as possible and as fully integrated with the knowledge available to him at the time as he could make them. In this context, his metaphor about verbal associations – as being comparable to a large amount of ore he had to sift through to find the "precious metal" of unconscious processes – acquires a new meaning. Freud was searching for one thing and determined that nothing should distract him from this task. The "precious metal" had to be found and incorporated into a comprehensible and scientifically acceptable theory. Anything that would undermine his concentration on discovering and articulating the workings of unconscious processes had to be left unattended, since otherwise, the focus would become blurred and only confusion could follow. I do not mean to say that Freud intentionally neglected other functions of his patient's words and imagery. I am saying that to build his theory about the unconscious he had to focus almost exclusively on those aspects of the spoken word that guided the analyst in his search for unconscious sources of pathology. Attending theoretically to other aspects of how words and imagery function could have become a dangerous distraction. In brief, his life work and commitment as a scientist consisted in *translating* the unknown unconscious processes present in his patients' and contemporaries' minds into demonstrable conscious narratives, through the mediation of verbal interpretations.

Before we go on to examine his clinical presentations, we must make a detour to examine Freud's theoretical papers in relation to his understanding of the spoken word.

References

Breuer, Josef, and Sigmund Freud. *Studies on Hysteria*. Vol. 2 of *Standard Edition*. London: Hogarth Press, 1893–1895.

Freud, Sigmund. Analysis Terminable and Interminable. Vol. 23 of *Standard Edition*, 209–53. London: Hogarth Press, 1937a.

———. Constructions in Analysis. Vol. 23 of *Standard Edition*, 255–69. London: Hogarth Press, 1937b.

———. The Disposition to Obsessional Neurosis. Vol. 12 of *Standard Edition*, 311–26. London: Hogarth Press, 1913a.

———. The Dynamics of Transference. Vol. 12 of *Standard Edition*, 97–108. London: Hogarth Press, 1912a.

———. Fragment of an Analysis of a Case of Hysteria. Vol. 7 of *Standard Edition*, 1–122. London: Hogarth Press, 1905a.

———. Freud's Psycho-Analytic Procedure. Vol. 7 of *Standard Edition*, 247–54. London: Hogarth Press, 1904.

———. The Future Prospects of Psycho-Analytic Therapy. Vol. 11 of *Standard Edition*, 139–51. London: Hogarth Press, 1910a.

———. *The Interpretation of Dreams*. Vols. 4–5 of *Standard Edition*. London: Hogarth Press, 1900.

———. *Introductory Lectures on Psycho-Analysis*. Vol. 16 of *Standard Edition*. London: Hogarth Press, 1916–1917.

———. *Jokes and Their Relation to the Unconscious*. Vol. 8 of *Standard Edition*. London: Hogarth Press, 1905b.

———. Lines of Advance in Psycho-Analytic Therapy. Vol. 17 of *Standard Edition*, 157–68. London: Hogarth Press, 1919.

———. The Neuro-Psychosis of Defense. Vol. 3 of *Standard Edition*, 41–68. London: Hogarth Press, 1894.

———. *On Aphasia: A Critical Study*. Trans. Erwin Stengel. 1953. New York: International Universities Press, 1891.

———. On Beginning the Treatment. Vol. 12 of *Standard Edition*, 121–44. London: Hogarth Press, 1913b.

———. On Psychotherapy. Vol. 7 of *Standard Edition*, 255–68. London: Hogarth Press, 1905c.

———. An Outline of Psycho-Analysis. Vol. 23 of *Standard Edition*. 1938, 139–207. London: Hogarth Press, 1940.

———. Psychical (or Mental) Treatment. In *Die Gesundheit*, edited by R. Kossmann and J. Weiss, 368–84. Stuttgart: Union Deutsche Verlagsgesellschaft, 1890.

———. Psychical (or Mental) Treatment. Vol. 7 of *Standard Edition*, 281–302. London: Hogarth Press, 1905d.

———. Psycho-Analysis. Vol. 20 of *Standard Edition*, 259–70. London: Hogarth Press, 1926a.

———. The Question of Lay Analysis. Vol. 20 of *Standard Edition*, 177–258. London: Hogarth Press, 1926b.

———. Recommendations to Physicians Practicing Psycho-Analysis. Vol. 12 of *Standard Edition*, 109–20. London: Hogarth Press, 1912b.

———. Remarks on the Theory and Practice of Dream Interpretation. Vol. 19 of *Standard Edition*, 109–21. London: Hogarth Press, 1923.

———. Remembering, Repeating, and Working-Through. Vol. 12 of *Standard Edition*, 145–56. London: Hogarth Press, 1914.

———. A Short Account of Psychoanalysis. Vol. 19 of *Standard Edition*, 191–212. London: Hogarth Press, 1924.

———. Three Essays on the Theory of Sexuality. Vol. 7 of *Standard Edition*, 123–243. London: Hogarth Press, 1905e.

———. "Wild" Psychoanalyis. Vol. 11 of *Standard Edition*, 219–27. London: Hogarth Press, 1910b.

Lewin, Bertram D. The Train Ride: A Study of One of Freud's Figures of Speech. *Psychoanalytic Quarterly* 39 (1970): 71–89.

Strachey, James, ed. Editor's Note to "Psychical (or Mental) Treatment (1890)." Vol. 7 of *Standard Edition*, 281. London: Hogarth Press, 1953.

7

FREUD'S THEORIES

Repression as gaps in consciousness and the words to fill them

> The theory of repression is the corner-stone on which the whole structure of psycho-analysis rests.
>
> (Freud 1914, 16)

In his posthumously published *Some Elementary Lessons in Psycho-Analysis*, Freud repeats that: "The psychical . . . is in itself unconscious" (Freud 1940b, 283) while "consciousness is only a *quality* . . . of what is psychical, and moreover an inconstant one" (pp. 285–86). Yet, it "remains the *one light* which illuminates our path and leads us through the darkness of mental life. In consequence . . . our scientific work . . . will consist in *translating* unconscious processes into conscious ones, and thus *filling in the gaps* in conscious perception. . . ." (p. 286, my italics). Consciousness is "a fact without parallel, which defies all explanation or description" (Freud 1940a, 157). Nonetheless "if anyone speaks of consciousness we know immediately and from our most personal experience what is meant by it" (p. 157). Freud's entire theoretical enterprise rests on his efforts to create a scientific explanation of unconscious phenomena and to find the means of *translating* into conscious awareness the repressed material that created *gaps* in his patient's psychic life.

Conscious awareness is a *subjective* phenomenon that is apprehended only by the experiencing individual and cannot be shared directly with others. Freud asked how we can know the consciousness of others and answered his own question in *The Unconscious*: "That other people, too, possess a consciousness is an inference which we draw by analogy from their observable utterances and actions, in order to make this behaviour of theirs intelligible to us" (Freud 1915b, 169). He continues in a parenthesis: "We attribute to everyone else our own constitution and therefore our consciousness as well" (ibid.).

The subjective certainty of consciousness has a significant advantage and a great shortcoming. The advantage is the capacity to know ourselves; the shortcoming is the limitation of its scope that leaves large sectors of our psyche unknown to us. Freud committed himself to creating theoretical models to comprehend the phenomena of accessing unconscious processes by the mediation of spoken words. In *On Aphasia* he created a model that remained the foundation of all his later efforts to understand the interdigitation between unconscious and conscious processes.

In *The Neuro-Psychosis of Defense* Freud describes the splitting of consciousness in conflicting moments and the formation of separate psychical groups as *"the result of an act of will on the part of the patient"* (Freud 1894, 46). When confronted with an experience, an idea, or a feeling that aroused distressing affect and finding himself unable to deal with it, he "decided to forget about it" (p. 47). The ego defensively transforms the idea into one that is weak and that will make "no demands on the work of association" while it remains as part of a defended unconscious psychical group (p. 49). These processes that are not consciously recognized create a *gap* in consciousness.

In 1895 Freud wrote a "Psychology for Neurologists" (Freud 1950) with the aim of exploring the economics of nerve forces and of creating a mental machine that would "run of itself" (Strachey 1950, 285). He mailed the manuscript to his friend Wilhelm Fliess on October 8 and never asked to have it returned to him. Marie Bonaparte, a faithful follower of Freud, found it in 1937 and protected it against Freud's wish to destroy it. It was published in 1950 as *Project for a Scientific Psychology*. It represents Freud's most systematic effort to create a bridge between neurology and psychology. He never returned to the manuscript but the ideas in it reappear in many of his theoretical writings, in particular Chapter 7 of *The Interpretation of Dreams*. Strachey concludes: ". . . the *Project*, or rather its invisible ghost, haunts the whole series of Freud's theoretical writings to the very end" (Strachey 1950, 290).

The *Project* is a rich but difficult document; its writing style is compact in exploring ideas of a staggering complexity. I will select from it what Freud said about conscious and unconscious processes and the function of speech in relation to them. Consciousness reveals "the subjective side of one part of the physical processes in the nervous system" that represent the registrations of perceptual neurons and sensory processes (p. 311). They leave behind *facilitations* that do not undergo changes so as not to "falsify the traces of reality" (p. 335). That means that perceptions must preserve their original registration and facilitations without alteration.

In the *Project* Freud gives his first description of primary and secondary processes. Early in life primary processes attempt to obtain satisfaction by means of an internal *hallucination*, which is followed by the unpleasure caused by the absence of relief, leading the child to scream. He remarks that the infant's screaming acquires another "function . . . that of *communication*" (p. 318 and also p. 366). The secondary process involves the ego employing *indications of reality* about what is there in the world to satisfy the need.

In discussing perception Freud seems to return to a thought he had expressed in *On Aphasia*: *"Perceptual cathexes are never cathexes of single neurones but always of complexes. So far we have neglected this feature"* (p. 327, my italics). He adds that perceptual complexes of *thing*s are composed of two neurons related to language: "Neurone *a*, which on the whole remains the same, and a second component portion, neurone *b*, which for the most part varies" (p. 328). Freud continues "[language] will call neurone *a* the *thing* and neurone *b* its activity or attribute – in short, its *predicate*" (p. 328). He seems to be talking about object-representation and word-representation.

In considering thought and reality Freud proposes that what is brought into the organism by perceptual neurons must become part of ψ, the system of impermeable neurons capable of memory, that is, reproducible thought. In the end through the mediation of thought processes the individual manages to recognize the identity between what he wished for and the *idea* of what he has perceived in reality.

Freud is also concerned with distinguishing between perceptions and thoughts. This is done by "indications of quality" that "come about normally only from perceptions" (p. 364). Freud indicates here his commitment to the notion that perception is the foundation of psychic life. Thought also needs indications of quality that are provided by speech:

> This purpose is fulfilled by *speech association*. This consists in the linking of ψ neurones with neurones which serve sound-presentations [*Vorstellungen*] and themselves have the closest association with motor speech-images . . . from the sound-image the excitation reaches the word-image and from it reaches discharge. . . . If now the ego precathects these word-images as it earlier did the images of ω [perception] discharge, then it will have created for itself the mechanism which directs the ψ cathexis to the memories emerging during the passage of Qη [quantity]. This is *conscious, observing thought*.
>
> *(p. 365)*

In sum the "*indications of speech-discharge* help . . . put thought-processes on a level with perceptual processes, lend them reality and *make memory of them possible*" (pp. 365–66). When the encounter with an object causes pain "the *information of one's own scream* serves to characterize the object" and the unpleasure it brings about and thus "the first class of *conscious memories* has been created. Not much is now needed in order to invent speech" (pp. 366–67). It is striking that Freud seems to link the "invention" of speech to the child's screaming with pain. He also suggests that *cognitive thought* is achieved through directing attention to indications of *speech discharge*. The scream that started the process of attempting to obtain actual satisfaction has contributed to the formation of facilitations and memories and the organization of the ego and its perceptual experiences. It must be noted that there is *a time gap* here between the foundational experiences of satisfaction and a child's capacity to speak.

Next Freud describes two *biological* rules. The first is the nervous system defense against unpleasure (p. 370) and the second is the rule of attention: "*If an indication of reality appears, then the perceptual cathexis which is simultaneously present is to be hypercathected*" (p. 371). He then addresses the *cognitive* process of thought, which is not prompted by wishful cathexes. Here he returns to the function of speech associations: "During this passage [of associations] the indications of quality (of speech) are generated, as a result of which the passage of association becomes *conscious* and *capable of being reproduced*" (p. 372, my italics). Attention can now be applied to thought: "Indications of discharge through speech are also in a certain sense indications of reality – but of thought-reality not of external reality" (p. 373). This represents Freud's first theoretical reference to a psychical reality that differs from perceptual reality. *The field of psychoanalytic exploration has been defined.* It follows that attention to internal reality is as important as attention to external reality if unpleasure is to be avoided. Furthermore, the passage [of associations] occurs *automatically* as part of our ordinary unconscious thought "with occasional *intrusions* [*Einfälle*] into consciousness" (p. 373). We have here Freud's earliest conception of how the mind works and of psychoanalytic technique. The "intrusions" have meaning. When they emerge in the patient's mind, their import can be ascertained by giving words to them and linking them to their source. This is *the first theoretical antecedent of free association and interpretation.*

Freud concludes: "*Thus thought accompanied by a cathexis of the indications of thought-reality or of the indications of speech is the highest, securest form of cognitive thought-process*" (p. 374). He repeats what he had said in *On Aphasia*: "Conscious thought takes place to the accompaniment of slight motor expenditure" (p. 367) of the muscles of pronunciation, thus including the body as part of consciousness.

Thought processes that cause unpleasure prompt a reaction and "the passage of thought is interrupted" (p. 380), thus creating a *gap*. A disagreeable "*untamed mnemic* image," as Freud describes it, would be countered by ego-binding processes to stop the unpleasure (p. 381) and to maintain the gap.

In 1896 Freud used the term 'metapsychology' for the first time in a letter to Fliess and "psychoanalysis" in a paper written in French and published that same year in the *Revue neurologique* (Freud 1985, 171, n.2). In sum, between 1895 and 1896 Freud devised the basic terminology for discussing conscious and unconscious processes.

The psychic machine of the *Project* that would "run of itself" could not function alone. In the experience of satisfaction, the baby's screams summon a helpful adult to provide the needed care. The crying introduces communication between them and leads the relieved infant to cathect the person and the action that brought relief. People had been tacitly introduced into the machine to oil it and keep it running. Yet, Freud did not reflect at that point that such a process must also create *facilitations* to register the exchanges with the satisfying external object to transform it into a psychical object.

When speech emerges it serves critical *intrapsychic* functions beyond communication with others in that it makes thought and memory accessible to consciousness. While thought may exist without speech, the reality of thought – its own independent realm of internal existence – is detected *consciously* only through its connection with speech. Furthermore, the indications of speech discharge make thought conscious and accessible for further thought and memory. To put it briefly, *the indications of speech create a perceptible internal reality* and permit access even to 'untamed' mnemic images, that is, an object-representation. Speech associations mediate the binding of such images by the ego until they can be tamed, that is, restrained from causing unpleasure. As I see it, Freud is describing psychoanalytic technique and the ways in which talking progressively makes painful memories available to conscious awareness. The intrapsychic realm of *thought reality* can be accessed only through the intervention of speech associations. Even though Freud does not say so explicitly in *The Project*, we live our lives in this *reality of thought*, regardless of our external circumstances. Our cognition, our understanding of ourselves and of the world takes place there, in our *unknown* unconscious and our *subjectively* conscious reality. We can only reach thought reality by the mediatory function of speech associations.

The Interpretation of Dreams

In Chapter VII of *The Interpretation of Dreams* Freud devotes the final section to the unconscious and consciousness and asserts: "The unconscious is the true psychical reality; *in its innermost nature it is as much unknown to us as the reality of the external world, and it is as incompletely presented by the data of consciousness as is the external world by the communications of our sense organs*" (Freud 1900, 613). We are limited by our senses in our ability to know external reality; we are prevented by our narrow conscious awareness from knowing our full psychic reality: "The unconscious is the larger sphere, which includes within it the smaller sphere of the conscious. Everything conscious has an unconscious preliminary stage" (pp. 612–13). The dominance of the unconscious rests on the nature of perception itself, which "provides our consciousness with the whole multiplicity of sensory qualities" (p. 539). Our perceptions, however, are conscious only transiently; they do not remain in our awareness but for a brief moment. The modifications effected by each perception are part of our unconscious memories (p. 539), yet they remain psychically effective as *facilitations* and find their most common manifestation in our 'character', where our past is inscribed. The perceptual memories are not isolated but "linked with one another in our memory – first and foremost according to simultaneity of occurrence. We speak of this fact as 'association'" (p. 539). This is the same process that Freud described as unconscious and 'automatic' in the *Project* (p. 373) and it is a repetition of his assertion in *On Aphasia* that to perceive is to associate. Together with repressed thoughts, memories "are left to themselves and can become charged with the uninhibited energy from the unconscious which is striving to find an outlet" (p. 605). This means that they are seeking to achieve "perceptual identity," that is, to come by an actual perception that replicates the original satisfaction (pp. 565–66). In their search for conscious expression, unconscious memories encounter the all-encompassing pleasure/unpleasure principle, which requires that unpleasure be inhibited. A certain limited unpleasure, however, "must be allowed, since that is what informs the second system of the nature of the memory concerned and of its possible unsuitability for the purpose which the [unconscious] thought-process has in view" (p. 601).

How do we manage to retrieve the memories we need to live our daily lives and to become aware of ourselves? It is the task of the Pcs. [preconscious] system that provides the only means available to the Ucs. for gaining access to conscious awareness. It "stands like a screen between the system Ucs. and consciousness" (p. 615). Guided by the pleasure principle it turns away thoughts capable of releasing wishes that would cause unpleasure. It offers thoughts "psychical quali-ties" *linked to speech* capable of accessing consciousness. Through this connec-tion, Freud concludes "consciousness, which had hitherto been a sense organ for [external] perceptions alone, also became a sense organ for a portion of our thought-processes. Now, therefore, there are, as it were, *two* sensory surfaces, one directed towards perception and the other towards the preconscious thought-processes" (p. 574). Freud added a further clarification in a footnote in 1925, where he explicitly noted that "the essential feature of a preconscious idea was the fact of its being connected with the residues of verbal presentations" (p. 611). Such "residues of quality are sufficient to draw the attention of consciousness to them and to endow the process of thinking with a new mobile cathexis from consciousness" (p. 617). The goal of psychoanalysis consists in bringing the Ucs. under the domination of the Pcs. by connecting apt words to the memories whose absence had left gaps in conscious memory.

Freud is certain that unconscious processes endure forever:

> They share this character of indestructibility with all other mental acts which are truly unconscious. . . . These are paths which have been laid down once and for all, which never fall into disuse and which, whenever an unconscious excitation re-cathects them, are always ready to conduct the excitatory process to discharge. If I may use a simile, they are only capable of annihilation in the same sense as the ghosts in the underworld of the Odyssey – ghosts which awoke to new life as soon as they tasted blood.
>
> (footnote to p. 553)

The ghosts were already present in *On Aphasia*; there Freud talked about their revival when similar neural conditions made them appear as "the psychical." Their persistence may create a problem if they would bring about unpleasure; in such case their awakening must be prevented. In ordinary circumstances an avoided memory "does not possess enough quality to excite consciousness and thus attract fresh cathexis to itself" (p. 600). This is the prototype of "*psychical repression*" (ibid.). Such situation has consequences: "If things remained at that point, the thought-activity of the second system would be obstructed, since it requires free access to *all* the memories laid down by experience" (p. 600, italics in the original). A *gap* is being formed as a result of the inhibition. Freud insists that this "is the key to the whole theory of repression: *the second system can only cathect an idea if it is in a position to inhibit any development of unpleasure that may proceed from it.* Anything that could evade that inhibition would be inaccessible to the second system as well as to the first; for it would promptly be dropped in obedience to the unpleasure principle" (p. 601). Repression has entered the dialectics between conscious and unconscious processes and has created a *gap* in the conscious memory of the person. Freud knew from working with hysterics that only a complete narrative of a repressed thought or experience could bring memories to a rest.

When Freud refers to primary processes's investment in revival of the psychical we must remember that in *On Aphasia* he said that all stimulation to speak arises from the area of object associations. Now we must *add* that speech involves overcoming the opposition to unpleasure together with a *translation* into meaningful words, that is, a linking of the unconscious processes to words that have been heard and psychically integrated. In other terms, we must acknowledge that the core of our psychic life is not ordinarily accessible to speech, and what is repressed least of all. *Speech about psychical life is always a translation. Psychoanalytic technique is the optimal tool for assisting a person to translate unconscious processes into affectively tolerable spoken words shared with the analyst.* Repressed experiences have achieved representational form, yet since they were recognized once, although transiently, they are *capable* of gaining access to the preconscious. Experiences that have never been articulated beyond the level of sensory impressions such as early events or profoundly traumatic occurrences need to be first articulated into some representational form, with some visual component, before the preconscious can facilitate their access to the spoken word. The analyst must assist the patient in gaining access to his repressed representations and finding the words to describe them while at the same time skirting excessive unpleasure.

Finally, we need to remember that words are embedded in complex networks of meaning. As Freud pointed out repeatedly their actual significance at a given moment calls for interpretation or *translation* of their meaning in the context in which there are located. In brief, *we live our psychical life as a series of translations. Conscious life is always a translation.*

Freud was proud of his discovery of repression as a mechanism of defense. In his paper *On the History of the Psycho-Analytic Movement*, he states that "the theory of repression quite certainly came to me independently of any other source" (Freud 1914, 15) and continues: "The theory of repression is the cornerstone on which the whole structure of psycho-analysis rests" (p. 16). It was an extraordinary scientific innovation and the key that opened the door to the newly discovered unconscious. The concept of repression stemmed from Freud's renunciation of hypnosis and its replacement by his instruction to patients to tell him whatever came to mind, thus changing their habitual use of speech. His method attempted to deprive speech of the normal conscious and non-conscious censorship present in verbal communications aimed at well-organized, conscious, goal-directed, and socially acceptable exchanges. Freud's request created an opportunity for unwanted mental processes (*Einfälle*) to emerge. The patients protected themselves against these unwelcome intrusions by resisting doing what Freud wanted them to do, namely, to put into words what came to their minds. It was this *resistance* that made repression obvious. In his essay *Repression* Freud concludes that "*the essence of repression lies simply in turning something away, and keeping it at a distance, from the conscious*" (Freud 1915c, 147).

He distinguishes between two kinds of repression: *primal repression* denies access to consciousness to the ideational representative of an instinct (p. 148), while *repression proper* denies access to conscious awareness to any *mental derivative* that has an associative connection with the instinct's ideational representative. These psychical maneuvers are palliative measures that do nothing to change the instinctual representative seeking satisfaction. On the contrary, "the instinctual representative develops with less interference and more profusely if it is withdrawn by repression from conscious influence. It proliferates in the dark, as it were, and takes on extreme forms of expression" (p. 149), elaborated by uninhibited fantasy and supported by the frustration of not finding satisfaction. Freud describes what then happens during analysis: "When they [the repressed thoughts] are *translated* and presented to the neurotic [they] are not only bound to seem alien to him, but frighten him" (p. 149, my italics). Psychoanalysis allows access to those derivatives by *deceiving* conscious awareness: "In carrying out the technique of psycho-analysis, we continually require the patient to produce such derivatives of the repressed as, in consequence either of their remoteness or of their distortion, can pass the censorship of the conscious. Indeed, the associations which we require him to give without being influenced by any conscious purposive idea and without any criticism, and from which we reconstitute a *conscious translation* of the repressed representative – these associations are nothing else than remote and distorted derivatives of this kind" (pp. 149–50, my italics). The *conscious translation* consists in putting into words the repressed material the patient had been unable to tolerate, that is, in naming and describing it. It also involves reuniting the psychical representative with its essential companion, the *quota of affect* that *belongs* to the representative (p. 153), which was separated from it at the moment of repression.

The change in technique to effect a *conscious translation* of the psychical representative continues to be a form of *tricking* the ego by replacing the earlier techniques with the analyst's attentive gathering of derivatives presented in the patient's words until she is able to approach and reconstitute the repressed representative and communicate it to the patient. Freud had learned to *translate* unconscious mental processes into ordinary, personal words.

In *Formulations on the Two Principles of Mental Functioning* Freud explores "the psychological significance of the real external world into the structure of our theories" (Freud 1911, 218). He returns to the experience of satisfaction as a sequence consisting first of a hallucination of the satisfaction and the ensuing unpleasure caused by its failure to satisfy the need. He suggests that, at this junction, "the psychical apparatus had to decide to form a conception of the real circumstances in the external world and to endeavour to make a real alteration in them" in order to obtain what is needed (p. 219). A new principle of mental functioning, the *reality principle*, becomes established, to include what is real, even if it is not agreeable. This new principle returns to the significance and value of consciousness, regulated by the sense organs' perceptions of reality. The quality of what is perceived contributes to the automatic regulation of the unpleasure principle. In this process attention was established, as a way of searching for what is needed instead of waiting for it to be provided. Finally, memory appeared as a system to register what attention had been able to locate. The function of judgment emerged in order to decide whether an idea [*Vorstellung*] was true or false, that is, whether perceived reality coincided with memory-traces of that reality. Under the guidance of the reality principle, motor activity was no longer followed by immediate discharge, but converted instead into an action for the "appropriate alteration of reality" (p. 221). The restriction of automatic discharge of motor activity led to a form of thinking "developed from the presentation of ideas" (p. 221). This is how Freud arrived at his conception of thinking as "an experimental kind of acting" (p. 221). In this manner, freely displaceable cathexes became 'bound' cathexes. Obviously, in this description he is conflating some Darwinian concepts of evolution and child development and incorporating them into his theory.

At this point Freud reintroduces the function of words and unconsciously registered impressions: "It is probable that thinking was originally unconscious, in so far as it went beyond mere ideational presentations and was *directed to the relations* between impressions of objects, and that it did not acquire further qualities, perceptible to consciousness, until it became bound to verbal residues" (p. 221, my italics). Freud reiterates what he had said from the beginning, namely, that *verbal expressions make conscious awareness possible*. Given the extraordinary importance of speech for obtaining knowledge and mastery over reality as well as for inhibiting action in order to gain time for thinking, I find myself surprised that Freud has nothing more to say about speech in a paper on the reality principle. In his introduction to the papers on metapsychology, Strachey mentions that Freud had intended to write a paper on consciousness, which I assume would have dealt with the connections between words and consciousness. Such paper was either lost or never sent for publication (Strachey 1957b, 106).

A relevant point about the reality principle is Freud's description of fantasizing and daydreaming as activities of thought that, in complete disregard of reality-testing and the "dependence on real objects" (Freud 1911, 222), respond to the call of the pleasure principle. In them the subject is involved in vivid *imaginary scenes* where he is the main actor. Conscious daydreams differ from unconscious fantasies in that the person knows they are fantasies and does not believe in them (Freud 1900, 535). Unconscious fantasies are distinct both in quality and topographic location: "On the one hand, they are highly organized, free from self-contradiction, have made use of every acquisition of the system *Cs.* and would hardly be distinguished in our judgement from the formation of that system. On the other hand they are unconscious and are incapable of becoming conscious. Thus *qualitatively* they belong to the system *Pcs.*, but factually to the *Ucs* . . . [and] remain repressed and therefore cannot become conscious" (Freud 1915b, 190–91). They are at the core of the neurotic's pathology and must be unearthed and verbalized for them to lose their dynamic power. Once more the *gap* created by the unconscious fantasy in conscious awareness must be filled by *translating* it into conscious words that the patient can integrate into the narrative of his life.

In *Psychoanalytic Notes on an Autobiographical Account of a Case of Paranoia* (Freud 1911), Freud elaborates the mechanisms of the defenses involved in the paranoid process, namely, the use of internal language and of projection. The paranoid's defensive maneuvers involves the patient's undoing of his *intolerable internal language* about his loved or hated objects by contradicting his internal propositions about such emotions. Freud explains: "The mechanism of symptom-formation in paranoia requires that *internal* perceptions – feelings – shall be replaced by *external* perceptions by *projection* into another: 'He *hates* (persecutes) *me*, which will justify me in hating him'" (p. 63). Similar undoing takes place in erotomania, jealousy, or alcoholic delusions. Freud does not state explicitly that this peculiar external reality is a matter of *belief* and its verbalization.

Paranoid defenses follow grammatical sentence structure: "Delusions of jealousy contradict the *subject*, delusions of persecution contradict the *verb*, and erotomania contradicts the *object*" (pp. 64–65), while all three depend on projection. It works in this manner: "An internal perception is suppressed, and, instead, its content, after undergoing a certain kind of distortion, enters consciousness in the form of an external perception" (p. 66). In this defense, the clear differentiation between internal and external reality is undone because the projection transposes the *location* of the subject, of the object, and of the feelings of both. Freud promised to discuss the nature of projection in a later occasion, but he never did. I reason that the *gap* in the continuity of consciousness in the paranoid person is filled up by the 'perceived' projection. The *internal speech* offers a psychical defense in relation to the self in the same manner that the perception error of displaced attribution supports the paranoid's pathological beliefs.

In *A Metapsychological Supplement to the Theory of Dreams*, Freud returns to the perception of what is real in dreams and in waking life. He needs to explain how the dreamer who "plays the chief part in their scenes" (Freud 1917a, 223) perceives them as real and returns to the hypothesized experience of satisfaction that eventuates in a hallucination: "The reversal of the course of the excitation from the *Pcs.* through the *Ucs.* to perception is at the same time a return to the early stage of hallucinatory wish-fulfilment" (pp. 227–28). Freud describes the regression of preconscious day's residues in dreams: "Thoughts are transformed into images, mainly of a visual sort; that is to say, word-presentations are taken back to the thing-presentations which correspond to them, as if, in general, the process were dominated by considerations of *representability*" (p. 228). In discussing the mediatory function of words (word-presentations), Freud says that they are *taken back* to the corresponding thing-presentations, implying that they belong together, just as he had described in *On Aphasia*. There are different ways of using word-presentations. If they are linked to thought processes they go back to their own thing-presentation. If they are residues of perceptions, however, they are given the value of thing-presentations and become susceptible, as all memories of things are, to condensation and displacement under the influence of the primary process, in order to form the manifest dream-content. He asserts "that words and speeches in the dream-content are not freshly formed, but are modelled on speeches from the day preceding the dream (or on some other recent impressions . . .). It is very noteworthy how little the dream-work keeps to the word-presentations; it is always ready to exchange one word for another till it finds the expression which is most handy for plastic representation" (p. 228). He concludes that in dreams "all operations with words are no more than a preparation for a regression to things" (p. 229).

In the end, the dream process forms a wishful fantasy that is hallucinated as a sense perception and *believed* in the reality of the dream. To explain such belief Freud resorts to regression: "When once a thought has followed the path to regression as far back as to the unconscious memory-traces of objects and thence to perception, we accept the perception of it as real. So hallucination brings belief in reality with it" (Freud, p. 230). This belief confronts Freud with the need for mental tools to discriminate between what is actually real and what is perceived in the hallucinatory belief. He reasons: "Hallucination must therefore be something more than the regressive revival of mnemic images that are in themselves *Ucs.*" (p. 231). Once more he returns to the experience of satisfaction and reflects that when the hallucination failed to deliver what was needed "we gave up hallucinatory satisfaction of our wishes at a very early period and set up a kind of 'reality-testing'" (p. 231), which he considers among "the major institutions of the ego." He describes how it comes about: "The *Cs.* must have at its disposal a motor innervation which determines whether the perception can be made to disappear or whether it proves resistant. Reality-testing need be nothing more than this contrivance" (p. 233). Freud had used the same concept in the *Project,* Part I, section 15, suggesting that when muscular action prompts a perception to disappear, it is an indication that it is external.

What have we learned about how Freud understands the function of speech, words, and images – particularly visual images – in this essay? We notice the persistence of the terminology and model from *On Aphasia* in describing regression, yet many things remain puzzling. In *On Aphasia* Freud intended to create a model of the speech apparatus and the ways in which a word is formed. The term "object-representation" – called "thing-presentation" in the *Metapsychological Supplement* [as in *The Unconscious*] – refers to the multisensory organization of perceptions that converge in forming the representation of a thing perceived, a single thing. But what happens, we must ask, when what is perceived (either in reality or in dreams) is not a single thing but *a whole experience*, such as the satisfaction of a need or complex scenes? It seems to me impossible to speak any longer in terms of "thing-representations" because what we perceive is entire events, which of necessity include the meaning of what is perceived along with a minimal narrative structure. A dream never uses single things but rather complex scenes organized around the self of the dreamer. If Freud is correct when he says in *On Aphasia* that the words we speak link the thing-presentation to the word-presentation, we must ask whether all the words we use have links only to unconscious presentations, as he seems to imply in the essay? If this is in fact correct, should we conclude that speech and words belong to conscious experience, but encounter their meaning in the unconscious presentations to which we have managed to connect them?

At this point it is important to recall that Freud uses the term "unconscious" with three meanings: (1) as an adjective to describe what is phenomenologically unconscious; (2) as a topographic/systemic component of the mental apparatus; and (3) as the dynamic unconscious comprising what has been repressed by defenses. Ordinary words may link to representations in the descriptive unconscious as a result of perception. Dynamically repressed representations come to be linked with words through the laborious interpretative work of the analyst, as she traces the many and convoluted derivatives of the representation to its unconscious source. Most words carry unintended disguised derivatives of repressed imagery and thoughts as well as hints of unconscious wishes, or to put it differently: because of most words' connections with conscious and unconscious representations, they frequently join with derivatives of the descriptive, systemic, and dynamic unconscious *simultaneously*. This process makes psychoanalysis possible and is compatible with Freud's notion of an ego whose foundations sink deep into unconscious processes. In ordinary conversations we attend to the meanings linked to the descriptive unconscious while, *subliminally*, we may register the other unintended meanings and messages. The greatest contribution of psychoanalysis consists in paying exquisite attention to those unintended meanings in order to hear the whispers of unconscious wishes and repressed material.

I must now ask another question: is it true that imagery is mainly the realm of regression? Are there aspects of imagery that are not only conscious but a normal part of ordinary thinking? Again, it seems necessary to make a distinction similar to the one made above. There is imagery that is descriptively unconscious and available for thinking, for the imagination, and for the anticipation of unknown realities. Then there is the imagery related either to early experiences that are not accessible to conscious awareness, or to repressed material that remains guarded and kept unconscious by the defenses.

Finally, I would like to explore another intriguing point. When we manage, be it in dreams or during analysis, to gain access to a repressed pathogenic event or scene, how do we 'look' at them to describe and name them with the words we have? To me this is a translation, a way of *selecting* what we 'see' and how to name or describe it because regardless of how simple it may be, it is never a 'thing', but a complex dream event, thought, or memory of *experiences* and *scenes*. It bears repeating that the only option in conscious psychic life is to live in translation because, as Freud said, we live between two unknown realities: the world and the unconscious.

Papers on metapsychology

I have already examined Freud's paper on the metapsychology of dreams. Here I will explore his understanding of speech and words in the remaining four papers.

In *Instincts and Their Vicissitudes* Freud says practically nothing about speech, but it does offer his clearest definition of an instinct: "An 'instinct' appears to us as a concept on the frontier between the mental and the somatic, as the psychical representative of the stimuli originating from within the organism and reaching the mind, as a measure of the demand made upon the mind for work in consequence of its connection with the body" (Freud 1915a, 121–22). In this text Freud uses the German term *Repräsentant*, with the legal and constitutional meaning of representing as an elected official or lawyer would do. In other essays, Freud uses 'drive representation' [*Triebrepräsentanz*, my translation]. In *The Unconscious*, Freud clarifies that: "An instinct [*Trieb*] can never become an object of consciousness – only the idea [*Vorstellung*] that represents [*repräsentiert*] the instinct can. Even in the unconscious, moreover, an instinct cannot be presented otherwise than by an idea" (Freud 1915b, 177). This bodily representation has its *source* in somatic processes, *aims* at obtaining satisfaction, and finds it in the adequate *object*. I see here another instance of the many processes of *translation* that are needed for the establishment of psychical life: biochemical and physiological processes are trans-ported and trans-lated into an unconscious psychical 'drive representation'.

Freud describes two types of primal instincts: the ego instinct of self-preservation and the sexual instincts. This is not the place to comment on them, but there is one point I wish to stress: in talking about the *content* of the instincts Freud mentions love and hate. He observes that "the attitudes of love and hate cannot be made use of for the relations of instincts to their objects, but are reserved for the relations of the *total ego* to objects" (Freud 1915a, 137, my italics). I have selected this remark because it seems to me that the same can be said about the attitude of the someone who speaks. Even when the speaker may not fully know what he is saying, the *act* of speaking requires the participation of the total ego, body and mind. Freud seems to take this point for granted: no one part of the psyche is in charge of speaking, the whole person is.

The Unconscious (Freud 1915b) presents a comprehensive elaboration of Freud's ideas about what he called the true psychical reality. He used the term "unconscious" for the first time in 1895, in a footnote in *Studies on Hysteria* (Breuer and Freud 1893–1895, 166) where he discusses his patient Frau Cäcilie's symptoms: "On each occasion what was already present as a finished product in the unconscious was beginning to show through indistinctly" (p. 76, n.1). That early sentence is already loaded with meaning that became progressively clearer in later works. Here I will focus only on Freud's conception of the use of the speech function in analytic theory and practice.

Freud asks: "How are we to arrive at a knowledge of the unconscious? It is of course only as something conscious that we know it, after it has undergone transformation or *translation* [*Übersetzung*] into something conscious. Psycho-analytic work shows us every day that *translation* of this kind is possible" (Freud 1915b, 166, my italics). Of course, resistances have to be overcome in order to achieve the goal of filling in the obvious *gaps* in consciousness. Freud repeats that we assume that other people are conscious by inferring that they are as we are. He suggests that we should apply the same procedure to ourselves and presume that we cannot fully know ourselves either: "All the acts and manifestations which I notice in myself and do not know how to link up with the rest of my mental life must be judged as if they belonged to someone else: they are to be explained by a mental life ascribed to this other person" (p. 169). Freud returns, now on technical grounds, to his foundational philosophy: mental processes are in themselves unconscious and their conscious perception is like that of the external world by means of the "sense-organs," that is, by 'looking' at what appears in our minds.

It is in this essay that Freud describes the three types of unconscious mental processes mentioned above: the temporarily unconscious [descriptive], the repressed dynamic unconscious, and the topographic unconscious. He explicitly notes that our "psychical topography has . . . nothing to do with anatomy"; "topography" refers rather "to regions in the mental apparatus, wherever they may be situated in the body" (p. 175).

Analytic practice prompted Freud to reflect about the *location* of representations (*Vorstellungen*). When he uncovered a representation and communicated this discovery to the analysand he realized that the "patient has in actual fact the same idea [*Vorstellung*] in *two forms* in different places in his mental apparatus: first, he has the conscious memory of the *auditory trace of the idea*, conveyed in what we told him; and secondly, he also has – as we know for certain – the unconscious memory of *his experience* as it was in its earlier form" (p. 175, my italics). Once more Freud is revisiting an idea from *On Aphasia* in which the sound component of the word-presentation had to be linked to the visual component of the object-presentation to acquire meaning; here, the sound of the analyst's words are in the patient's conscious memory while in his unconscious there are memories of his experience. Freud calls them two *forms* of the same idea. This situation does not lift the repression until the resistance has been overcome, at which point the conscious idea presented by the analyst's words enters "into connection with the unconscious memory-trace" (p. 176). Freud explains that "the identity of the information given to the patient with his repressed memory is only apparent. To have heard something and to have experienced something are in their psychological nature two quite different things, even though the content of both is the same" (p. 176). Hearing is not enough; if repression is to be lifted, the words have to revive the patient's experiences themselves, what is called "the psychical" in *On Aphasia*. This revival is complicated by the affect of the experience which has remained consciously available, even though displaced onto another idea. Freud concludes that "to suppress the development of affect is the true aim of repression and that its work is incomplete if this aim is not achieved" (p. 178). If repression is to be lifted through the mediation of conscious words, the *unity* between the affect and the *experience* must be restored, brought to its *status nascendi*, as Breuer and Freud had determined much earlier.

Topographic repression indicates that repressed ideas remain active and cathected in the unconscious. The process of repression proper "can only consist in withdrawing from the idea the (pre)conscious cathexis which belongs to the system *Pcs.*" (linked to words), while the idea retains the unconscious cathexis (p. 180). Freud concludes that "repression is essentially a process affecting ideas on the border between the systems *Ucs.* and *Pcs.* (*Cs.*)" (ibid.). Having reviewed repression from three angles Freud feels he has reached the "consummation of psycho-analytic research . . . [and] in describing a psychical process in its dynamic, topographical and economic aspects, we should speak of it as a *metapsychological* presentation" (p. 181).

"The nucleus of the *Ucs.* consists of instinctual representatives which seek to discharge their cathexis; that is to say, it consists of wishful impulses" (p. 186). In the unconscious, reality does not count, only wishes count. Freud concludes: "*Exemption from mutual contradiction, primary process* (mobility of cathexes), *timelessness, and replacement of external by psychical reality* – these are the characteristics which we may expect to find in processes belonging to the system *Ucs.*" (p. 187). We must recall from *On Aphasia* that the instantaneous associations coterminous with perceptive process become the reality of the perceiver. The only means to access our unconscious is the preconscious which "has taken over access to consciousness and to motility" (ibid.), uses secondary processes, and inhibits "the tendency of cathected [unconscious] ideas towards discharge" (p. 188). The preconscious also establishes communications between ideational [*Vorstellung*] contents, gives them order in time, and establishes censorships, reality-testing, and memory: "Conscious memory, moreover, seems to depend wholly on the *Pcs.*" (p. 188). Freud clarifies that these conscious memories "should be clearly distinguished from the memory-traces in which the experiences of the *Ucs.* are fixed" (p. 189).

The systems interact with each other beyond the repressive struggle: "the *Ucs.* is alive and capable of development and maintains a number of other relations with the *Pcs.*, amongst them that of co-operation" (p. 190). Furthermore, Freud states that the "*Ucs.* is continued into what are known as derivatives, that it is accessible to the impressions of life, that it constantly influences the *Pcs.*, and is even, for its part, subjected to influences from the *Pcs.*" (ibid.). We must remember that conscious perceptions are registered, leave facilitations behind, and remain in the unconscious as storage of experiences which, through primary processes, will be recombined, condensed, and displaced into each other with various degrees of cathexes capable of forming derivatives accessible to the preconscious. This conception – a germ of which is already present in *On Aphasia* – is the foundation of Freud's notion of psychic determinism, and, in the end, of the analytic technique itself.

The preconscious regulates the access of ideational contents to consciousness, entry that is controlled by two censorship barriers. The first, placed between the unconscious and the preconscious, may bar access to the preconscious, while the second stands between the preconscious – that is, preconscious derivatives of unconscious ideas – and consciousness. At this point in his paper *The Unconscious* Freud returns to psychoanalytic technique. The patient has to pay *attention* to unconscious derivatives now emerging in his conscious mind [*Einfälle*] and cathect them enough to describe them in words to the analyst. He may resist by disregarding what he has in mind, ceasing to talk or repressing it again. It is obvious, therefore, that the "psycho-analytic treatment is based upon an influencing of the *Ucs.* from the direction of the *Cs.*" (p. 194), by the mediation of attention and speech.

In the last section of the paper Freud returns to objects and words, synthesizing his views:

> What we have permissibly called the conscious presentation of the object (*Objektvorstellung*) can now be split up into the presentation of the *word* (*Wortvorstellung*) and the presentation of the *thing* (*Sachvorstellung*); the latter consists in the cathexis, if not of the direct memory-images of the thing (*Sacherinnerungsbilder*), at least of remoter memory-traces (*Erinnerungsspuren*) derived from these. We now seem to know all at once what the difference is between a conscious and an unconscious presentation (p. 201). . . . The conscious presentation comprises the presentation of the thing (*Sachvorstellung*) plus the presentation of the word (*Wortvorstellung*) belonging to it, while the unconscious presentation is the presentation of the thing alone (*Sachvorstellung*). The system *Ucs.* contains the thing-cathexes of the objects, the first and true object-cathexes; the system *Pcs.* comes about by this thing-presentation being hypercathected through being linked with the word-presentations corresponding to it. It is these hypercathexes, we may suppose, that bring about a higher psychical organization and make it possible for the primary process to be succeeded by the secondary process which is dominant in the *Pcs.*
>
> (pp. 201–2)

I read in this citation an expansion of the psychic word in *On Aphasia*; this amplification of the term's meaning permits Freud to include the process of repression: "It denies to the presentation its *translation* into words which *shall remain attached to the object*. A presentation which is not put into words, or a psychical act which is not hypercathected, remains thereafter in the *Ucs.* in a state of repression" (p. 202, my italics). Next, Freud addresses the relations between things in the unconscious, an issue he had mentioned earlier: "By being linked with words, cathexes can be provided with quality even when they represent only *relations* between presentations of objects and are thus unable to derive any quality from perceptions. Such relations, which become comprehensible only through words, form a major part of our thought-processes" (p. 202). Once more Freud attributes a significant part of thinking to the function of words. We must recall that in *On Aphasia* he had considered only substantives. Now in *The Unconscious*, the phrase "*relations* between presentations" seems to refer to other grammatical functions. Finally, Freud considers the role of the preconscious in these processes: "Being linked with word-presentations is not yet the same thing as becoming conscious, but only makes it possible to become so; it is therefore characteristic of the system *Pcs.* and of that system alone" (pp. 202–3).

I have cited from these paragraphs at length because they represent the core of Freud's understanding of how words function in psychical life. The similarity of this section of *The Unconscious* to the description of the word in *On Aphasia* prompted Strachey to reprint the corresponding pages of the monograph as

"Appendix C," in his own translation. There he draws attention to the changes in terminology. The object-presentation of *On Aphasia* has now become the thing-presentation. Furthermore, in *The Unconscious*, Strachey notes, "'object-presentation' denotes a complex made up of the combined 'thing-presentation' and 'word-presentation' – a complex which has no name given to it in the *Aphasia* passage" (Strachey 1957a, 209). The *term* did not exist in the monograph, but the *concept* did exist, as suggested by the conclusion that a word's meaning comes from its being linked to an 'object-presentation'. Therefore – as I understand it – the thing-presentation of *The Unconscious* is equivalent to the meaningful 'word' in the monograph. In either case the *meaning* of words is related to the conscious awareness of what *we* think or say, an activity of the total person.

The theoretical issues addressed in these dense sentences call for reflection. I object to the notion of linking a word to a single *thing*-presentation. In the unconscious the thing/object presentation is too rich and historically too complex to be fully encompassed by a single word. Nonetheless, when a word links consciously to a thing/object representation it must have in its background the other components that form it and may appear as 'derivatives' coming from it. The word naming an object/thing representation carries such echoes with it. In analysis and in life, we do not deal with single objects but with complex *events and scenes* described by our words in their context and psychical meaning. A rose is a rose, but it never comes alone. Passed from the hand of a man to a woman it is a message; for a mourner, it may be a farewell. These examples make the point that in psychic life objects and words take their meaning from the *context* in which they appear. Such concepts apply to Freud's notion of cathexis of both memory-images of things and memory traces whose cathexes are a measure of their affective value in the internal and external context in which they are used.

I would like to end this section with a final comment. Freud focused attention on the intrapsychic function of words and left unattended their communicative significance, the obvious fact that we use words to engage in practical and emotional interactions both with others and ourselves. We may ask: how does such engagement affect and modify the conscious and non-conscious function of words? This is not the place to answer the question. Suffice it to say that analysts of many persuasions and scholars in the field of linguistics are exploring these dimensions of the spoken word.

Mourning and Melancholia

Mourning and Melancholia is the last paper of the metapsychology series. In it Freud reflects about "the melancholic's many and various self-accusations" and suggests that "the self-reproaches are reproaches against a loved object which have been shifted away from it on to the patient's own ego" (Freud 1917b, 248) as a result of identification. The melancholic's ambivalence about the lost object lead him to oscillate between love for and hatred of the lost person. In melancholia "the unconscious (thing-) presentation [*Dingvorstellung*] of the object has been abandoned by the libido" (p. 256). Freud says explicitly: "The location of these separate struggles cannot be assigned to any system but the *Ucs.*, the region of the memory-traces of *things* (as contrasted with *word*-cathexes)" (pp. 256–57). In normal mourning the effort to detach the libido from the object reaches the preconscious and consciousness; in melancholia "this path is blocked" (p. 257), and as a result the melancholic continues a repetitious struggle with his investment of love for and hatred of the dead object. While the struggle is in the unconscious, the patient resorts to speech and words to give form to complaints about the dead person, which are now displaced onto himself.

Freud comments that perhaps "the ego may enjoy in this the satisfaction of knowing itself as the better of the two, as superior to the object" (p. 257), in other words the bereft person may experience a narcissistic triumph that is the counterpart of the self-reproaches. He does not comment about this peculiar use of language, except to say that the reproaches are in fact directed at the absent object. What does this have to do with words? It seems that melancholia requires a developmental level in which the function of *speech communication* has not only been consolidated but has become the main tool for loving and hating between the mourner, now bereft, and the deceased. The complaints and self-reproaches indirectly address the dead person and represent the affective load of their relationship transformed into defensive identification. In other words, the process that Freud describes as happening in the unconscious does find expression in repetitious speeches to the deceased.

Freud's papers from 1915 to 1923

I will review here only those papers that offer a contribution to the understanding of speech in analysis.

Introductory Lectures on Psycho-Analysis

In Lecture I, entitled *Introduction*, Freud gives his most vivid description of the patient's verbal communications and illustrates the spoken procedures the analyst employs to entice him to explore his psychic reality. Psychoanalysis is possible because speech is possible. Freud repeats: "Nothing takes place in a psycho-analytic treatment but an interchange of words between the patient and the analyst. The patient talks, tells of his past experiences and present impressions, complains, confesses to his wishes and his emotional impulses. The doctor listens, tries to direct the patient's processes of thought, exhorts, forces his attention in certain directions, gives him explanations and observes the reactions of understanding or rejection which he in this way provokes in him" (Freud 1915–1916, 17). Freud also observes that "Words provoke affects and are in general the means of mutual influence among men" (ibid.).

Psychoanalytic listening differs from that of everyday life: "The talk of which psycho-analytic treatment consists brooks no listener; it cannot be demonstrated"

(p. 17) and "you cannot be present as an audience at a psycho-analytic treatment. You can only be told about it . . . at second hand, as it were" (p. 18). The analyst learns the procedure by undergoing analysis herself with a competent practitioner. Freud does acknowledge that the manner in which analysis uses speech and listening is a new way of attending to words and to the people who speak them. Listening to the whispering derivatives of unconscious processes without specific goals is as original as is the patient's speaking without conscious intentions. Both processes open the window for capturing unconscious derivatives coming from the mouth of the unsuspecting patient.

In Part III of Lecture XXIII, *A General Theory of the Neuroses*, Freud proposes that a "symptom, like a dream, represents something as fulfilled: a satisfaction in the infantile manner" (Freud 1915–1916, 366). A surprise awaits the analysts who listens to the patient's description of childhood experiences: sometimes they reveal a historical event, sometimes a fantasy. "When he brings up the material which leads from behind his symptoms to the wishful situations modelled on his infantile experiences, we are in doubt to begin with whether we are dealing with reality or phantasies" (p. 368). It is no easy task to ascertain which is which. He says that in analysis the best approach is to "equate phantasy and reality and not bother to begin with whether the childhood experiences under examination are the one or the other" (p. 368). The theoretical foundation is clear: "The phantasies possess *psychical as contrasted with material* reality, and we gradually learn to understand that *in the world of the neuroses it is psychical reality which is the decisive kind*" (p. 368). Following the fantasies to the libidinal points of fixation and the desires that motivate them opens the way to their infantile sources and the wishes they fulfill. These considerations alert the analyst to the need to listen without concern for the actual *truth* of the words. What the analyst is listening to is not primarily the words, but the avenues they open to the *psychical reality* in which the patient lives out the symptomatic fulfillment of wishes.

Two Encyclopaedia Articles

In the first article, *Psycho-Analysis*, Freud reports that his "strong belief in the strict determination of mental events certainly played a part in the choice of this technique as a substitute for hypnosis" (Freud 1923a, 238). The patient is invited to follow the 'fundamental technical rule' and to become "an attentive and dispassionate self-observer, merely to read off all the time the *surface of his consciousness*, and on the one hand to make a duty of the most complete honesty while on the other not to hold back any idea from communication" (ibid., my italics). The surface refers to the spontaneous appearance [*Einfälle*] of unconscious derivatives, which Freud expects will contribute to fill in the *gaps* in the patient's conscious awareness. He takes it for granted that they are strictly determined by pre-existing mental processes (the *facilitations* they left behind as he said in his early theorizing). The physician works by surrendering "to his own unconscious mental activity, in a state of *evenly suspended attention*, to avoid so far as possible reflection and the construction of conscious expectations, not to try to fix anything that he heard particularly in his memory, and by these means to catch the drift of the patient's unconscious with his own unconscious" (p. 239). All the analyst has to do is "to go a step further in order to guess the material which was concealed from the patient himself and to be able to communicate it to him" (p. 239). I find this elegant description at odds with the one on page 17 of the Introduction to the *Introductory Lectures in Psycho-Analysis* cited above, where the doctor 'directs', 'exhorts', 'forces the patient's attention', all of them very active *verbal* interventions in which the doctor's words are enticements and, at times, orders. Perhaps, they are not as incompatible as they seem, especially if one places them sequentially at different moments in the treatment.

Symbols are significant components of mental life. Freud suggests here that their *"translation* has to be provided by the analyst, who can himself only discover it empirically by experimentally *fitting it into the context"* (p. 242, my italics) of the patient's communications. In *The Interpretation of Dreams*, Freud says that only the patient can give the full meaning of a symbol in the dream.

The Ego and the Id

In *The Ego and the Id* (Freud 1923b) Freud introduces his structural theory as distinct from the earlier topographical theory. The id, the ego, and the superego, each with its own distinctive functions and relations to the others, constitute the structural components. In the essay the concept of consciousness once again has its early descriptive meaning. The superego is presented as derived from the earliest relationship with the parents. The ego is in the first instance a structure of the mind, but in some instances it seems to stand for the total person.

In ordinary circumstances and in Freud's writings the first person pronoun *I*, *ich*, refers to the conscious aspects of an individual's mental life and also to the executive aspects of the person as a whole. The introduction of the article "the," *das*, before the pronoun to create *das Ich* is as much of a grammatical innovation as is *das Es*, *the it*, the indefinite pronoun. Confronted with this new coinage, Strachey opted to resort to the Latin pronouns *ego* (*I*) and *id* (*it*), to make the psychical entities sound scientific, as Freud had done by adding the gender-neutral article *das*. This peculiar use of language suggests that Freud wanted to find a way of including in his terminology a structure that had the power of an agent, an *Ich*, and another that eluded that agency. A name would not do. *Only a pronoun could carry the agent's function*. There is a paradox in the terminology, because Freud considered the unconscious, now called *das Es*, as the true psychical reality. Now, having reflected about the essay's title, I want to discuss what Freud says in it about speech and words.

In the opening section "Consciousness and What Is Unconscious," Freud repeats the core idea of all his work: "The division of the psychical into what is conscious and what is unconscious is the fundamental premise of psycho-analysis; and it alone makes it possible for psycho-analysis to understand the pathological processes in mental life" (p. 13). He describes the ego and its functions: "We have formed the idea that in each individual there is a coherent organization of mental processes; and we call this his *ego* [*das Ich*]" (p. 17, italics in original). The ego is conscious, regulates motility and discharge, supervises its own processes, sleeps at night without relinquishing the censorship of dreams, and is in charge of repressing what is not fit for conscious awareness. I am surprised that Freud did not include in this list the critical fact that the ego regulates speech both as a conscious and as a motor activity. If he considered speech critical for transforming internal processes and thoughts into conscious perceptions of the individual's ego, how could he have omitted this function from the list of the ego's activities?

In Freud's understanding of it, the ego extends further than consciousness: "A part of the ego, too – and Heaven knows how important a part – may be *Ucs.*, undoubtedly is *Ucs*. And this *Ucs*. belonging to the ego is not latent like the *Pcs.*" (p. 18). The unconscious part of the ego is not repressed, but *qualitatively* unconscious, which leads Freud to a critical conclusion: "All that is repressed is *Ucs.*, but not all that is *Ucs*. is repressed" (p. 18). Consciousness "is the *surface* of the mental apparatus" (p. 19). The ego is conscious from the start of its sense perceptions of the external world. These processes are automatic and need no other mediation than the exposure to a material reality. The ego also has to deal with another reality as well, namely, that of the internal processes of thought, some of which need to become conscious in order to serve psychical life. This is the task of the preconscious. Freud asks: "'How does a *thing* become preconscious?' And the answer would be: 'Through becoming connected with the word-presentations corresponding to it'" (p. 20, my italics). Once more Freud refers to 'a thing', a singular type of object, and repeats what he had already said in *On Aphasia*, namely, that a complex object-presentation acquires meaning by being linked to *a* word-presentation, suggesting that they belong to each other on account of that meaning. Freud reflects that "word-presentations are residues of memories; they were at one time perceptions, and like all mnemic residues they can become conscious again. . . . it dawns upon us like a new discovery that only something which has once been a *Cs*. perception can become conscious, and that anything arising from within (apart from feelings) that seeks to become conscious must try to transform itself into external perceptions: this becomes possible by means of memory-traces" (p. 20). These memory traces are mainly visual and potentially able to become conscious and to participate in giving consciousness to some thoughts. But they also have limitations: they present the "concrete subject-matter of the thought" (p. 21) only up to a certain point because, in Freud's appraisal, "the *relations* between the various elements of this subject-matter, which is what specially characterizes thoughts, cannot be given visual expression. Thinking in pictures is, therefore, only a very incomplete form of becoming conscious" (p. 21, my italics). Once more Freud asserts that imagery is "ontogenetically and phylogenetically" (p. 21) older than speech. As mentioned above, he had discussed aspects of this matter in *The Unconscious* but never resolved the issue of the *relations* present in thought processes.

Freud's description of vivid events and the use of the term *scenes* rather than individual things in his clinical presentations convinced me that we do not perceive 'things', but rather complex *scenes* and *events* and that such perception implies the almost immediate understanding of the *relations* between their component parts. Are relations embedded in the perceptions?

In the section "Consciousness and What Is Unconscious," Freud returns to perception and draws a critical conclusion: "The part played by word-presentations now becomes perfectly clear. By their interposition internal thought-processes are made into perceptions. It is like a demonstration of the theorem that all knowledge has its origin in external perception. When a hypercathexis of the process of thinking takes place, thoughts are *actually* perceived – as if they came from without – and are consequently held to be true" (p. 23, my underlining). What is undoubtedly true is that most of the words we have available for capturing our thoughts have come from perceiving and registering the words of others. Neologisms provide little service to thought processes. The question remains, however – at least in my mind – whether the constant preconscious/unconscious function of imagery is *unavoidably* connected to the *meaning* of words. If this is so and Freud is correct about perception, then imagery must sustain the process of thought, even the most abstract thoughts.

Following Georg Groddeck, Freud calls "the other part of the mind . . . which behaves as though it were Ucs., the 'id [*das Es*]'" (p. 23). The ego rests upon its surface (p. 24) and "is not sharply separated from the id; its lower portion merges into it" (p. 24). In developmental terms, "the ego is that part of the id which has been modified by the direct influence of the external world through the medium of the *Pcpt.-Cs.*; in a sense it is an extension of the surface-differentiation" (p. 25). The external world exercises its influence upon the ego by the senses' perception of reality. This conception led Freud to conclude: "The ego is first and foremost a bodily ego; it is not merely a surface entity, but is itself the projection of a surface" (p. 26). We must recall that all object representations originate in bodily perceptions that remain unconscious after the initial perceptive moment until word-representations originating in acoustic registrations manage to link to them and make them conscious. A consequence follows from this conception: "we shall have to say that not only what is lowest but also what is highest in the ego can be unconscious" (p. 27).

In Chapter III, "The Ego and the Super-Ego (Ego Ideal)," Freud describes the superego as a "differentiation within the ego" (p. 28) using as scaffolding the ideas he had presented in *Mourning and Melancholia*: "When it happens that a person has to give up a sexual object, there quite often ensues an alteration of his ego which can only be described as a setting up of the object inside the ego" (p. 29). There is an identification with the object that leads Freud to "suppose that the character of the ego is a precipitate of abandoned object-cathexes and that it contains the history of those object-choices" (p. 29). This identification also affects the id because it is "a method by which the ego can obtain control over the id and deepen its *relations* with it – at the cost, it is true, of acquiescing to a large extent in the id's experiences" (p. 30, my italics). At this point Freud introduces a fascinating 'dialogue' between the ego and the id: "When the ego assumes the features of the object, it is forcing itself, so to speak, upon the id as a love-object and is trying to make good the id's loss by saying: '*Look*, you can love me too – I am so *like* the object'" (p. 30, my italics).

The metaphoric statement has a profound truth. What I find especially interesting is that the ego 'talks' to the id to 'seduce' it into loving the ego with the same love it had for the object. The "too" of the sentence indicates the intention to use *similarity* to get the id's love. In my reading of it, the sentence implies more than a single instance of identification. Such an internal dialogue between aspects of ourselves is an everyday event that colors not only our relationship with ourselves, but also with all the objects that pertain to our psychic reality. In my appraisal, as in the sentence addressed by the ego to the id, words do not stand alone: visual imagery also enters the conversation as when the ego insists on being loved because of its visual ["look"] resemblance to the object. The imperative request for love is not enough: the id has to 'see' that the ego resembles the object.

Freud traces the origins of the ego ideal to the earliest identifications with the parental figures and during the oedipal period. They leave their permanent mark on the ego by forming the superego, a *"precipitate in the ego, consisting of these two identifications in some way united with each other. This modification of the ego retains its special position; it confronts the other contents of the ego as an ego ideal or super-ego"* (p. 34). The confrontation takes the form of verbal commands to the ego from the superego: "'You *ought to be* like this (like your father),' including prohibitions 'You *may not be* like this (like your father) – that is, you may not do all that he does; some things are his prerogative'" (p. 34, italics in the original). Once more the 'speech' of the superego is not limited to words but it needs to *compare* the likeness of the child to the father and infer from the comparison what is acceptable and what is forbidden. Without such 'looking' at the father and the desires of the child's ego, the command loses its meaning. From the moment the superego emerges to the end of life, it will continue to 'talk' to the individual as a representative of the parents in the internal world, reflecting "the contrast between what is real and what is psychical, between the external world and the internal world" (p. 36). Once it has been exposed to social institutions such as religion and social authorities, the ego ideal takes "the form of conscience, to exercise the moral censorship" (p. 37). In this manner, "As the child was once under a compulsion to obey its parents, so now the ego submits to the categorical imperative of its superego" (p. 48). It is worth remembering that Kant's *categorical imperative* is an internal *verbal command* that uses the imperative mode.

Freud gives some thought to the deep connection between the unconscious components of the superego and its origin in primary objects and asks: "Having regard, now, to the importance we have ascribed to preconscious verbal residues in the ego, the question arises whether it can be the case that the super-ego, in so far as it is *Ucs.*, consists in such word-presentations and, if it does not, what else it consists in. Our tentative answer will be that it is as impossible for the super-ego as for the ego to disclaim its origin from things heard: for it is a part of the ego and remains accessible to consciousness by way of these word-presentations (concepts, abstractions). But the *cathectic energy* does not reach these contents of the super-ego from auditory perception (instruction or reading) but from sources in the id" (pp. 52–53). What is Freud saying here? First, it should be noticed that in parentheses he has enlarged the notion of word-presentation to include concepts and abstractions without giving any explanation. Second, he reiterates the origin of ego and superego in words heard from others. Finally, he makes a very significant point: the *investment* (cathexis) in the objects of the internal reality instigates the categoric verbal imperatives not because the words were heard, which they were once upon a time, but because the internal object is still affectively and dynamically alive.

Freud lists the many strengths of the ego and also its limited mastery: "we see this same ego as a poor creature owing service to three masters and consequently menaced by three dangers: from the external world, from the libido of the id, and from the severity of the super-ego" (p. 56). He describes a series of graphic, dramatic *intrapsychic scenes* about the ego's difficulties in serving three masters. Freud's rich portrayal of the ego's struggles deserves a full citation.

> As a frontier-creature, the ego tries to mediate between the world and the id, to make the id pliable to the world and, by means of its muscular activity, to make the world fall in with the wishes of the id. In point of fact it behaves like the physician during an analytic treatment: it *offers itself*, with the attention it pays to the real world, as a *libidinal object* to the id, and aims at attaching the id's libido to itself. It is not only a helper to the id; it is also a submissive slave who *courts his master's love*. Whenever possible, it tries to remain on good terms with the id; it clothes the id's *Ucs.* commands with its *Pcs.* rationalizations; it *pretends* that the id is showing obedience to the admonitions of reality, even when in fact it is remaining obstinate and unyielding; it *disguises* the id's conflicts with reality and, if possible, its conflicts with the super-ego too. In its position midway between the id and reality, it only too often yields to the temptation to become *sycophantic, opportunist and lying*, like a politician who sees the truth but wants to keep his place in popular favour.
>
> (p. 56)

Freud had said earlier that his case histories read like short stories. I would like to add that his theorizing about that "poor creature," the ego, can also be read as theater, a complex plot of love-seeking and maneuverings by an entity willing to lie to keep itself libidinally invested. I find this description not only delightful but also very useful. It confirms that if psychical life is to be depicted in connection with the need for love, even intrapsychic love, technical terms do not suffice. Scientific language must resort to *scenes* of human interactions to portray the relationships of intrapsychic agencies.

In *The Economic Problem of Masochism* (Freud 1924) Freud describes how the masochist uses the fantasies to exchange roles and *impersonated himself* as a female.

In Freud's understanding, the *imaginary scenic* transmutation of gender in sexual exchanges constitutes the core of male masochists' perversion.

In *Negation* Freud examines the function of the particle 'no' in psychic life. "Negation is a way of taking cognizance of what is repressed; indeed it is already a lifting of the repression, though not, of course, an acceptance of what is repressed" (Freud 1925, 235–36). The repression persists even though there is an intellectual acceptance of the repressed. The 'no' "affirms or disaffirms the possession by a thing of a particular attribute; and it asserts or disputes that a presentation has an existence in reality" (p. 236). 'No' is used to protect the "pleasure-ego [that] wants to introject into itself everything that is good and to eject from itself everything that is bad" (p. 237), thus acknowledging a thought or a fact while denying that it pertains to oneself such as when the obsessive says about one of his ideas: "But no; that can't be true, or it could not have occurred to me" (p. 235), thus keeping repressed the *affective* component of the idea.

Negation, as a linguistic function, is an activity of the ego: "We never discover a 'no' in the unconscious and . . . recognition of the unconscious on the part of the ego is expressed in a negative formula" (p. 239). It is as though the user of the word 'no' has found a way of simultaneously reaching some [object-]representation in the unconscious and denying the disturbing components of what it has found. This is how I read Freud's following sentence: "There is no stronger evidence that we have been successful in our effort to uncover the unconscious than when the patient reacts to it with the words 'I didn't think that'" (p. 239). In this case the *gap* in consciousness has found its missing part, but the ego refuses to own it as part of itself, because it would cause unpleasure.

In *An Outline of Psycho-Analysis*, Freud revisits the psychoanalytic method as a way of filling in the *gaps*, "the breaks in the sequence of 'psychical' events: we fill in what is omitted by making plausible inferences and *translating* it into conscious material. In this way we construct, as it were, a sequence of conscious events complementary to the unconscious psychical processes" (Freud 1940a, 159). These assertions *imply* that psychical life requires that events complete their sequential organization in conscious life. If this is correct, I could suggest that psychoanalysis is a discipline that serves to complete defensively interrupted *narratives* of our lives. Or to put it more daringly, *psychical life is based on the struggle between the need to complete personal narratives and the defenses against grasping their meaning.*

In a surprising move, Freud modifies what he had said all along about the preconscious. Here he says explicitly that the quality of being preconscious is independent of the connection with "mnemic residues of speech" (p. 162). Nonetheless, he reaffirms that consciousness "is the work of the function of speech, which brings material in the ego into a firm connection with mnemic residues of visual, but more particularly of auditory, perceptions" (p. 162), as he had said in 1891 in *On Aphasia*.

Constructions in Analysis describes all the "raw material" – memories, dreams, ideas, allusions, affects, transferential phenomena – which the analyst assembles to help the patient. Freud describes how he proceeds: "What we are in search of is a *picture* [*Bild*] of the patient's forgotten years that shall be alike trustworthy and in all essential respects complete" (Freud 1937, 258, my italics). The patient must be induced to remember what he has repressed; the analyst's "task is to make out what has been forgotten from the traces which it has left behind or, more correctly, to *construct* it" (pp. 258–59). After the analyst has given the construction sufficient form in his mind, he communicates it to the patient to link his part of the work with the patient's part. A construction presents the patient with "a piece of his early history that he has forgotten" (p. 261).

Freud believed that no harm follows if the construction does not correspond to the *historical truth*. The analyst must admit to having made a mistake and start over. The proof that a construction is correct comes when the patient brings up new memories that complete it or associations similar to the one offered. The patient's rejection of a construction may represent a defensive move or indicate that it is incomplete. The final confirmation must await the further course of analysis because at the time a construction is presented, it is no "more than a conjecture which awaits examination, confirmation or rejection" (p. 265). If accepted, the construction (or reconstruction) becomes the patient's conviction. Such conviction presents a dilemma: "The path that starts from the analyst's construction ought to end in the patient's recollection; but it does not always lead so far. Quite often we do not succeed in bringing the patient to recollect what has been repressed. Instead of that, if the analysis is carried out correctly, we produce in him an assured conviction of the truth of the construction which achieves the same therapeutic result as a recaptured memory" (pp. 265–66). Freud clarifies that the effectiveness of the construction is due to the fact that "it recovers a fragment of lost experience" (p. 268), of a *historical truth*, in the attempt to explain the patient's past.

In this context I want to re-examine Freud's example of reconstruction that was discussed in Chapter 6:

> 'Up to your *n*th year you regarded yourself as the sole and unlimited possessor of your mother; then came another baby and brought you grave disillusionment. Your mother left you for some time, and even after her reappearance she was never again devoted to you exclusively. Your feelings towards your mother became ambivalent, your father gained a new importance for you,' . . . and so on.
>
> (p. 261)

This construction intertwines two types of events, the *subjective experience* of the child and the *objective events* synchronous with it. It begins with the foundational psychic event of how the child *regarded* himself. This is an illustration of the ego's division as subject and object. The ego as subject regarded itself as an object ego who was the sole possessor of the mother, equivalent to an intrapsychic portrayal of a believed exclusive *relational scene* between mother and child. Then two *objective events*, the birth of a sibling and the temporary disappearance of the mother, appear as historically undeniable and experiential situations that confront the subject's ego with a direct contradiction of what he believed. The subjective ego can no longer maintain the earlier belief, and the loss of it brings disillusionment, a private experience accessible only to the child in relation to what he had *believed* about his mother. The earlier internal relational scene must be relinquished, because the mother who returned in historical reality was a sharply *different mother* from the one the child had experienced before: "she was never again devoted to you exclusively." This fact forces the subjective ego to revise the feelings toward the mother, from the sense of being her sole possessor to one of ambivalence. The mixed feelings result from having a mother changed into the mother of another child, a dramatic transformation not only of the relational scene but also of the kind of mother she is. Finally, the construction introduces the father as a person who has gained importance in relation to the child's feelings.

What can we learn from this construction? I would suggest that at its core it consists not just in the external events (birth, loss, and changed mother), but in the transformations of *belief, reality-testing, object and self-representation, and feelings*; the subjective ego of the child had to find *a new narrative* for itself and a new stance in relation to his mother and his desires in the context of a given historical reality. The point I can hardly overemphasize is that the thought processes of the adult in analysis in reorganizing his experience as a child and the constructions offered by the analyst both make use of relational and self-evaluative *intrapsychic scenes*. A therapeutically effective "conviction of the truth of the construction" depends on the reconstruction of this past *psychical reality*, a reality that strikes the patient as believable even if it may have left behind no apparent memories. What it would have left behind, however, are ways of experiencing oneself subjectively and in relational contexts. In this effort, the task of the analyst consists in progressively using *words* to reawaken and connect with the patient's early subjective beliefs about himself and others, and with the feelings those beliefs aroused. This is how I understand the reference to a *"picture of the patient's forgotten years."*

In summary: I hope to have demonstrated that Freud's theories built upon the core ideas presented in *On Aphasia*. He used new concepts to expand and elaborate the dialectic between representations and words while two key concepts organized the entire theoretical edifice: representational *gaps* create pathology; verbal *translation* of the repressed material restores the integrity of the ego in the process of articulating personal meaningful words about what could not be affectively tolerated before the treatment.

After this long detour through Freud's technical and theoretical papers, it is time to address the question: How did Freud talk with his patients?

References

Breuer, Josef, and Sigmund Freud. *Studies on Hysteria*. Vol. 2 of *Standard Edition*. London: Hogarth Press, 1893–1895.

Freud, Sigmund. *The Complete Letters of Sigmund Freud to Wilhelm Fliess 1887–1904*. Trans. and ed. Jeffrey Moussaieff Masson. Cambridge, MA: Belknap Press of Harvard University Press, 1985.

———. Constructions in Analysis. Vol. 23 of *Standard Edition*, 255–69. London: Hogarth Press, 1937.

———. The Economic Problem of Masochism. Vol. 19 of *Standard Edition*, 155–70. London: Hogarth Press, 1924.

———. The Ego and the Id. Vol. 19 of *Standard Edition*, 1–66. London: Hogarth Press, 1923b.

———. Formulations on the Two Principles of Mental Functioning. Vol. 12 of *Standard Edition*, 213–26. London: Hogarth Press, 1911.

———. Instincts and Their Vicissitudes. Vol. 14 of *Standard Edition*, 109–40. London: Hogarth Press, 1915a.

———. *The Interpretation of Dreams*. Vols. 4–5 of *Standard Edition*. London: Hogarth Press, 1900.

———. *Introductory Lectures on Psycho-Analysis*. Vol. 15 of *Standard Edition*. London: Hogarth Press, 1915–1916.

———. A Metapsychological Supplement to the Theory of Dreams. Vol. 14 of *Standard Edition*, 217–35. London: Hogarth Press, 1917a.

———. Mourning and Melancholia. Vol. 14 of *Standard Edition*, 237–58. London: Hogarth Press, 1917b.

———. Negation. Vol. 19 of *Standard Edition*, 235–39. London: Hogarth Press, 1925.

———. The Neuro-Psychosis of Defense. Vol. 3 of *Standard Edition*, 41–68. London: Hogarth Press, 1894.

———. On the History of the Psycho-Analytic Movement. Vol. 14 of *Standard Edition*, 1–66. London: Hogarth Press, 1914.

———. An Outline of Psycho-Analysis. Vol. 23 of *Standard Edition*. 1938, 139–207. London: Hogarth Press, 1940a.

———. Project for a Scientific Psychology. Vol. 1 of *Standard Edition*, 283–397. London: Hogarth Press, 1950.

———. Psycho-Analytic Notes on an Autobiographical Account of a Case of Paranoia (Dementia Paranoides). Vol. 12 of *Standard Edition*, 1–84. London: Hogarth Press, 1911.

———. Repression. Vol. 14 of *Standard Edition*, 141–58. London: Hogarth Press, 1915c.

———. Some Elementary Lessons in Psycho-Analysis. Vol. 23 of *Standard Edition*. 1938, 279–86. London: Hogarth Press, 1940b.

———. Two Encyclopaedia Articles. In Vol. 18 of *Standard Edition*, 233–59. London: Hogarth Press, 1923a.

———. The Unconscious. Vol. 14 of *Standard Edition*, 159–215. London: Hogarth Press, 1915b.

Strachey, James. Appendix C to Freud's *The Unconscious*. Vol. 14 of *Standard Edition*, 209–15. London: Hogarth Press, 1957a.

———. Editor's Introduction to "Project for a Scientific Psychology." Vol. 1 of *Standard Edition*, 283–93. London: Hogarth Press, 1950.

———. Introduction to "Papers on Metapsychology." Vol. 14 of *Standard*, 105–7. London: Hogarth Press, 1957b.

8
HOW DID FREUD TALK WITH HIS PATIENTS?

Introduction

There is no simple and direct answer to this question. We only have what Freud *wrote* about what he said to his patients and what his patients *wrote* about what he said to them. Furthermore, Freud's written cases have multiple theoretical and educational intentions besides presenting his clinical work. His reported words are *transcriptions* of words he said aloud to them. The printed words cannot convey the tone of voice, the feelings, and the manner in which he spoke them, all those affective imponderables that are crucial for effective dialogue and analytic exploration.

Several of Freud's well-known patients have written about what he said to them. Among these memoirs we have Abram Kardiner's book *My Analysis with Freud: Reminiscences* (Kardiner 1977) and Hilda Doolittle's *Tribute to Freud* (Doolittle 1974). Kardiner was a New York psychiatrist who in 1921 went to Vienna to be analyzed by Freud. Upon his return to the United States, he became a practicing psychoanalyst and a stern critic of the orthodox technique.

Kardiner describes his disappointing experience with Freud while acknowledging his positive feelings for him: "In our hours together, there were many personal interchanges. I was enormously fond of him. This was a very likable and dear person. He was a charming man, full of wit and erudition. One could not tell from his behavior in the office what a real giant he was, because he was unassuming and quite natural" (p. 71). These feelings contrasted with his analytic disappointment in Freud who, in Kardiner's appraisal, failed to understand his transferential suppression of self-assertion "in order to maintain his favor and support" (p. 100), and who insisted unnecessarily on his unconscious homosexuality (p. 99). Such emphasis "makes the patient address himself to a non-existent state of affairs and augments his sense of helplessness, thereby confirming his feeling that he cannot direct his own life" (p. 99). In spite of these criticisms, Kardiner was grateful to Freud for his dream interpretations that "finally freed me from my resistance to analysis itself" (p. 98).

Kardiner reports some instances of Freud's verbal communications that are not as neutral as the technique required such as raising his voice when he disagreed with Kardiner about the significance of his stepmother to him and also several occasions in which Freud was "infuriated" by Kardiner's observation that "you could do no harm with psychoanalysis" (p. 69). Freud responded by showing him two pictures of Horace W. Frink, a fellow American and analysand of a colleague, who in one photograph before analysis was looking well and another in which he appeared "haggard, emaciated and looked twenty years older" (p. 67). He wanted to prove to Kardiner the harm that analysis could cause to a person. Kardiner reported Freud's inclination to comment about analytic events, to gossip, and talk about contemporary analysts (p. 70). One day Kardiner asked Freud what he thought about himself as an analyst. He quotes him as saying: "I'm glad you ask, because, frankly, I have no great interest in therapeutic problems. I am much too impatient now. I have several handicaps that disqualify me as a great analyst. One of them is that I am too much the father. Second, I am much too much occupied with theoretical problems all the time . . . rather than paying attention to the therapeutic problem. Third, I have no patience in keeping people for a long time. I tire of them, and I want to spread my influence" (pp. 68–69). After his analysis, Kardiner thought that psychoanalysis needed many changes to be viable.

The American poet Hilda Doolittle – who published as "H.D." – was in analysis with Freud for some months in 1933–1934. After the analysis ended, they became friends and remained so until his death. Her book *Tribute to Freud* is exactly that.

H.D. saw Freud first in March 1933 for five weeks and then from October 1934 to December 1 of that year. Freud was in his late seventies and H.D. in her late forties. Doolittle developed a deep affection for Freud and her tribute shows it. She describes how Freud sometimes used the statuettes in his office to make an analytic point, as when he handed his small bronze statue of Athena to her and said: "*This* is my favorite" ". . . She is perfect, . . . *only she has lost her spear*" (pp. 68–69). The patient did not grasp the allusion to female castration. In her memoir she follows the story with a description of Freud's "beautiful" manner of speaking: "The tone of his voice, the singing quality that so subtly permeated the texture of the spoken word, made that spoken word live in another dimension, or take on another color . . . ripped from the monotonous faded and outworn texture of the language itself, into the bubbling cauldron of his own mind . . ." (p. 69). It is easy to recognize the poet in her words, yet they present her perception of his *spoken* words. During her sessions in March 1933 Freud also talked about himself. He said that "if he lived another fifty years, he would still be fascinated and curious about the vagaries and variations of the human mind or soul" (p. 171). At another time he spoke at length about his grandchildren (p. 62) or gave some information about other analysands H.D. met on the staircase going to the office. She knew a great deal about the family life of "the Professor" – as she called him – and occasionally had tea with his daughter Anna and Mrs. Dorothy Burlingham in the latter's apartment in the same building. This description suggests a relaxed atmosphere in which analysis was carried out in the context of everyday life in an extended family. Freud interpreted, explained, and lectured a bit while she offered her dreams and associations. She did not relinquish her own opinions: "I was a student, working under the direction of the greatest mind of this and of perhaps many succeeding generations. But the Professor was not always right" (p. 18).

The correspondence between Freud and his colleagues and disciples – in particular Karl Abraham, Sándor Ferenczi, and Carl Jung – offers further evidence that Freud did far more than to interpret his patients' associations and dreams. He advised them, told them stories, referred to objects in his office, made revelations about himself, commented on psychoanalytic politics, the actions of colleagues, and other non-analytic events. There is no need to be scandalized because the physician of that time was *the* authority, the agent of the cure, who mingled with families and ruled the patients' lives while under his care. Freud changed the focus of attention from the doctor to the patient because he understood that the illness and the cure could only come from the psychic life of the patient and from finding the *meaning* of the disease in his life. The transition from the old form of practicing medicine to the new analytic mode did not happen all at once. For a long time Freud continued to offer patients the standard treatments of the day even when he was in the process of becoming a full-time analyst. This process of transformation can easily be followed by reading in chronological order his own reports about what he did and said to his patients, and what he requested they tell him about what was in their minds. I have presented in Chapters 2 and 3 the evolution of Freud's procedures in working with his first hysterical patients. We saw Freud in his transition from massages and hypnosis to the *analytic situation* in which the ordinary conversation was replaced by the patient's obligation to report in words to the analyst what came to his mind, what he saw during his sessions on the analyst's couch. Freud listened for the derivatives of unconscious representations until he was able to uncover a potential meaning and communicate it to the analysand while hoping for further elaboration of the psychic material.

This new manner of speaking between patient and analyst was an extraordinary innovation that substituted the ordinary referent of everyday words for their intrapsychic and repressed referent, thus establishing *a new use* of spoken exchanges between people and a new category of psychical words with their idiosyncratic personalized meaning for each individual.

Freud based his manner of talking with his analysands on the conviction that there had to be a causal story, a set of internal representations that would reveal the meaning of their symptoms, if he assisted the patients to give words to what appeared in their minds [*Einfälle*] during the hour. In brief, he was trying to help them to revive and experience their internal representations and articulate them into conscious psychical words, the 'meaningful words' of *On Aphasia*. At first he tried to force the appearance of representations by hypnotizing them, pressuring their foreheads, insisting they describe what they were *seeing* until he learned that

.hey would become available through the associative process. In all cases he favored he visual component of what kept emerging in the patients' mind as the condition)f connecting it to words. He concluded that at the end of the analysis he could see hat there was "an intimate connection between the story of the patient's sufferings ind the symptoms of his illness" (Breuer and Freud 1893–1895, 161).

I will now examine Freud's major cases – Dora, the Rat Man, and the Wolf Man – to explore how they talked to each other during their analyses. The reader s invited to return to Freud's original report of the cases to asses if my observa-ions describe accurately how he worked with them. Here I can present only the)asic facts to underscore the main points I wish to make.

Dora

)ora's father brought her to Freud in October 1900, after reading her letter saying 'she could no longer endure her life." She had also experienced an episode of "loss)f consciousness" (p. 23). She had seen Freud before and had refused treatment. This time, however, "it was determined, in spite of her reluctance, that she should :ome to me for treatment" (p. 23). The father pleaded with Freud: "Please try and)ring her to reason" (p. 26). Her last attack had followed upon a conversation in which she insisted her father break off the relationship with their friends, the K.s, n particular Frau K.

Freud had met Dora's father several years earlier when Herr K. brought him .o consult for a grave condition, which Freud diagnosed as syphilitic and treated .uccessfully. Dora's father and the Ks. were entangled in a complex web of rela-ionships going back to 1888, when the family moved to Tyrol for the sake of the ather's tuberculosis. There they befriended the K. family. Frau K. became Dora's ather's caretaker while Dora frequently took care of the K.'s young children. She ind Frau K. became close friends and confidantes. Dora's mother refused to have .exual relations with her husband, while Frau K. tried her best to avoid having hem with her husband. Dora's father and Frau K. started an affair that was still ;oing at the time her father brought Dora to Freud. Each man, Herr K. and Dora's ather, let it be known that "I get nothing out of my wife." Dora's father asked ™reud to tame Dora's disruption of the adults' sexual entanglements.

Herr K. had been very attentive to the young Dora, giving her gifts, visiting ier, and writing to her. Neither parent seemed to have registered the significance)f such behavior in a man besieged by sexual dissatisfaction.

Two critical episodes marked the relationship between Dora and Herr K. In 1896, when Dora was thirteen and a half, not fourteen as Freud says (Mahony, P. J. 1996, 19), Herr K. clasped and kissed her on the lips in his place of business where ie had arranged to be alone with her. In 1898, Frau K. invited Dora to a resort on l lake. On June 30 of that year, Herr K. made a proposal to the sixteen-year-old)ora, while on a walk together at the lake's side. She slapped him and ran away.)uring the next three nights she had a recurring dream about a burning house. Two days later when her father left the resort, she departed with him. A few days before Herr K.'s proposal to her, Dora had learned from the young governess of the K.'s children that he "had made violent love" to her (Freud 1905a, 105) with the excuse that "he got nothing from his wife" (p. 106) and that "after a little while he had ceased to care for her" (ibid.).

Dora's treatment started in October 1900, when she was a month short of her eighteenth birthday and ended by her decision on December 31 of the same year. On October 14, 1900, Freud wrote to Wilhelm Fliess: "It has been a lovely time and it has brought a new patient, an eighteen-year-old girl, a case that has smoothly opened to the existing collection of picklocks" (Freud 1985, 427). A picklock is an instrument for opening locks without a key, frequently used by burglars. The metaphor insinuates phallic imagery and *violation* of what is closed, which Freud wants to open with his special analytic picklock, as one more for his collection. It implies an action *analogical* to what we will soon learn Herr K. wanted to do with Dora, suggesting that Freud had already identified with him. Freud finished writing up the case on January 24, 1901, but did not publish it until 1905. Mahony asserts that during that period Freud was treating either Herr or Frau K. (Mahony 1996, 141). On January 25, 1901, he wrote to Fliess that the case was organized around two dreams "so it is really a continuation of the dream book. In addition it contains resolutions of hysterical symptoms and glimpses of the sexual-organic foundation of the whole thing. It is the subtlest thing I have written so far" (Freud 1985, 433).

Freud clarifies that he has "not reproduced the process of interpretation to which the patient's associations and communications had to be subjected, but only the results of that process" (Freud 1905a, 12–13). Even so, there is enough material to ascertain how Freud and Dora spoke to each other during the analysis. He also tells the reader: "My object in this case history was to demonstrate the intimate structure of a neurotic disorder and the determination of its symptoms" (p. 13). In saying this, Freud declares that his focus is intrapsychic and theoretical – the *structure* of the neurosis – while Dora's enmeshment with sexually dysfunctional adults is taken simply as the context of her life. The fact that she was an adolescent entrapped in a situation in which her father was sexually involved with her close friend whose husband wanted to be sexually involved with her appears as no more than the background for her intrapsychic processes.

We do not hear Dora's voice in the report until page 28 and then only in an indirect citation. In the previous pages Freud indicates that he let her talk freely, select the subject of the day, and offers the reader details of her life along with some theoretical considerations. We hear Freud referring to the episode that Dora had kept "secret till her confession during the treatment" as "the little scene," when Herr K. "suddenly clasped the girl to him and pressed a kiss upon her lips" in his shop (Freud 1905a, 28). Dora felt "a violent feeling of disgust, tore herself free from the man, and hurried past him to the staircase and from there to the street door" (ibid.). Freud comments: "This was surely just the situation to call up a distinct feeling of sexual excitement in a girl of fourteen who had never before been approached. *But* Dora had at that moment a violent feeling of disgust" (ibid.,

ny italics). Freud's "but" implies that she should have responded with excitement, even though she was a thirteen-year-old and perhaps had not yet started
her periods (Glenn 1980), he was married, much older than she, and a family
friend. Freud's calling the episode "the little scene" disregards *her* experience of
the moment while he also *assumed* that "during the man's passionate embrace she
felt . . . the pressure of his erect member against her body. This perception was
revolting to her; it was dismissed from her memory, repressed, and replaced by
the innocent sensation of pressure upon her thorax" (p. 30). She denied feeling his
erect member. Freud also *imagined* that Dora's clitoris responded with an erection.
He concluded: "the behaviour of this child of fourteen was already entirely and
completely hysterical" (p. 28). At this point Freud writes in a footnote that Herr K.
". . . was still quite young and of prepossessing appearance" (note 3, p. 29), implying she should have been glad and excited that such a handsome man had given
her a sexual kiss. Freud *assumed* her disgust about his supposedly erect penis (p. 30)
and also *imagined* Dora's clitoris responding with an erection. Dora denied feeling
such sensations. The reader does not hear Dora's voice but Freud's explanations to
himself about *her* experience.

Freud wanted Dora to talk about Herr K. She wanted to talk about her father
and told Freud the whole story of his affair with Frau K. Dora criticized her father
bitterly and felt that "she had been handed over to Herr K. as the price of her tol-
erating the relations between her father and his wife" (p. 34). Freud acknowledges
that the father was among those capable of "falsifying their judgement upon one of
the conflicting alternatives" (p. 34). When Dora talked about what she considered
her father's malingering, Freud felt the need to show her that she too was malingering: "There could be *no doubt*, I said, that she had *an aim* in view which she hoped
to gain by her illness. That aim could be none other than to detach her father from
Frau K. . . . Yet if her father refused to give way to her, *I was quite sure* she would
not let herself be deprived of her illness so easily" (p. 42, my italics). He is talking *at*
Dora and not *with* Dora. He sounds like a stern task master who has caught the person in his care being at fault and needs to set her straight. The absence of empathy
is painful. Without transition, Freud goes on into three and one half pages of theoretical considerations about the intentions present in the formation of symptoms.

Dora was capable of free associating and more than once she confirmed some
of Freud's interpretations with memories of past or recent events. He used them
to validate his hypothesis and theories against her reticence as illustrated when
he reports the day that Dora was very upset and they discovered it was Herr K.'s
birthday. This was "a fact" – Freud says – "which I did not fail to use against her"
(p. 59). He shows himself in *combat* with Dora; he is sure she is in love with Herr
K. and insists that she accept his conclusion. His victory over her is intended to
prove *his theories* correct. All this is contained in Freud's narrative presenting *his*
understanding of Dora's psychical life. Her voice has been almost drowned by the
assured and clever *explanations* he gives of what she harbors in her unconscious.
This conclusion does not mean that they did not talk to each other or collaborate to understand her first dream ("*A house was on fire*") and other issues. At the

end of such period of collaboration, however, Freud could not resist giving her a very long-winded speech about *his own construction* of Dora's internal narrative. He added that "the re-appearance of the dream in the last few days forces me to the conclusion that you consider that the same situation has arisen once again, and that you have decided to give up the treatment – to which, after all, it is only your father who makes you come" (p. 70). Freud said he was talking with Dora, but I believe he was also – and perhaps more important – talking to himself, reasoning like a prosecuting attorney.

Freud wanted to unveil the true motive of her dream. Further elaboration of what he knew led him to conclude that Dora had "fled *to* her father because she was afraid of the man who was pursuing her; she summoned up an infantile affection for her father so that it might protect her against her present affection for a stranger" (p. 86). He was pleased with the conclusion; his dream theory about infantile wishes in dreams had been confirmed: "The wish to replace Herr K. by her father provided the necessary motive power for the dream" (p. 86). Freud continues with a complex elaboration of the significance of the words 'wet' and 'jewel-case' in sexual life.

Freud attributes to Dora revengeful motives in relation to her father and Herr K. as well as himself even though there is no indication she used the word. When Dora announced that she was leaving the treatment, he commented: "For how could the patient take a more effective revenge than by demonstrating upon her own person the helplessness and incapacity of the physician?" (p. 120). He went further by placing these words in her mouth: "Men are all so detestable that I would rather not marry. This is my revenge" (p. 120). It is a fact, however, that Dora married exactly three years after the end of the treatment.

Much more could be said about how they talked with each other. In the end I concur with Mahony (1996), Gay (1988), Marcus (1976), Spence (1986), Blos (1972), Erikson (1962), Langs (1980), Scharman (1980), Sachs (2005), and others that Freud mishandled Dora, seemed not to like her, and ignored her adolescent condition in order to further his theories. In fact, when she returned to him for further treatment fifteen months after the interruption, he did not accept her as a patient. It would be unfair to suggest that he did not wish to help Dora. Yet it is all too obvious, at least in the written case, that his main concern was to advance his own knowledge and to confirm that his theory of dreams was a therapeutic tool. In spite of it all, I cannot help but admire Freud's brilliance in putting disparate elements together, while I regret that his compulsion to make analytic sense of the clinical facts left little room for him to hear Dora, the adolescent betrayed by the adults in her life, and to engage her in listening to herself in a meaningful analytic dialogue.

The Rat Man

On October 1, 1907, Freud received in consultation a self-referred patient, Ernst Lanzer, age twenty-nine, who presented a long history of obsessive ideas and their increase after participating in military maneuvers. He had been awarded a Doctor

Juris degree from the University of Vienna in July of that year. Freud accepted him immediately for analysis and they worked together "for more than eleven months" (Freud 1909, 186). He wrote up the case in a month in the summer of 1909 and sent it to the printers on July 7. It was his first analytic report of an adult male. After Freud's death his daily hand-written notes dating from the initial consultation up to January 20, 1908, were found among his papers. The part of the treatment presented in the published case after such date is not documented in these notes. Strachey translated and published the notes in 1955 in the *Standard Edition*, as *Addendum: Original Record of the Case*. He omitted the first ten sessions because Freud used them almost unaltered in his published case history. Elza Ribeiro Hawelka (Freud 1974) published a French translation of the full text. She had obtained a photocopy of the manuscript from Anna Freud and published the German text of Freud's notes and the French translation on the facing page. I have used her publication to better understand his work.

Lanzer, who had consulted eminent psychiatrists to no avail, had glanced at one of Freud's works and its sexual referents and felt he could obtain help from him. Freud describes him as a: "youngish man of university education ['*von akademischer Bildung*']" and says Lanzer "introduced himself to me with the statement that he had suffered from obsessions ever since his childhood, but with particular intensity for the last four years" (p. 158). He was afraid of harming his father (already dead) and the lady he admired. Freud commented: "He gave me the impression of being a clear-headed and shrewd person" (ibid.). His condition had exacerbated when he participated in military maneuvers in Galicia (Mahony, 1986, 27). During a halt in the maneuvers a Czech captain whose inclination for cruelty frightened his subordinates described a horrible punishment used in Eastern countries. The story entered forcefully into Dr. Lanzer's obsessive ideas and plunged him into a crisis.

They began the analysis the following day, Wednesday, October 2, 1907. Freud reports that he made Lanzer pledge to say everything no matter how unpleasant or unimportant it might appear to him and then allowed him to start with "any subject he pleased" (p. 159). In the notes Freud observes, "I set him free from the start [*ihm den Beginn freigestellt*] (Freud 1974, 32). This seems to be the first time that Freud tried to let a patient associate freely, yet he could not stop himself from asking questions. At the start Lanzer presented to Freud "the first great blow [*Erschütterung*] of his life" (Freud 1909, 160). A medical student and dear friend had duped him by making him feel well liked, when all he wanted was access to one of his sisters. Was he warning Freud not to betray him? Then, he launched into the description of his sexual life starting with the fourth or fifth year of his life. He mentioned fingering the genitals of one governess and watching another attending to abscesses on her buttocks. He gave the surname of the women, both male names. Freud asked his *first* question about the room he slept in at the time and Lanzer said that he slept "mostly with my parents" (p. 161). The patient went on with stories about his governesses and his great wish to see nude women in their baths. Freud was not only listening but attending to his own thoughts about potential homosexuality, so he interrupted the patient to ask a *second* question about the first names of the governesses, which the patient didn't know. Lanzer went on to tell Freud about his erections at age six, his belief that his parents knew his thoughts, and his fear that his wish to see women naked would bring about bad consequences. Freud asked a *third* question requesting an example. The answer was rich and promising: "(. . . 'For instance, *that my father might die.*') 'Thoughts about my father's death occupied my mind from a very early age and for a long period of time, and greatly depressed me'" (p. 162). Freud learned with "astonishment that the patient's father . . . had died several years previously" (p. 162), but the fears about his death persisted. Freud's three questions point to what he was thinking about: primal scene, sexual orientation, and the need for a concrete example. In spite of his best intentions to let Lanzer talk freely, Freud could not stop himself from constructing clinical theories even in the first analytic hour.

The patient opened the next hour by telling the story of the Czech captain: "I had a kind of dread of him, *for he was obviously fond of cruelty*" (p. 166). He reported "The captain told me he had read of a specially horrible punishment used in the East" (ibid.). At this point he got up and begged Freud to spare him describing the details. He responded in a threefold manner. First, "I *assured him* that I myself had no taste whatever for cruelty, and certainly had no desire to torment him, but that naturally I could not grant him something which was beyond my power" (p. 166, my italics). Then, in the same breath, Freud gave him a *theoretical comment* about overcoming defenses, and finally, he made a *promise*: "I would do all I could, nevertheless, to guess the full meaning of any hints he gave me. Was he perhaps thinking of impalement? – 'No, not that'" (p. 166). The patient proceeded to describe in mumbling and agitated words that a prisoner was tied up an inverted pot with rats in it was attached to his buttocks and they "'. . . bored their way in . . .' – Into his anus, I helped him out [*durfte ich ergänzen*, I permitted myself to complete (1974, p. 44]" (p. 166). Freud had fulfilled his promise to guess his patient's words. Lanzer continued: "'At that moment the idea flashed through my mind that *this was happening to a person who was very dear to me*,'" and after prompting from Freud, he said it was his lady friend (p. 167). Finally, in response to another question, he said that the punishment was not applied by him. He declared the thoughts repugnant to him and described the formulas he used to prevent the fantasy from becoming reality and asserted that "he had just succeeded in warding off *both* of them" (p. 167). The word 'both' indicated that his [dead] father also received the punishment. Then, the patient launched into an extremely complicated story of a dilemma of how to repay a Lieutenant A the charge of 3.80 kronen he had laid out for Lanzer's glasses. If he paid the money back, however, he feared the punishment threatening his lady friend and his father would actually come true. Freud describes how at the end of the session, the patient "behaved as though he were dazed and bewildered. He repeatedly addressed me as 'Captain'" (p. 169), in spite of Freud's assurance that he was not cruel. The patient concluded the hour by talking about punishment in the next world and his religious devotion as a youth. This dramatic hour illustrates how *actively* Freud participated in his patient's associations, from reassuring him about his non-cruel disposition to completing the associations himself, although he was unable to allay the Rat Man's fears that he could be another cruel captain.

In the published case, the third session starts and continues with Lanzer's convoluted story about repaying the money he owed. The hand-written notes say, "He responds *to my questions* by saying that his father died when he himself was 21 years-old. The inclusion of the hereafter did not come to him until a certain time later" (Freud 1974, 54). After that, Freud let him talk for the rest of the hour, with the exception of another question about the feasibility of catching the trains to make the payment. Freud comments: "The true technique of psychoanalysis requires the physician to suppress his curiosity and leaves the patient complete freedom in choosing the order in which topics shall succeed each other during the treatment. At the fourth session, accordingly, I received the patient with the question: 'And how do you intend to proceed to-day?'" (Freud 1909, 174). A literal translation would read: "How would you continue now?" (1974, p. 62). I believe that this question contradicts Freud's assertion about suppressing his curiosity. Lanzer described how he was not at his father's bedside when he died and unable to believe his father was dead. Eighteen month after his father's death, on the occasion of the death of an aunt, he began to see himself as a criminal and became incapacitated in his work. A friend consoled him by saying that his self-reproaches were exaggerated. Freud used the occasion to refute the friend's opinion in the light of psychoanalysis: "When there is a *mésalliance*, I began, between an affect and its ideational content (in this instance, between the intensity of the self-reproach and the occasion for it), a layman will say that the affect is too great for the occasion – that it is exaggerated. . . . On the contrary, the [analytic] physician says: 'No. The affect is justified. The sense of guilt is not in itself open to further criticism. But it belongs to some other content, which is unknown (*unconscious*), and which requires to be looked for'" (Freud 1909, 175–76). This excerpt gives the flavor of Freud's words.

In the fifth session Freud explained the unconscious, the infantile, guilt, affect, and other analytic concepts to Lanzer. When the patient doubted that his symptoms could be modified, Freud reports: "I told him . . . that his youth was very much in his favour as well as the intactness of his personality" and continued: "In this connection I said a word or two upon the *good opinion I had formed of him*, and this gave him visible *pleasure*" (p. 178, my italics). This remark suggests a mixture of seduction and reassurance on Freud's part and does not hide his pleasure at having Dr. Lanzer as a patient.

In the sixth session Lanzer made revelations about his childhood, his first non-sensual love at age twelve, and the desire that the girl would be affectionate [*liebevoll*] with him, which might come about if he suffered a misfortune, perhaps if his father died, but he could not admit ever having wished for his father's death. Through objections and explanations Freud tried to get him to admit he had had such a thought and that he had had it more than once. The patient admitted that it had crossed his mind six months before his father's death, when it occurred to him that he would then be rich enough to marry, thus creating the internal debate about whom he loved more, his father or his lady friend. At this point Freud "thought it advisable to bring a fresh piece of theory to his notice" (p. 180), namely, that unconsciously repressed wishes have a contrary conscious counterpart. The patient became agitated and claimed to have loved his father. Freud retorted that it was "such intense love as his that was the necessary precondition of the repressed hatred" (p. 180) and illustrated it with the story of Brutus's love and hatred of Julius Caesar. Lanzer provided several arguments supporting his doubts about such an explanation. Freud gave him a lawyer-like response, suggesting that whoever asked questions like that "was already prepared with an answer" (p. 181).

The patient described his friendship with his father as more intimate than with his lady friend, for whom he felt no sensual desire. Freud gave him a direct interpretation, saying that he must have felt that his father was an interference to his sensual desires, and constructed the evolution of Lanzer's desires sustained by a sort of legal self-defense: "I then got him to agree that I had not led him on to the subject either of childhood or of sex, but that he had raised them both of his own free will" (p. 182). Lanzer retorted with a question about the relationship between his love for his father and his love for his lady. Freud gave him an answer (sixteen lines long in the text) that started with another legal point, namely, that "it was scarcely possible to destroy a person in *absentia*" (p. 182, italics in the original) and went on to offer Lanzer a detailed construction of the evolution of his wish (pp 182–83). As a reader I cannot help but witness their efforts to understand, but also to outwit, each other and I must confess feeling a certain voyeuristic joy in reading about such a contest between a lawyer and a doctor who uses legal arguments to analyze him.

In the seventh hour Lanzer doubted that he had death wishes toward his father and told the story of a woman who committed suicide after having a bad wish, a step that would be right for him to take if he harbored death wishes for his father. He reported a criminal act he had committed as a child when he shot a toy gun directly into the eye of his younger brother with the intention of hurting him; the gun failed, however, and nothing happened. Freud jumped in: "I took the opportunity of *urging my case*" (p. 185, my italics) suggesting it was possible that something similar had occurred at a still earlier age, but in relation to his father. Lanzer responded by describing some vindictive fantasies toward his lady friend. Freud *reassured* him by saying that "he ought logically to consider himself as in no way responsible for any of these traits in his character" (p. 185) because they came from "his infantile disposition" and added that "a man, with his moral responsibility, grew up out of the sum of his infantile predispositions" (p. 185). In a footnote Freud admits that reassuring words were useless. The patient doubted that his impulses stemmed from such a source and Freud retorted: "I promised to *prove* it to him" (p. 186, my italics) and added that the abnormal mourning of his father's death found expression in his illness.

Freud's chronological presentation of the case ends here. He continues to document what happened but not the details of the analysis. The early daily notes reveal how Freud worked with a patient he obviously liked. Freud respected

Lanzer's intelligence and trusted he could participate in the analytic process. His explanations address a person capable of theoretical understanding. Sometimes the reader has the feeling that Freud wants to win a legal case by using theoretical arguments to convince him, to encourage him to go on, while letting him know that he knows what the patient is talking about. If Lanzer does not *believe* him, he promises to offer him the right proof. Freud does not hesitate to interrupt the patient to ask questions related to his own thoughts. There is a certain camaraderie between them, perhaps as graduates of the University of Vienna, a sort of a man-to-man alliance that is not present in the reports about his women patients. At the personal level they also had in common a dead sibling in childhood and fathers that were nineteen years older than their mothers.

From this point on I alternate between the notes and the published text to bring out significant points in Freud and Lanzer's work together. On October 11, the notes say: "Violent struggle, bad day. Resistance, because I requested him yesterday to bring a photograph of the lady with him – i.e. to give up his reticence about her. Conflict as to whether he should abandon the treatment or surrender his secrets" (p. 259). Free association did not call for photographs. What could have prompted Freud to demand to *see* the lady's photograph?

In the published text, Freud offers a lengthy presentation of his theories about obsessional ideas and continues with the exploration of the precipitant of Lanzer's illness and his father complex. The patient described a ritual act: at midnight he would open the front door "as though his father were standing outside it; then, coming back into the hall, he would take out his penis and look at it in the looking-glass" (p. 204). Freud reflected about the patient acting as though his father's ghost would visit him and explored Lanzer's ambivalence toward him. Freud offered him a 'construction' about himself as a young child: "he had been guilty of some sexual misdemeanour connected with masturbation and had been roundly castigated for it by his father" (p. 205). The patient told a story reported by his mother that when he was very small "he had done something naughty, for which his father had given him a beating. The little boy had flown into a terrible rage and had hurled abuse at his father" (p. 205). He was never beaten again. Soon he repeated the behavior in the transference: "he began heaping the grossest and filthiest abuse upon me and my family" (p. 209) and, frightened that Freud would hit him "he would get up from the sofa and roam about the room" (p. 209). Freud comments that from his behavior "the patient won the sense of *conviction* which he had lacked" (ibid.).

Freud then examines the dynamic organization of the neurosis: "We may regard the repression of his infantile hatred of his father as the event which brought his whole subsequent career under the dominion of the neurosis" (p. 238). In his adult life, Freud notes: "His hatred of his lady was inevitably coupled with his attachment to his father, and inversely his hatred of his father with his attachment to his lady" (p. 238). Freud writes that "the love has not succeeded in extinguishing the hatred but only in driving it down into the unconscious; and in the unconscious the hatred, safe from the danger of being destroyed by the operations of consciousness, is able to persist and even to grow" (p. 239). He concludes that "a relation between love and hatred . . . is among the most frequent, the most marked, and probably, therefore, the most important characteristics of obsessional neurosis" (p. 239).

The hand-written notes provide many more examples of the events and verbal exchanges between patient and analyst. In the note of October 27, 1907, Freud observes that "so long as he makes difficulties over giving me the lady's name his account must be incoherent" (p. 272), and proceeds to list the disjointed stories the patient has presented to him. He continues: "After I had persuaded him to reveal the name of Gisa Hertz and all the details about her, his account became clear and systematic" (p. 273). Again, Freud wants factual data about the lady. Only her first name was important because it had become part of a prayer-formula the patient had created to handle his ambivalence.

They continue their work together with Freud pointing things out to Lanzer particularly in relation to Lanzer's sexual feelings, fantasies, and the new material he had presented. He had many sexual fantasies about his sisters that even included copulating with them, and at times he attempted to enact some of his wishes Freud thought that his being chastised by his father [p. 265] "was related to assaulting [*Vergehen gegen die Schwestern*] his sisters" (p. 278).

On November 21 the notes describe the patient in a deep crisis. He could not say what came to his mind, the cure would not be worth such a sacrifice, Freud would turn him out. Explanations about the transference had no results. "It was only after a forty minutes' struggle [*Kampf*] and after I had revealed the element of revenge against me and had shown him that by refusing to tell me and by giving up the treatment he would be taking a more outright revenge on me than by telling me – only after this did he give me to understand that it concerned my daughter" (p. 281). The ideas involved Freud's family, his daughter, and bizarre sexual and anal fantasies and wishes about them.

The treatment was at stake. Lanzer *interpreted* Freud's assertion that "my undertaking to show that all the material concerned only himself looked like anxiety on my part" (p. 281) and decided to continue the analysis. He produced many fantasies about Freud's daughter and mother, some gruesome, such as his mother's genitals having been "entirely eaten up by me and the children" (p. 282) and Freud's daughter performing fellatio on Lanzer. Freud closes the note of the day saying "I repeated my *lecture* [*Vorlesung*] . . . on the perversions" (p. 283, my italics). Lanzer continued to bring up bizarre fantasies about Freud's family and when Freud offered an interpretation he accused the analyst of *taking revenge* on him while Freud claimed that it was Lanzer who wanted revenge. Meanwhile he was walking around the room afraid that Freud would beat him up for his "confessions" while he was punning about Freud's daughter being a "'*Freudenhaus-Mädchen*' ['girls belonging to a house of pleasure' – i.e. prostitutes, a play on Freud's name]" (p. 284). He mentioned a Leopold Freud in Budapest who had been executed for a crime. Freud *laughed* and assured him he had no relatives there (p. 285). Lanzer accused him of being "a filthy swine" who picked his nose and "refused to shake hands with me" (p. 293). He continued to pile insults and sexual fantasies upon Freud's wife, daughter, and Freud himself. Freud documented no response on his part to these offenses. Later in the analysis the patient started a "historical account of his obsessional ideas" (p. 300) and Freud "pointed out to him that this attempt to deny the reality of his father's death is the basis of his whole neurosis" (p. 300).

In the notes from December 28, the reader is shocked to read: "He was hungry and was fed" (p. 303). Freud himself brought out the meal that included herrings. Lanzer later thought that it had been prepared by two women. During the hour he brought out his childhood thoughts about suicide and how "on his mother's account, he would never kill himself" (p. 306). Freud writes: "I gave him Zola's *Joie de vivre* to read" (p. 306), a book in which the hero is constantly preoccupied with thoughts of death. Freud must have been in the grip of complex counter-transferential feelings as suggested by the mistaken date of the next session as December 2, when it should have been January 2. The meal prompted Lanzer to spin bizarre sexual fantasies, to allude to the story of a man copulating for another when he offered to pay for the meal, and – with Freud's help – to establish some links with childhood worms and the enema treatments to eliminate them.

On January 3 Freud told him: "If the rat is a worm, it is also a penis" (p. 311) and explained that the patient's urge for intercourse was related to rage and desire and the infantile fantasy of intercourse by the anus. The patient followed with "a whole flood of associations" (p. 311) and offered *ironic* praise: "It was my science that was the child which solved the problem with the gay superiority of 'smiling virtuosity', peeled off the disguises from his ideas and so liberated the two women from his herring-wishes" (p. 311).

The notes for January 6 and 7 record Freud's observation that Lanzer "was smiling with sly amusement, as though he had something up his sleeve" (p. 315). The patient reported a dream about a pulled tooth. After much effort on Freud's part he acknowledged that it had to do with "a very large penis," – namely, his father's (p. 318). Then, he "finally admitted this as being a *tu quoque* and a revenge against his father" (pp. 317–18). The last note from January 20 comes after a "long interruption" and reports that the patient rejected Freud's interpretation about his running (p. 318). After this we have the published text to follow the analysis.

At the end of the clinical presentation Freud writes: "When we reached the solution that has been described above [about obeying his father], the patient's rat delirium disappeared" (p. 220). Lanzer married his lady after the analysis and died during his military duty early in the First World War.

Conclusions

Freud and Lanzer did talk *with* each other, *to* each other, and *about* each other. In spite of the difference in age they talked as man to man. Each stood his ground, agreed or disagreed, listened or managed not to listen, without losing their capacity to cooperate in furthering the analytic process. Neither was bothered by the bizarre sexual fantasies the patient concocted about Freud and his family. The reader senses the mutual respect doctor and patient had for each other. Lanzer was an articulate, intelligent man, a professional gifted with the capacity to develop free association and run with it. Freud was all ears for his obsessive fantasies to the point that he lost his neutrality when he expressed "the good opinion I had formed of him" (p. 178).

Freud, the master narrator, must have been greatly pleased with the unique series of plots emerging from the Rat Man's mouth. They brought much confirmation to his theories, illustrating them in the most graphic detail. His fascination with the case is best illustrated by the fact that he presented it to the Wednesday meetings of the Vienna Psychoanalytic Society on five occasions while the treatment was ongoing. He also gave an oral presentation of the case to the First International Psycho-Analytical Congress held at Salzburg, April 27, 1908, that lasted over four hours (Strachey 1960, 154).

Freud's listening stance involves his overall attitude to what the patient *had to say*. His clinical curiosity and theoretical commitment disposed him to be intensely attentive to the convoluted and confusing stories of events, thoughts, feelings, beliefs, doings and undoings of the Rat Man. Precision with some detail was critical to understanding the confusing accounts of his obsessive and dramatically inclined patient. Freud gave every indication to Lanzer that he was willing to listen no matter what he had to say. The patient must have *felt* the depth of this commitment because he entrusted Freud with his most bizarre feelings and ideas. That said, it does not mean that Freud was willing to hear *all* the patient had to say or even capable of it. Here is a good example: on January 2, the Rat Man was depressed and "he apparently had only trivialities to report and I was able to say a great deal *to him* to-day" (p. 308, my italics). When the Rat Man began to associate and described that "he felt a rat gnawing at his own anus and had a visual image of it," Freud brought "out his own associations in connection with the rats. After all, he had had worms as a child . . . he must have had a period of itching in his anus. . . . I told him that the story about the herring reminded me very much of the enemas," and so on (p. 308). This example illustrates how they worked together a good part of the time. Freud was making *his* own connections, giving him some explanations, and Lanzer agreed, confirmed, or disagreed, but continued bringing up more associations. The hours seem to move smoothly between moments when Freud might remind him of past associations and moments when the patient would add more stories and details. The last example illustrates how Freud favored reconstruction and bringing up memories from the past over attending to transferential components of the moment because he said nothing about having given the herrings to the patient at the office.

Freud's most frequent non-listening interventions took the form of short or long lectures to Lanzer about psychoanalysis and theoretical concepts all aimed at educating him. What emerges from the report is the *urgency* Freud felt to make sense of what he was hearing, in both theoretical and clinical terms. He interrupts the patient in mid-sentence to complete his associations for him; he searches for opportunities to introduce his ideas and actively further the patient's learning from him. In inviting the patient to associate freely Freud frequently ceded the analyst's place to the investigator and theoretician who were almost running ahead of the patient. The analyst in him tries to wait, but the other two urge him to intervene to convince Lanzer before he has time to grasp the nature of his experience. As Raymond de Saussure points out "one rapidly sensed what special theoretical question preoccupied him, for often during the analytic hour he developed at length new points of view he was clarifying in his own mind" (Saussure 1973, 359). Saussure attributes Freud's difficulties as a clinician to the fact that he had never been analyzed by another person.

As far as the transference is concerned, Freud frequently dismisses it with firm reassurances: no, he is not a cruel captain; no, he has no intention to harm Lanzer; no, he has nothing to do with the criminal Freud in Budapest. This attitude contrasts sharply with his calm acceptance of the gruesome sexual fantasies and wishes about him and his family that Lanzer offered or his accusations about Freud picking his nose, a clear paternal transference.

Freud and Lanzer resorted at times to humor. Freud *laughed* when Lanzer brought up the murderous Freud from Budapest. The patient made a good pun – with plenty of dynamic meaning – when he suggested that Freud's daughter lived in a brothel while on another occasion he gave Freud mocking praise about his science. I sense a certain pleasure between doctor and patient derived from doing something meaningful together – Freud spinning out theories and lengthy interpretations while Lanzer brings out a multitude of complex associations. It feels to me like a pleasure akin to participating in a good tennis match. Each seems to be pleased with himself and with the other. No other patient Freud reported about had made such creative and bizarre use of imagery. Good and intelligent obsessive that he was – Lanzer displayed imagination and devised machinations that filled the consulting room with drama, horror, terrifying images, and a sense that no one could bear to hear his thoughts and wishes. To my mind, Freud's true capacity to listen and the encouragement he offered Lanzer to speak must have represented a tremendous relief for his thought-spinning mind while it offered Freud a unique opportunity to hear an articulate patient unveil so many derivatives of unconscious processes in his presence.

Freud's language at times echoes Lanzer's military experience and also resorts, as noted above, to *legal* arguments. Freud insists to his doubting patient that his infantile impulses are the cause of his problems: "I promised to prove it to him" (p. 187). When Lanzer reveals an early childhood memory, Freud presses him ("I took the opportunity of urging my case"), insisting that he could have other memories. I am inclined to conclude that Freud was doing his best to find a way of talking to his patient – in a certain mimetic military or legal language – in order to convey his intention to reach out to him.

As for the issue of revenge, Freud seems to have felt that Lanzer *owed it to him* to remain in treatment just as he had with Dora when she announced her intention to leave. When his lawyer patient insinuated that he might terminate the analysis, Freud replied that giving up the treatment would be taking a greater revenge on him than by communicating a supposedly unspeakable fantasy. Accusations were made on both sides. Lanzer retorted to Freud's interpretation that if his mother died he would be freed from conflicts and able to marry: "'You are taking a revenge on me' he said. 'You are forcing me into this, because you want to revenge yourself on me'" (p. 283).

Comparison of the published case and Freud's hand-written notes opens our eyes to what Freud included for publication and what he omitted. The analyst and master-narrator intent on creating a solid analytic theory took the lead in the official version. As Mahony points out: "In those instances where Freud's case histories did not factually conform to his process notes, we notice that he retained his role as effective storyteller, aesthetically guiding his fabled reconstruction by narrative principles" (Mahony 1986, 213). We should be grateful to Freud the writer because without his incomparable ability to organize a case as complex and confusing as the Rat Man's, we would not have been able to grasp obsessive neurosis and the dynamic principles that bring it about. Freud's published case report gives a comprehensive theoretical analysis of the characteristics of obsessional psychical structures. The description sets the standard for all future understanding of obsessional neurosis as based on a conflict of love and hatred for the same sexually invested object.

Infantile neurosis: The Wolf Man

From the History of an Infantile Neurosis offers Freud's clinical evidence about the existence of infantile sexuality, the primal scene, and deferred action; it also contains his response to Adler and Jung's modification of his ideas regarding "the significance of the infantile factor" (Freud 1918, 54). The case centers on the early sexual life of Serge Pankejeff, the Wolf Man (1887–1979), who in his twenties offered Freud the possibility to reconstruct it from the patient's dreams and associations.

Freud wrote up the case from September to early November 1914 (Mahony 1984, 86) soon after the termination of the analysis on July 10 and published it after the end of the First World War in late 1918. In Pankejeff's analysis he encountered an unexpected problem. He had taken it for granted in *On Aphasia* that a person's words naturally link to internal representations, and came to believe that eliciting meaningful speech would eventually lead to the unveiling of a patient's unconscious reality. Pankejeff was certainly able to speak to Freud but as Freud described the situation his words did not give access to his private world:

> The patient with whom I am here concerned remained for a long time unassailably entrenched behind an attitude of *obliging apathy*. He listened, understood, and remained *unapproachable*. His unimpeachable intelligence was, as it were, cut off from the instinctual forces which governed his behaviour in the *few relations* of life that remained to him. It required a long education to induce him to take an independent share in the work; and when as a result

of this exertion he began for the first time to feel relief, he immediately gave up working in order to avoid any further changes, and in order *to remain comfortably in the situation* which had been thus established. *His shrinking from a self-sufficient existence* was so great as to outweigh all the vexations of his illness.

(p. 11, my italics)

Words were not enough to engage Pankejeff on an emotional level. Something else was needed. The analysis was into its fourth year when Freud decided to confront his patient's inertia. He waited until "his *attachment* to myself had become strong enough" to announce that "the treatment must be brought to an end at a particular fixed date" (ibid., 11, my italics). Freud's maneuver paid off:

Under the *inexorable pressure* of this fixed limit his resistance and his fixation to the illness gave way, and now in a *disproportionately short time* the analysis produced all the material which made it possible to clear up his inhibitions and remove his symptoms. All the information, too, which *enabled me* to understand his infantile neurosis is *derived from this last period* of the work, during which resistance temporarily disappeared and the patient gave an impression of lucidity which is usually *attainable only in hypnosis*.

(ibid., my italics)

Freud's case report presents *exclusively* the work of this time when he says "we succeeded in descending into the deepest and most primitive strata of mental development" (p. 10). He also acknowledges that the analysis had been "most terribly disjointed," and that "feeling one's way into his mind [was] a laborious" task (p. 104).

I am convinced that most of the work was done on Freud's part, as he describes: "I have therefore *been obliged* to put it together from even *smaller fragments* than are usually at one's disposal for purposes of synthesis" (p. 72, my italics). Freud's masterful narrative voice dominates the presentation while the reader hears Pankejeff's voice directly only three times. All the rest is a combination of what Freud reports about Pankejeff's communications: "These *scenes* from infancy are not reproduced during the treatment as recollections, they are the products of *construction*" (pp. 50–51, my italics). They "have to be divined – constructed – gradually and laboriously from an aggregate of indications" (p. 51), such as recollections, hints, and dreams, which are also forms of recollecting. The whole case represents Freud's effort to create a sequential narrative showing the internal transformations in the organization of a young child's sexuality. The case he said "*enabled me* to understand his infantile neurosis" (p. 11, my italics) without revealing whether Pankejeff grasped it himself.

At the age of twenty-one Serge Pankejeff was the heir and only surviving child of one of the wealthiest landowners in Russia. He had no notion of how much he owned and left all business to his mother's care while he took to painting for pleasure. Psychopathology and tragedy abounded in his family. On his father's side the wife of his grandfather committed suicide; his father had been hospitalized severa. times in Germany for depression when Pankejeff was young. His only sister and older sibling committed suicide when she was nineteen years old. His father took his own life through an overdose two years later while in Moscow on business. In *The Memoirs of the Wolf-Man* he said about his early years: "As our parents were often away, my sister and I were left mostly under the supervision of strangers, and even when our parents were home we had little contact with them" (Gardiner 1971, 8). He says of his mother "she did not have much time left for us. But if my sister or I was ill, she became an exemplary nurse . . . as a child I sometimes *wished I would get sick*, to be able to *enjoy* my mother's being with me and looking after me" (p. 9, my italics). Little is known about his relationship with his father except that as a small child he liked him.

Pankejeff's difficulties with human encounters started early. When the family moved to Odessa he cried because "now I would have to get used to a large and *strange* city" (p. 11, my italics). Earlier, he had experienced the country fairs a. creating in him "an impression of indescribable confusion, and I thought to mysel that the goings-on in hell must be pretty much like this" (p. 5). On the other hand he described his experience on his father's estate in White Russia as idyllic: "This was the perfect place to *recover* from what Freud called 'civilization and its discontents'" (p. 12, my italics). There is no evidence he had friends as a child or as an adolescent. He only had tutors, female and male, and was in contact with many servants on the estate. Before his father's suicide, while he was with his mother or their estate, she *hired* a law student to keep him company. The image emerges of a lonely and forlorn child and adolescent hidden behind the life style of an aristocrat.

At the same time he was incapable of enduring real solitude, as is perhaps bes exemplified by the period he spent in Munich for psychiatric treatment. His desperate letters so alarmed his mother that she decided to join him. He improved at once: "No longer alone, and in my mother's company, I felt somehow *sheltered and safe* from the tempest to which I had been exposed. The pain, so severe only a shor time before, lost its sharpness and made room for a wistful, almost elegiac mood" (p. 61, my italics). I believe that this episode illustrates what Freud described as hi being "totally incapacitated," that is, his inability to be alone. In other respects he was functional enough.

In a footnote he added to the case study in 1923 (p. 121), Freud documented the significant childhood landmarks related to Pankejeff's psychopathology and treatment: at one and a half years old, Freud believed he witnessed parental intercourse (the primal scene); before two and a half, he saw Grusha scrubbing the floor on her knees, urinated in her presence, and she replied "with a threat of castration" (p. 93); at three and a quarter, his sister played with his penis. Shortly after hi Nanya threatened him with castration; immediately before his fourth birthday he had the wolf dream, signaling the origin of his phobia; at four and a half he learned about the Bible and Christ and developed religious compulsions; before five he had a transient hallucination of losing his "little finger" (p. 85); finally a eighteen he contracted gonorrhea from intercourse with a country girl.

After being infected with gonorrhea Pankejeff became depressed and could not continue his studies, "could not be interested in anything" (Gardiner 1971, 41), and found himself in a "desolate emotional state" (p. 43). His father arranged consultations with top Russian and German psychiatrists, but they were not able to provide relief. Professor Kraepelin recommended a "prolonged stay in a sanatorium" in Munich which did not help Pankejeff either. There, however, he met a nurse, "an extraordinarily beautiful woman" (p. 49) named Therese, who would become his wife. Upon returning to Russia he found a Dr. Drosnes who, after some attempt at treatment, suggested a consultation with German doctors. While they were in Vienna they consulted with Freud who found Pankejeff "suitable for psychoanalytic treatment" (p. 137).

Freud wrote to Ferenczi on February 8, 1910: "I have taken on a new patient from Odessa, a very rich Russian with compulsive feelings" (Freud and Ferenczi 1996, 132). Five days later, in another letter to Ferenczi he added: "A rich young Russian . . . admitted the following transference to me after the *first session*: Jewish swindler, he would like to use me from behind and shit on my head" (1996, p. 138). Freud did not include in the case presentation this dramatic opening documenting the earliest words Pankejeff addressed to him.

Pankejeff was twenty-three years old at the start of the analysis. Freud describes him as "entirely incapacitated and completely dependent upon other people" (Freud 1918, 7). In 1952, Pankejeff confirmed his condition at the time, describing his emotional life as "'inadequate,' inappropriate to outer reality" (Gardiner 1971, 135). He also said: "I found life empty, everything seemed 'unreal,' to the extent that people seemed to me like wax figures or wound-up marionettes with whom *I could not establish any contact*" (p. 50, my italics).

Freud gained Pankejeff's confidence, and later in life his grateful patient wrote: 'The way in which *he listened to me* differentiated him strikingly from his famous colleagues" (p. 137, my italics). He added how relieved he had been "when Freud asked me various questions about my childhood . . . and listened with the greatest attention to all I had to say" (p. 138). He cherished the "sacred peace and quiet" (p. 139) he experienced in Freud's office.

Pankejeff's earliest childhood dream became the central piece of the analysis. In response to a letter from Freud he confirmed on June 6, 1926: "I narrated the dream of the Wolves to you near the beginning of my analysis, to the best of my recollection within a month or two after the start. The solution came then, as you state entirely accurately, only at the end of the treatment" (Pankejeff 1957, 449). When Freud reports his patient's dream, the reader hears Pankejeff directly for the first time:

I dreamt that it was night and that I was lying in my bed. (My bed stood with its foot towards the window; in front of the window there was a row of old walnut trees. I know it was winter when I had the dream, and night-time.) Suddenly the window opened of its own accord, and I was terrified to see that some white wolves were sitting on the big walnut tree in front of the window. There were six or seven of them.

The wolves were quite white, and looked more like foxes or sheep-dogs, for they had big tails like foxes and they had their ears pricked like dogs when they pay attention to something. In great terror, evidently of being eaten up by the wolves, I screamed and woke up. My nurse hurried to my bed, to see what had happened to me. It took quite a long while before I was convinced that it had only been a dream; I had had such a clear and life-like picture of the window opening and the wolves sitting on the tree. At last I grew quieter, felt as though I had escaped from some danger, and went to sleep again.

(Freud 1918, 29)

Prolonged analysis of this dream and the patient's associations to it led Freud to reconstruct the internal history of Pankejeff's childhood neurosis, his sexual development, the primal scene he believed to be the antecedent of the dream, and the fairy tales that contributed to the dream's imagery.

Freud admired his patient's sharp intelligence, high education, and multilingual skills. The question to be pondered is how they talked to each other to find the "solution" to the dream. In his writings later in life Pankejeff describes "discussing all manner of things" with Freud (Gardiner 1971, 142) from literature to gossip. As an old man, he said to the Viennese journalist Karin Obholzer: "I always talked about something. But he [Freud] didn't find *what he was after, whatever it was*" (Obholzer 1982, 48, my italics). Freud wanted access to the internal representations in his patient's mind, yet Pankejeff's words did not allow Freud to "approach" him as the subject of his inner reality. Freud's model of the spoken word favored the *representational content* in the patient's mind but it had no room for the affective person. Pankejeff's pathology could not allow access to his internal reality; he tried his best by giving Freud many words while he was at a loss as to his analytic intent. As he listened, Freud was always ready to grasp in the "smallest fragments" of his patient's words a coherent narrative of his earliest experiences which he considered foundational for his pathology. The case is exceedingly complex and I can select only brief sections of it to explore how they talked to each other.

In Section III of the case report, in a phase when they *seemed* to be working together, Freud realized that some "of these ostensible reminiscences . . . could only be a question of phantasies" (Freud 1918, 19). Soon after the patient remembered two events: his sister inviting him to show each other their bottoms and her playing with his penis while telling him his nurse did the same with the gardener. Upon learning that the sister had done a similar thing with an older male cousin Freud concludes: "His seduction by his sister was certainly not a phantasy" (p. 20). Pankejeff developed aggressive fantasies toward her as compensation to "efface the memory of an event [the playing with his penis] . . . offensive to the patient's masculine self-esteem" (ibid.) and reported that during puberty he had approached her sexually. After being rejected he became involved with a servant girl with the same name as his sister. Freud draws the conclusions that his heterosexual choice of object had been fixed upon *peasant girl servants*, a true compulsion that represents Pankejeff's clear "intention of debasing his sister" (p. 22) who had always outshone him with her intellectual superiority. Soon after, he began playing with his penis in the presence of his Nanya who told him that children who do that "got a 'wound' in the place" (p. 24). Castration had entered into the boy's scheme of things and came up in his associations about cut-up snakes, a wolf that lost its tail, and other allusions. He reported that after his Nanya's threat "he gave up masturbating." Immediately, Freud draws a dynamic and theoretical conclusion: "*His sexual life, therefore, which was beginning to come under the sway of the genital zone, gave way before an external obstacle, and was thrown back by its influence into an earlier phase of pregenital organization*" (p. 25). Now his sexual life became anal-sadistic, and the boy tormented his Nanya, insects, small animals, and other living creatures. The description fits Freud's theory of regression to an earlier period of sexual development.

Freud presents Pankejeff's next intrapsychic move as the selection of his father as a sexual object, following the renewal of "his first and most primitive object-choice, which, in conformity with a small child's narcissism, had taken place along the path of identification" (p. 27). I wonder how his father could have been "his first and most primitive object-choice" when Freud documents that as a small child he "was looked after by a nurse, an uneducated woman of *peasant* birth, with an untiring affection for him" (p. 14, my italics). His sister's seduction and his Nanya's castration menace, Freud concludes, contributed to transforming his sexual desires and behavior into passive attempts at seducing his father, a tactic that achieved the aim of obtaining masochistic satisfaction through inviting his father to beat him: "His screaming fits were therefore simply attempts at seductions" (p. 28). Once more I notice Freud's certainty in reporting his *construction* of Pankejeff *motivations*. No reported words from Pankejeff confirm Freud's conclusions, yet they are presented as actual psychical facts.

We don't know how they talked to each other up to this moment. There is not a single instance – except the dream – in which we hear directly what Pankejeff said to Freud or Freud to him. What we have is not a documented analytic process but a reconstructive narrative of his sexual development that conforms with the concepts in *Three Essays on the Theory of Sexuality* (Freud 1905b), whose third edition Freud was revising at the time. My impression is that under the pressure of the termination Pankejeff was giving him as much *information* as he could about his childhood while Freud was using his words to construct *in his own mind* what he thought was going on in his patient's mind. There is no indication of a joint construction. They had different tasks. The model of the spoken word had taken an interesting turn: Pankejeff's words found their meaningful completion for the analysis not in the representations in his mind but in those in Freud's mind. Freud offered no theorizing about the representational activity of the analyst's mind in giving meaning to the patient's words. He presents his conclusions about the patient's psychic transformations as factual childhood transformations.

In Section IV, "The Dream and the Primal Scene," Freud presents the core of the case interpretation. Pankejeff had commented how from the time he had the dream "'until my eleventh or twelfth year I was always afraid of seeing something terrible in my dreams'" (p. 29). He gave Freud a drawing of the tree with five wolves and told him how he had been so tremendously afraid of the picture of a wolf in a book of fairy tales and that his sister used it to make him scream in terror. Pankejeff associated the dream to the fairy tales *Little Red Riding-Hood* and *The Wolf and the Seven Little Goats*, as well as to the story of the tailor, who fought a wolf by pulling off the animal's tail.

Freud considers that his "fear of his father was the strongest motive for his falling ill," and for the wolf phobia. He concludes "if in my patient's case the wolf was merely a first father-surrogate" (p. 32), then Pankejeff could have linked the wolves of the fairy tale to his own father. Freud draws a conclusion about the source of the dream, asserting that it "relates to an occurrence that really took place and was not merely imagined" (p. 33). Then, Freud makes another move: "If it was to be *assumed* that behind the content of the dream there lay some such unknown *scene* – one, that is, which had already been forgotten at the time of the dream – then it must have taken place *very early*" (p. 33, my italics) and he becomes specific about the scene: "We *must naturally* expect to find that this material [of the dream] *reproduces* the unknown material of the *scene* in some distorted form, perhaps even *distorted into its opposite*" (p. 34, my italics).

The analysis of the dream required hard work. Freud quotes Pankejeff briefly saying that the opening of the windows must have meant "'my eyes suddenly opened' and . . . 'I saw something: the tree with the wolves'" (p. 34). Freud adds three reversals to the dream: Pankejeff said that the wolves "had riveted their whole attention upon me" (p. 29); Freud concludes: "The attentive looking . . . should rather be shifted on to him" (p. 34). The wolves sitting on the tree transposed the story of the wolves "unable to climb on to the tree" (p. 35), while their immobility is the opposite of the "scene of violent movement at which he looked with strained attention" (p. 35). Freud is referring to the primal scene the child purportedly witnessed.

Using his earlier reconstruction of the child's sexual development, Freud concludes that the wish for the formation of the dream must have been "the wish for sexual satisfaction . . . from his father" (p. 36), a wish so strong that "it made it possible to *revive* a long-forgotten trace in his memory of a scene" that brought about terror and "a conviction of the reality . . . of castration" (p. 36). Freud believed that the primal scene took place when he was "one and a half years" of age (ibid.). The word "revive" echoes a passage in *On Aphasia* where Freud says that when the same region of the representational cortex is stimulated, the memories that have left indelible traces are revived. The stimulant in this case is the child's wish for sexual satisfaction from his father.

As Freud presents Pankejeff's mental representations he clarifies that he "must abandon the support I have hitherto had from the course of the analysis" (p. 36) and that he had constructed them himself from meager fragments: what "*sprang into activity* that night . . . was the picture of copulation between his parents. . . a coitus *a tergo* [from behind] . . . he was able to see his mother's genitals as well as his father's organ; and he understood the process as well as its significance" pp. 36–37, my italics). Freud thought that the child had interrupted the parents by passing a stool and says that Pankejeff accepted this interpretation "when I had constructed it" (p. 80). Soon after this Freud takes the "*fact* that our little boy passed a stool as a sign of his sexual excitement" (p. 81, my italics). He described his identification with the sexual role of the woman, which under the threat of castration, prompted Pankejeff to decide "in favour of the intestine and against the vagina" (p. 79) and *repress* what he had witnessed.

In footnote 6 to page 37, Freud clarifies that the patient received "the *impressions* [of the parental coitus] when he was one and a half; his understanding of them was *deferred*" until the time of the dream. He was providing evidence for the existence of the primal scene and its later *revival* as a deferred action [*nachträgliches Verständnis*, i.e., "retroactive understanding"]. At this point Freud believed that he had "exhaustively explained" (p. 42) Pankejeff's anxiety-dream at age four.

To document Pankejeff's castration fears Freud cites *verbatim* the story of his transient hallucination at age five about cutting his hand's little finger. He also reports that at the time of the primal scene the patient "had observed the penis disappear, that he *had felt compassion* for his father on that account, and *had rejoiced* at the reappearance of what he thought had been lost" (p. 88, my italics). Freud said he had used small fragments of information to ascertain the primal scene but here he seems to offer his patient's direct observations and feelings at the time. Was Pankejeff giving Freud what he assumed he "wanted"? A sort of retrospective hallucination to give form to a moment he seemed not to remember?

We hear Pankejeff's voice for the third time when he reported a dream during the analysis about "'a man tearing off the wings of an Espe.'" The word he wanted was *Wespe* ["wasp"]. He realized that the word contained his initials, S. P., suggesting that "Espe" was a mutilated *Wespe* (p. 94). This exchange gives a glimpse of the changes that had taken place in Pankejeff. He seems to be making himself available to Freud, engaging him in an analytical dialogue; he no longer appears "unapproachable." They connected the dream to the nurse story as "the first experience that he could really remember" and that his urinating in front of Grusha constituted "the earliest effect of the primal scene" (p. 94). Freud's conclusion offer no confirmatory words from Pankejeff, however.

From that moment on Pankejeff seemed to have co-operated and all Freud had to do was "to collect and co-ordinate" (p. 95) the material they had already uncovered: "the problem of the treatment had every appearance of having been solved" (p. 94) and the reality of the primal scene proven in the case (p. 96). Freud's reconstruction of the primal scene and its consequences had contributed to the completion of the analysis and had "made it possible to clear up his inhibitions and remove his symptoms" (p. 11). However, in *Analysis Terminable and Interminable* Freud says, "When he left me in the midsummer of 1914, . . . I believed that his cure was permanent" (Freud 1937a, 217) but adds in the next page, "I was mistaken."

Pankejeff showed improvement. He returned to Russia, married Therese, completed his law degree, and settle into his married life. After the Russian revolution, however, he returned to Vienna as a destitute Russian emigré. He went back into analysis with Freud for a few months in the spring of 1919, ostensibly to work out some remnants of a paternal transference. Freud treated him for free and after the treatment collected money for six years to support his ex-patient. Freud wrote that "the patient has felt normal and has behaved unexceptionably . . . fifteen years have past . . . , but . . . his good state of health has been interrupted by attacks of illness which could only be construed as offshoots of his perennial neurosis" (Freud 1937a, 218). The truth is that Pankejeff continued to see psychiatrists and analysts as well as many medical doctors and dentists until his death at the age of ninety-two. He had many somatic complaints – intestinal, dermatological, dental – as well as anxiety, despair, and insomnia. Eminent analysts of the time including Ruth Mack Brunswick, Muriel Gardiner, and Kurt Eissler offered him help; the latter two also aided him and provided assistance in other respects. Eissler saw him as a patient each time he went to Vienna and tried to analyze him with the patient sitting up. During Pankejeff's final illness he paid for his care until his death.

As for his relationship with women, the Austrian journalist Karin Obholzer, who interviewed the Wolf Man in 1973, reports that Pankejeff could not be without a woman but could not stop complaining about her. He said to the journalist "If Freud had cured me, I would not have been stuck with this woman" (Obholzer 1982, 141). He was referring to Luise, with whom he had a relationship for over thirty years. He continued to pursue women impulsively until very late in his life. He would see a woman in the street, fall instantly for her, invite her to a hotel, pay her, and leave her without any emotional involvement. This compulsive pattern was present even during the years he was married and having some sex with his wife.

Reflections and conclusions

Freud tried to carry out an ordinary analysis but his "unapproachable" patient had his "instinctual forces" cut off from their conversation and from his self-awareness while they remained present in his behavior. Freud was confronted with an unexpected problem. He decided that the way to overcome his patient' avoidance of talking about himself was to end the treatment at a fixed date. The patient responded positively and produced "all the material which made it possible to clear up his inhibitions and remove his symptoms" (Freud 1918, 19). His later life confirms the persistence of problems, however, such as the absence of insight and his incapacity to open himself to others.

Pankejeff's *attachment* to Freud was deep and life-long. He wrote to Muriel Gardiner: "I had found in the person of Professor Freud *a new father* with whom I had *an excellent relationship*. And Professor Freud had also a great deal of personal *understanding for me*, as he often *told me* during the treatment, which, naturally strengthened *my attachment* to him" (Gardiner 1971, 88–89, n.3, my italics). Later in life he said to Obholzer: "The bad thing about an analyst is that one *clutches* on to him" (Obholzer 1982, 173). He reflected: "There is the danger that you will then transfer to others and no longer make your own decisions. I think that was my situation. Because the tie to Freud was too strong, I then transferred to other figures who could somehow stand for the father" (ibid., p. 59). He compared his relationship to the analysts who helped him after Freud with that of a child looked after by seven nannies, only one of whom can be trusted: "And that is really the situation in which I find myself after Freud's death. Because I don't know whom to believe now" (ibid., p. 173). These citations point in the same direction: Panke- jeff had found in Freud a parental object for deep and lasting *attachment*, perhaps a combination of the mother who had taken care of him when he was sick, his beloved 'Nanya', and the father of his infancy, the one he loved and who had liked him. As had been the case in his childhood, illnesses allowed him "to *enjoy* my mother's being with me and looking after me." Pankejeff commented further that "Freud's sharp way of expressing his opinion . . . , afforded one *great enjoyment*" (Gardiner 1971, 141, my italics).

I conclude that Freud offered him what he most needed: a competent adult he could attach himself to and who would listen to him with the deepest attention and care while he was lying on the analyst's couch saying anything he liked. A critical element was missing, however, namely, Pankejeff himself as the active subject of the encounter with Freud. His cultured linguistic competence permitted him to talk endlessly without saying much about himself. This grave psychological limitation remained with him to the end of his life. Gardiner, documented that with her "he was amazingly unreserved, no doubt putting me in the role of the analyst" (Gardiner 1971, 316) but with limited emotional engagement. Obhol- zer reports: "I did everything in my power to create a more personal, friendlier atmosphere than it is customary between analyst and patient. In spite of this, the Wolf-Man saw me as a new kind of analyst" (Obholzer 1982, 8–9). It is as though he had to repeat with all his helpers the type of conversation he had with Freud.

Freud also seemed to have felt attached to Pankejeff. He waited *four years* before confronting him with irrevocable termination and after he returned to Vienna as an impecunious emigré, he helped to support him financially for six years.

Let us return now to our central question: what happened to their manner of talking during that brief period of analysis that permitted Freud first to articulate Pankejeff's sexual development and second to identify the organization of his neu- rosis around the primal scene (as manifested in his dream by the effect of deferred action)? What changed at that moment? Freud describes how, in this brief period before the termination, Pankejeff's "resistance temporarily disappeared and the patient gave an impression of lucidity which is usually attainable only in hypno- sis" (Freud 1918, 11) something alike the transient visual conviction of cutting his finger (reported during that period). For him to be able to give what Freud wanted he had to reach an altered state of consciousness. I conclude that the patient did manage to tell Freud about all kinds of childhood thoughts, fantasies, beliefs, and even actual events such as his memory of Grusha, the castration threat made by his Nanya, his sister's playing with his penis, as well as his own anal and sadistic activities. I am convinced that he offered all this to Freud without ever grasping the import these events had for him as a child and for his adult life. I am aware of two pieces of evidence that support my conclusion: first, it was Freud who had to *construct* not only the shape of some actual events but also their meaning. And second, none of Pankejeff's writings give the slightest indication that he had acquired any insight into his problems through analysis. The best he could do was to repeat the *concepts* he had learned from Freud and memorized.

Freud does not describe Pankejeff's feelings during the analysis, except affection for him: "Whenever he shrank back on to the transference from the difficulties of the treatment, he used to threaten me with eating me up and later with all kinds of other ill-treatment – all of which was merely an expression of *affection*" (pp. 106–7, my italics). This sentence opens a small window to see how Pankejeff talked to Freud and how Freud understood him. The analyst was intent on understanding his sexual life, while the patient wanted to express his childish affection. Nevertheless, he was able to give words to infantile experiences that *helped Freud* to find evidence for his theory of sexuality.

Now, I arrive at my most daring conclusion: Pankejeff was not the only one to enter into a state similar to hypnosis, for Freud's *visualization* of what the child *saw* in the primal scene did not come from the patient. Pankejeff never remembered anything about it: Freud *constructed* it in a frame of mind in which he truly wanted to *ascertain* the child's experience. In his visualizing efforts he too entered a particular frame of mind, a quasi-hypnotic state of free-floating attention and *mimetic ideational experience* that permitted him to attribute extraordinary perceptive capabilities to a one-and-one-half-year-old boy. They exceed by far what the child could have noticed or felt. What becomes clear to me is Freud's intended and intense identification with the little boy who, he thought, had witnessed parental intercourse. It led him to construct in his mind in a *visually hallucinatory manner* the internal representation the child *could have formed*, that is, a primal scene. This representation was constructed in *visionary identification* with the child of the past, the alleged witness, by using Pankejeff's childish descriptions of his sexual thoughts and experiences. As much as I believe that Pankejeff's primal scene is no more than Freud's analytic construction, I must do justice to Freud by noting my conviction that in that last period of their work patient and analyst entered together into a mode of working and of talking to each other that not only had *hypnotic* characteristics, but also let them plunge into the child's mode of thinking and unveil his oral, anal, phallic, sadistic, fearful, and loving experiences. They contributed greatly to *Freud's understanding* of Pankejeff's sexual pathology without having any effect on the patient's relational or sexual behavior or providing any indication that he gained insight from them. By delivering his childhood material Pankejeff was giving Freud what he thought he wanted and making his last and best effort to keep Freud as his doctor. Later in life he complained to Obholzer that "Freud praised the sexual to the skies. He extolled the sexual" (Obholzer 1982, 130). Pankejeff also shared with her his doubts about the Professor's conclusions: "All those constructs must be questioned. Do you believe in all these constructs of psychoanalysts?" (p. 40). Obviously, he did not believe in them.

In conclusion I want to note that Freud's model of the spoken word lacked the indispensable relational components that indicate that we intend to talk from within ourselves about ourselves to a listener. Most of the time Pankejeff talked to keep people – Freud included – with him. He wanted attachment, no deep relationships. He longed for the *enjoyment* of the care and company, but was not capable of making himself available. His words were the means for attachment, not a medium for achieving self-knowledge or obtaining a personal involvement. Freud's model of a word achieving meaning by linking to an internal representation had deep limitations in Pankejeff's case. Of course, he could not speak without using representations but, as Freud acknowledged very early on, they were separated in him from their emotional source and his capacity to be present in them. Nonetheless, I do believe that it was his minimal connection to internal scenes and representations that Freud used to make his constructions.

Freud's model of the spoken word served *him* well in another respect. Convinced as he was that words lead to scenes and representations he used every little scrap of information in Pankejeff's words that could lead his totally dedicated and almost hypnotic attention to form in *his mind* the type of scenes and events that were hinted at. In terms of the structure of Freud's model, Pankejeff's words acquired their meaning by finding in *Freud's mind* the representation that belonged to them. Freud would not articulate this idea until 1937, in *Constructions in Analysis*, where he says that the work of analysis "involves two people, to each of whom a distinct task is assigned" (Freud 1937b, 258). He does not say that two people are needed to construct the meaning of words, but that is precisely the greatest contribution of psychoanalysis, namely, to uncover unconscious processes and to give personal meaning to verbal exchanges between people.

References

Blos, Peter. The Epigenesis of the Adult Neurosis. *Psychoanalytic Study of the Child* 27 (1972): 106–35.

Breuer, Josef, and Sigmund Freud. *Studies on Hysteria.* Vol. 2 of *Standard Edition*. London: Hogarth Press, 1893–1895.

Doolittle, Hilda. *Tribute to Freud.* 1956. Boston: David R. Godine, 1974.

Erikson, E.H. Reality and Actuality. *Journal of the American Psychoanalytic Association* 10 (1962): 451–74.

Freud, Sigmund. Analysis Terminable and Interminable. Vol. 23 of *Standard Edition*, 209–53. London: Hogarth Press, 1937a.

———. *The Complete Letters of Sigmund Freud to Wilhelm Fliess 1887–1904.* Trans. and ed. Jeffrey Moussaieff Masson. Cambridge, MA: Belknap Press of Harvard University Press, 1985.

———. Constructions in Analysis. Vol. 23 of *Standard Edition*, 255–69. London: Hogarth Press, 1937b.

———. Fragment of an Analysis of a Case of Hysteria. Vol. 7 of *Standard Edition*, 1–122. London: Hogarth Press, 1905a.

———. From the History of an Infantile Neurosis. Vol. 17 of *Standard Edition*, 1–122. London: Hogarth Press, 1918.

————. *L'homme aux rats. Journal d'une analyse.* Trans. and ed. Elza Ribeiro Hawelka. Paris: Presses Universitaires de France, 1974.

————. Notes upon a Case of Obsessional Neurosis. Vol. 10 of *Standard Edition,* 151–318. London: Hogarth Press, 1909.

————. Three Essays on the Theory of Sexuality. Vol. 7 of *Standard Edition,* 123–243. London: Hogarth Press, 1905b.

Freud, Sigmund, and Sándor Ferenczi. *The Correspondence of Sigmund Freud and Sándor Ferenczi.* Vol. 1. Edited by Ernst Falzeder and Eva Brabant. Cambridge, MA: Belknap Press of Harvard University Press, 1996.

Gardiner, Muriel. *The Wolf-Man by the Wolf-Man.* New York: Basic Books, 1971.

Gay, Peter. *Freud: A Life for Our Time.* New York: W. W. Norton, 1988.

Glenn, Jules. Notes on Psychoanalytic Concepts and Style in Freud's Case Histories. In *Freud and His Patients,* edited by Mark Kanzer and Jules Glenn, 3–19. New York: Aronson, 1980.

Kardiner, Abram. *My Analysis with Freud: Reminiscences.* New York: W. W. Norton, 1977.

Langs, Robert. The Missalliance Dimension in Freud's Case Histories: 1. The Case of Dora. In *Freud and His Patients,* edited by Mark Kanzer and Jules Glenn, 58–71. New York: Aronson, 1980.

Mahony, Patrick. *Freud and the Rat Man.* New Haven, CT: Yale University Press, 1986.

Mahony, Patrick J. *The Cries of the Wolf Man.* New York: International Universities Press, 1984.

————. *Freud's Dora: A Psychoanalytic, Historical, and Textual Analysis.* New Haven, CT: Yale University Press, 1996.

Marcus, Steven. Freud and Dora: Story, History, Case History. *Psychoanalysis and Contemporary Science* 5 (1976): 389–442.

Obholzer, Karin. *The Wolf-Man Sixty Years Later: Conversations with Freud's Patient.* London: Routledge & Kegan Paul, 1982.

Pankejeff, Serge. Letters Pertaining to Freud's "History of an Infantile Neurosis." *Psychoanalytic Quarterly* 26 (1957): 449–60.

Sachs, David M. Reflections on Freud's Dora Case after 48 Years. *Psychoanalytic Inquiry* 2 (2005): 45–53.

Saussure, Raymond de. Sigmund Freud. In *Freud as We Knew Him,* edited by Hendrik M. Ruitenbeek. 1956, 357–59. Detroit: Wayne State University Press, 1973.

Scharman, Melvin A. Further Reflections on Dora. In *Freud and His Patients,* edited by Mark Kanzer and Jules Glenn, 48–57. New York: Aronson, 1980.

Spence, Donald P. When Interpretation Masquerades as Explanation. *Journal of the American Psychoanalytic Association* 34 (1986): 3–22.

Strachey, James. Editor's Note to "Notes upon a Case of Obsessional Neurosis." Vol. 10 of *Standard Edition,* 153–54. London: Hogarth Press, 1960.

9
CONCLUSIONS

In my beginning is my end.

T. S. Eliot, *Four Quartets*, "East Coker" (1940)[1]

have completed the journey of exploring the many functions of the spoken word
n Freud's texts. I hope I have been respectful, inquisitive, and challenging toward
both my subject and my readers. I have selected T. S. Eliot's words from his poem
"East Coker" to head this final chapter because they beautifully capture Freud's
ntellectual and creative evolution from his first publication on the subject of
words in the monograph *On Aphasia* to his last paper *An Outline of Psychoanalysis*.
The monograph and his discarded *Project for a Scientific Psychology* form the original pillars of the arch that would encompass his theories and technique until he
completed his life's work, creating a science capable of unveiling the mysteries of
he unconscious. The evolution of his theories is coterminous with his progressive
understanding of the function of words and affects in the organization of mental
ife. From the time of his conversation with Breuer about the treatment of Anna
O., Freud's self-assigned task of understanding the formation of symptoms and the
patient's pathology was taken over by the power of the spoken word. I daresay that
psychoanalysis as Freud left it to us resulted from his continuous re-elaboration of
he phenomena elicited by the words spoken between people.

Freud's first conception of words in *On Aphasia* makes it clear that he is not
alking about words as heard or pronounced sounds. A word acquires its *meaning*
when its sound finds an internal mental representation whose *visual component*
aptly links to it. To put it more strongly, *words do not exist* as a psychic reality until
he person who hears them is able to link their sound to an internal representation,
hus transforming sounds into *personally meaningful words*. This understanding of
he words we exchange with each other offers the bedrock that supports Freud's
ntire psychoanalytic theory and makes possible a technique capable of accessing
unconscious processes *for the first time in human history.*

I will now give an overview of the interconnections of Freudian conceptions and their implication in tracing the *intrapsychic function* of words. Freud's philosophy clearly states that we live our *conscious* life encircled by two unknown realities: the physical world and our unconscious. Perception is all we have to capture glimpses of what each has to offer and to build our experiences. Conscious sensory perception of the material world is psychically transient and can never be retrieved as a perception, yet, it always leaves its mark in the perceiver at several levels. The first and most striking point Freud makes in his understanding of the neural processes of perception proposes that from their start in the senses to their arrival in the cortex they are organized as a series of transformational relays whose final aim is to *serve the speech function*. They contribute to the formation of the multisensory complex in the cortex he called object-representation. Freud affirmed that this mental formation is always expandable in its richness of detail and connections to other representations because he was convinced that *to perceive is to associate*. Freud' later free associative technique would reverse this process: by progressive associative links – he postulated – the patient would uncover pathogenic representation that he had formed earlier but defensively repressed to his unconscious.

The never-ceasing processes of perception and association lead to the formation of an internal reality that remains in many respects consciously unavailable to its owner even though it does affect his character structure and the organization of his experiences. In ordinary life and during analysis the *sound* of words capable of linking to *representations* in the internal world convert the two – the sound and the unconscious representation – into an *experienced psychic word*, one that can be placed at the service of gaining conscious awareness of our private reality. In presenting this viewpoint, which integrates the contributions of the monograph and some of the concepts in the *Project* and subsequent works, I intend to show that Freud's *descriptive unconscious* – which is formed by the accumulated representations and associations in a person's mind – was already present as a seed ready to germinate as early as 1891. The future technique of free association was also delineated when Freud asserted in the monograph *On Aphasia* that "whenever the same cortical state is stimulated the psychical (*das Psychische*) emerges anew as a remembered image (*Erinnerungsbild*)" (Freud 1891, E. p. 56; G. p. 58, my translation). These theoretical considerations appear to me as the indispensable explanation for Freud's technical insistence to his patients at the beginning of his work and even in his later clinical exploration that they tell him what they *were seeing* in their minds. It also helps to understand why he wanted to know the *scenes* they saw internally, so he could use them as way stations toward grasping the meaning of the patient's experiences.

Psychoanalytic theory and technique are in fact based in three early Freudian premises: (1) the neural traces left by perceptions remain unmodified; (2) the pathways established by the formation of the traces create *facilitations* to revive in the present the representation formed in the past; and (3) the combination of neural pathways and their facilitation conditions and determines the emergence of psychical processes dependent on them. The critical notion of psychic determinism is upported by the three premises and in turn is the foundation of free association. Freud was faithful to these presuppositions when he insisted that patients look internally and see what had been revived in their minds in the form of scenes and thoughts. He was convinced that the connections between the descriptive and the dynamically repressed unconscious would combine in predetermined mental processes to bring to conscious awareness derivatives of the pathogenic material. These in turn would progressively converge to unveil the repressed experiences and thoughts.

The word *scene* calls for special exploration. Freud used it repeatedly to denote what he expected would appear in his patients' minds. He rarely if ever used the theoretical term *representation* in a clinical context. Yet Freud did not pay attention to the slippage of meaning between representation and scene when he asked patients what they were seeing in their minds. He took it for granted that the imagery and scenes were what they had to talk about that would give meaning to their symptoms and pathological beliefs and convictions. Tacitly, he was equating scenes with representations. It makes eminent sense that he would ask for scenes in the clinical setting because they, unlike representations, include the experiential subject while a representation describes a conceptual, objectively conceived reality. Scenes, like dreams, have the experiencing person at the center of their organization. In fact, I believe that we are unable to think about what pertains to us as persons without going from scene to scene in order to locate ourselves as experiential beings. Freud's dream analysis offers abundant illustrations of this point: one dreams about oneself and directly or in displacement locates oneself at the center of the dream and its scenes.

Freud uses the word *scene* throughout his works to refer to the private emergence of recollections of particular experiential or fantasized moments which he hoped would provide pointers and clues to the dynamically repressed material. He wanted to know what patients saw with their inner eye when the conditions of the analytic situation weakened the power of the defenses. And in those scenes he was searching for a pointer to the experiences and thoughts that had become repressed on account of the painful affect they would elicit if consciously recognized and understood. Freud wanted those scenes to be put into words as the means to make them and their implications innocent enough to be acceptable to the defended patient. Much to his satisfaction, he observed that when the patients had not fully described what they had seen with their inner eye the imagery and scenes kept reappearing, only to vanish later like ghosts once they were fully articulated in words to the analyst and accepted by the patient.

He knew that such reawakened experiences could not acquire meaning without the person feeling their emotional impact. The affect elicited by the psychically meaningful word was not considered in the monograph but emerged as a theoretical and *economic* issue in the *Project*. Freud's conception of object-representation evolved *silently* into scenes, memories, and thoughts capable of arousing *feelings* when they appeared in the patient's consciousness during analysis. He used the term "scene" to the very end of his writing. The expression is compatible with the fact that human perception involves experiential gestalts, even though they might be distorted or fragmented by defenses. We never perceive isolated object as the original conceptualization of representation implied; instead we locate wha we perceive in a contextual gestalt that facilitates recognition and assignation o meaning, and allows us to relate them to our stance as the perceiver.

Freud's last published paper, *Constructions in Analysis*, completes the theoretica arc by describing the analyst's work of constructing and communicating to the patient "a piece of his early history that he has forgotten" (Freud 1937, 261). Hi example of a construction presents a sequence of intrapsychic and historical scene to describe the young child's experience. The intrapsychic scene can be summe up as "up to your *n*th year you considered yourself as the sole and unlimited pos sessor of your mother," while the external historical scenes describe the child disillusionment when the mother returned with a new baby and saw she would n longer offer him exclusive devotion. The construction does not offer representa tions but describes psychical and actual *experiential scenes* the impact of which ha affected the patient throughout life. Freud concludes that if the patient can fee "an assured conviction of the truth of the construction" it would lead to "the sam therapeutic results as a recaptured memory" (p. 261).

This conclusion is convincing to me as an analyst who has followed Freud persistent efforts to understand the complex interactions between representa tions of experiences, their verbal communication to the analyst, and the affec felt by the patient as the key to their psychic significance. In fact, if psychical lif is to be depicted in connection with the need for love, even intrapsychic love technical terms do not suffice. Psychical processes and language must resort t *scenes* of human interactions. As I mentioned in Chapter 7, nothing illustrate this point better than Freud's dramatic description in *The Ego and the Id* of th *interaction* between the *agencies* of the mind. He presents a scenic encounter an 'dialogue' between the ego and the id: "When the ego assumes the features of th object, it is forcing itself, so to speak, upon the id as a love-object and is tryin to make good the id's loss by saying: 'Look, you can love me too – I am so lik the object'" (p. 30). The ego insists that the id form a representation of its visua "appearance," and compare it with the loved object; once that is done, the ego sure of the resemblance between them – "talks" to the id inviting it to bestow th old love for the object upon itself. The earlier love scene with the original objec is now repeated intrapsychically as a scene between the – supposed – two agencie of the mind that 'feel' compelled to present themselves as people.

A similar scenic situation can occur between the superego and the ego. Th superego 'talks' to the ego and commands: "You *ought to be* like this (like you father)." It also inflicts prohibitions: "You *may not be* like this (like your father) that is, you may not do all that he does; some things are his prerogative" (p. 34) The 'speech' of the superego is not limited to words: it involves 'looking' at bot child and father, 'comparing' the two and ascertaining their similarities and differ ences. Without such 'looking' at the father and the desires of the child's ego at th time, the command loses its meaning. Talking, looking, and desiring definitel onstitute intrapsychic scenes between agencies that are assumed to be mental tructures. Nonetheless, I agree with Freud that the portrayal is accurate. Psychic ife is bound to be a succession of scenes in which the subject *simultaneously* per- eives, relates, communicates, and feels where and how he stands in relation to imself and the external and internal objects that share the moment. Freud clearly understood the consequences of this phenomenon when he conceived of the defenses as interrupting such simultaneity between feeling and scenic representa- ion. The repression, he said repeatedly, intends to prevent conscious experience of painful feelings. The defenses fail frequently because the perceptual systems – nternal and external – never rest. Components of the event have already been reg- stered as simultaneous, and only the continuous reinforcement of the defenses can eep the pain at bay. He offered the beautiful demonstration of Fräulein Elisabeth's lesperate efforts to deny to herself that she was in love with her brother-in-law nd wanted to marry him when her sister died.

I have reached these conclusions after paying close attention to Freud's constant use of the term *scene* in his writings when he refers to the patient's experiences that need to be reawakened in analysis in order to bring them back to what he called he moment of origin (and also referred to as "the psychical" [*das Psychische*] in *On Aphasia*). As Breuer and Freud said clearly at the very beginning of psychoanalysis, 'the psychical process which originally took place must be repeated as vividly as ossible; it must be brought back to its *status nascendi* and then given verbal utter- nce" (Breuer and Freud 1893–1895, 6).

Freud's problems in dealing with these issues stem from three sources. The arliest is his conception of representation in *On Aphasia*, which he considers to be laborated from sensory perceptions as individual component processes – visual, actile, and auditory – that converge to form the representation of a *single* object. ̄he second problem emerges from his manner of understanding perception with- out a perceiving *subject* or self that grasps in a *simultaneous gestalt* the separate nput of the senses and to which he experiences an instantaneous *affective* response. ̄he third problem is the persistent discrepancy between *feelings* as experiences of atients and people on the one hand, and the economic theory of *affect* as a dis- harge of quantities of psychic energy on the other hand. There is no question that f one watches a person in an emotional moment attentively, one can observe the hysiological changes that appear to support the notion of a neural or endocrine lischarge. Furthermore, science has documented the neural and hormonal pro- esses present in emotional experiences.

The key question, however, is this: can a conscious affect be separated rom the person experiencing the particular scene or thoughts of the moment? ̄reud rejected the notion that unconscious affects exist. In *The Unconscious* he ays: "The whole difference arises from the fact that ideas [*Vorstellungen*] are athexes – basically of memory-traces – whilst affects and feelings correspond to rocesses of discharge [a mechanical process without subject], the *final manifesta- ions* of which are perceived as feelings [the subjective experience of a person]. n the present state of our knowledge of affects and feelings we cannot express this difference more clearly" (Freud 1915, 178). But, what causes what? In thi. description, Freud suggests that affects *discharge* their energy and *cause* the person to feel. The *agency* of the feeling belongs to the process of discharge. In clinical context, however, Freud clearly suggests that when the patient become *aware* again of a repressed representation he feels the whole emotional impact o the original experience (which was defended against precisely to avoid feeling psychic pain). The *agent* is the feeling person who has become *aware* of the ful impact of what has come to mind, such as Fräulein Elisabeth who loved and wanted to marry her widowed brother-in-law. Thus, even in Freud, the causality is located in the person's awareness of something painful to the experienc- ing self. In sum, Freud never developed the notion of scene, a conception tha carries – as dreams do – what is needed to assert that the feelings result from the awareness of the perceiving self about the personal meaning of the scene and no from an economic process of discharge in relation to conceptual representation and an economic theory of affect. The words exchanged between patient and analyst have the potential to restore the original scene, revive the pathogenic moment or a significant derivative of it and, most important, reactivate it in the transference with all its affective implications. In the here and now of the analysis the adult is not only able to revisit his childhood experiences and fee again the old pain but also to re-evaluate it with the analyst as *a new object tha accompanies him in the affective task of accepting his feelings and wishes and updating them to the situation in the present.*

Freud does not reflect on the affective, interpersonal meaning of the exchange of words between patient and analyst. Today we know that these words *mus simultaneously* convey empathy with both the child of the past and the adult on the couch; this is indispensable if they are to effect the necessary transformation of the analysand's feelings. The empathic power of words depends upon the analyst' capacity to experience in himself what the patient is not capable of grasping and articulating in his own mind. Empathy is defined as "the action of understand- ing, being aware of, being sensitive to, and *vicariously experiencing* the feelings thoughts, and experience of another of either the past or present without hav- ing the feelings, thoughts, and experience fully communicated in an objectively explicit manner" (*Merriam-Webster's 11th Collegiate Dictionary*, 2003). What Freud refers to as the analyst's constructions cannot be the result of cognitive processe alone, which articulate the hints and allusions present in the patient's associations They require the preconscious formation in the analyst's mind of scenes capable of capturing the *type of event* the analysand underwent in childhood or is experienc- ing during the analytic hour. The analyst's *imagination* responds to the patient' words and communications by forming scenarios – preconscious or conscious transient or persistent – that spontaneously capture aspects of what the patient i unable or afraid to articulate. I believe that this is what Freud meant to convey in *Constructions in Analysis*, when he said that interpretations refer only to single ele- ments while constructions represent "a piece of his [the patient's] early history tha he has forgotten" (Freud 1937, 261).

What mental processes made it possible for Freud to say to an adult patient "Up to your *n*th year you *regarded yourself* as the sole and unlimited possessor of our mother?" Obviously he had heard the patient's associations and had formed his own associations and images in response to them. Yet, to be able to say "you *regarded yourself*" he had to locate his imagination within the mind of his patient as a child in the act of *feeling* he possessed his mother. The word "regarded," once more points to the visual – even if metaphoric – component of the experience. There is no objective way of saying such a sentence except through the mediation of an act of empathic imagination in which the analyst *vicariously experiences* what the young child felt. I claim that this is what Freud means when he poses a rhetorical question about the analyst's task. He responds: "His task is to make out what has been forgotten from the traces which it has left behind or, more correctly, to construct it" and concludes that conveying such construction to the analysand constitutes "the link between the two portions of the work of analysis, between his own part and that of the patient" (Freud 1937, 259, my underlining). I daresay that "what has been forgotten" has to encompass episodes, events, experiences – in a word, scenes of the patient's past life, even those he is unable to retrieve.

We have returned in a broad sense to the process Freud described in 1891 when he conceived of the conscious meaningful word as being composed of two parts, the patient's spoken word and the representations/scenes to which it is linked. Our modern understanding differs in two respects from Freud's early formulations. The first is that we are no longer talking about single objects or words but complex experiences of the analysand's past life; the second is that *in analysis* this process of linking occurs as a result of the collaboration of *two persons, each of whom contributes one component of the wording* that will finally give meaning to the person's previously unconscious experience. I should add that *Constructions in Analysis* is the last work to be published during Freud's lifetime. It is my understanding of this process as described above that prompted me to select Eliot's line "In my beginning is my end" to head this chapter. I firmly believe Freud's conclusions in *Constructions in Analysis* clearly show that his beginning in *On Aphasia* implicitly anticipates the culmination of his life's work. The joint human process of creating meaning, any meaning – and especially making unconscious meaning conscious – can only occur by means of linking words to internal representations/scenes. To communicate with words requires the ability in the speaker to elicit a representational process in the mind of the listener *similar* to the one that prompted the utterance. As Freud said so clearly all along, only the spoken word has the power to bring to life the preconscious and unconscious realities harbored in the human mind.

Freud had a vivid imagination, as his masterful metaphors clearly illustrate. He used it clinically to ascertain what was going on in his patients' minds when they developed their symptoms. I described in Chapter 5 how Freud came to understand Dora's persisting tickling in her throat and her cough. After learning from Dora that she was aware of sexual acts besides intercourse Freud believed that "the conclusion was inevitable" that her cough had as a stimulus "a tickling in her throat" when "she pictured to herself a scene of sexual gratification *per os* between the two people whose love-affair occupied her mind so incessantly" (Freud 1905a 48). Dora did not say such a thing to Freud. It was he, the analyst, who *imagined* that Dora *imagined* her father's penis tickling Frau K.'s throat and using her own throat as a substitute for Frau K.'s.

In Chapter 8 I showed to what extent Freud used constructions and reconstructions of the purported earliest experiences of the Wolf Man to convince his readers and himself that his patient had actually witnessed the primal scene. He had affirmed that without fantasizing we cannot make progress in clinical or theoretical work. It is clear to me that his technique of free-floating attention creates the conditions under which unconscious processes in the analyst's mind can be activated in response to the patient's words. In ordinary circumstances, when we pay attention to the speech of another person we are intent on matching in our minds the representations in the mind of our interlocutor that have prompted him to select the words addressed to us. The analyst's attempt to suspend such a direct function facilitates the emergence in her mind of unconscious processes which can offer some hints about what the patient is trying to suppress. Freud assumed that the patient's unconscious intention to reveal what he simultaneously tries to suppress will in the end give some guidance to the analyst's preconscious activity in her efforts to make sense of the patient. The distortions that repression has inflicted on the original material find a tool in the analyst's free-floating attention to pick up the clues pointing to their original form. In this manner the analyst processes the patient's words and finds echoes in the vast region of her unconscious mind. Yet this is only the beginning of the analyst's interpretive or constructive work, for she must then convey to the patient in adequate spoken words what she has grasped about his internal processes and his internal experience, obscure or clear as they might be. At this level, patient and analyst return to a conversation in which the analyst addresses the patient with the intention of assisting him to understand and accept, or correct the analyst's construction of his internal reality in her own internal reality. Patient and analyst use their spoken words to avoid and/or awaken unconscious representations and intolerable scenes until they find a way to describe and name them jointly. They are also, then, able to accept these representations affectively, aided by their mutually recognized verbal descriptions with shared referents. Ultimately, thanks to the analyst's construction, such scenes no longer need to remain unconscious in the patient's mind.

Obviously, this is an idealized and paradigmatic description of the analytic process. It sums up the theory behind clinical work, which calls for alternation between unconscious and preconscious representations and scenes – both the analysand's *and* the analyst's psychic realities – and the words that mediate access to them. In actual clinical practice the process is never so clear and linear. It meanders between multiple strands of the patient's and the analyst's unconscious and preconscious processes while they continuously grope within the dark streams of associations and imagery to find what will make the patient's past, present, and transferential experiences meaningful.

In sum, analytic work uses all the powers of language as articulated in the spoken words exchanged between analyst and patient. Language itself, as a cultural creation, has to submit during analysis to what it finds in the minds of the participants. It has to keep *and* to surrender its referents to the calls of unconscious processes if – as Freud has instructed us – we want to gain access to aspects of the unknowable territory he called the unconscious. Words are the tool; their goal is to reach the unconscious – the true psychic reality – and bring it to the conscious light of the analysand's experience of himself, to the narrative of his psychic journey to become the person he is.

We must now consider the importance of the body in relation to the spoken word. Freud's conviction that perception is all we have at our disposal to deal with the unknowable external and internal realities makes it clear that the components of speech draw on all the sensory capabilities of the body for the elements needed to construct representations and associations. Because perception is the action of particular individual's body, the objects perceived and the words heard become *idiosyncratically colored*; they become *personal* without losing the accurate-enough registration of the perception. Freud did not make this extrapolation but it is clear to me that this is an obvious implication of his theorizing. A similar process occurs in the perception of words as sounds and as affective messages. I therefore conclude that according to psychoanalytic theory speaking always implies symbolizing in words a sentient bodily mind (Rizzuto 2001). Directly and indirectly we are always speaking with our body about our bodily organization of all perceptions, including those of ourselves.

Freud created the concept of *ideational mimetics* to illustrate how we express the attributes of largeness and smallness in the contents of our ideas. He made some fascinating observations on the subject, saying that we 'innervate' our bodies with the pictorial 'size' of our ideas. He describes how through posture and gesture the entire body participates in conveying the manner in which we want our words to be heard. The body participates in the communicative function of the words; we cannot help but speak with 'embodied' words. I have already mentioned the self-observations Freud drew on to illustrate how the body participates in communication: "When I speak of something sublime I innervate my speech in a different way, I make different facial expressions, and I try to bring the whole way in which I hold myself into harmony with the dignity of what I am having an idea of. I impose a solemn restraint upon myself" (Freud 1905b, 200). Neither at this point of his theorizing nor at any other time does Freud make a reference to this 'innervation' of speech as a critical component of analytic work, yet empathy must be present in the analyst's words and voice if they are to reach the patient's emotional stance and communicate that she understands his situation.

I have also cited Freud's description of his spontaneous reaction to the words he heard from others about themselves: "It is as if I were obliged to compare everything I hear about other people with myself; as if my personal complexes were put on the alert whenever another person is brought to my notice" (Freud 1901, 4–25) . Once again, he did not elaborate on the meaning of these observations but I draw a conclusion from them. Freud did not link ordinary personal comparisons upon hearing others speak about themselves to the comparative empathic process that an analyst must have available and use spontaneously to facilitate the understanding of the patient's experience. Yet today we know that how we convey in our words the preconscious or conscious introspection of our experience in relation to those of the analysand's constitutes an essential component of the analytic process. It is worth repeating that Freud's self-observations confirm that even when he did not theorize or made technical references to such comparisons he unequivocally understood that the total person, body and self, are involved in the acts of listening and speaking.

Finally, we must consider how the sentient body perceives its own appetites. Freud believed that "an instinct can never become an object of consciousness – only the idea that represents the instinct can" (Freud 1915, 177). This means that to become consciously available bodily needs must be *translated* into 'instinctual representatives'; they must be *perceived* internally, recognized, and named as hunger, thirst, or a wish to be touched, for example, if they are to be acknowledged and communicated to another person or even to oneself. We have therefore come back to the original composition of the word: an unconscious instinctual representative and a word capable of naming it. In brief, speaking involves not only the motor processes of mouthing sounds and conveying meanings but the participation of the person's body and self as the source of its perceptual representations of things and words, its desires, and its mode of communicating in ideational mimetics. The same conception applies to hearing the words of others.

In theoretical terms, as I mention in Chapter 7, Freud considers that "the ego is first and foremost a bodily ego" (Freud 1923a, 26). He reached such a conclusion by returning to the irreplaceable role of perception: "the ego is that part of the id which has been modified by the direct influence of the external world through the medium of the *Pcpt.-Cs.* [perception-consciousness]" (ibid., p. 25). Ordinary perceptions belong to the descriptive unconscious and they offer little difficulty in becoming conscious by being linked to words. It is the dynamically repressed representations, memories, and scenes that are in Freud's theory "the prototype of the unconscious for us" (ibid., p. 15). These are the mental processes that represent the pathological inability to tolerate external or internal reality and the feelings they will awake in their owner if they become conscious. They constitute the focus of analytic work. They are also bound to have associative connections with the more easily accessible descriptive unconscious which will be used to provide many distracting associations *and* a few leads to the dynamically repressed material. This must have been what Freud had in mind when he created the shocking expression about analytic work as "extracting the pure metal of the repressed thoughts from the ore of the unintentional ideas" (Freud 1904, 252).

The notion of words as *ore* brings to our attention Freud's understanding of the many functions of words. We have already learned how indispensable they are to make the repressed unconscious available to conscious psychic life. Such conception sums up *Freud's newly created use of words*, and his carefully elaborated description of the *intrapsychic* function of words in connecting the segregated representations, memories, and scenes to the patient's awareness. It was this use of words that permitted him to demonstrate that psychic life comprises the vast territory of the unconscious and a more restricted conscious awareness. He proved to his contemporaries that the core reality of their lives, their *psychic reality*, was to large extent beyond their grasp. He knew it was a Copernican revolution that would affect "the *naïve* self-love of men" (Freud 1916–1917, 284). As for him it deeply increased his well-earned self-satisfaction at having discovered a previously unknown reality by the simple device of *eavesdropping* on "the age-old dossiers of Nature" (Freud 1969, 424).

Words, however, as Freud so skillfully described, perform many other functions in everyday life and in the analytic process. Words can be intentionally or unconsciously deceptive, false, misleading, and distracting; they may hide or reveal double meanings, or express something other than what the speaker intended, for example. Freud simply said "words are a *plastic material* with which one can do all kinds of things" (Freud 1905b, 34). Obviously, he was talking about words as we encounter them in the language of our culture. In fact, however – and this is one of *Freud's core contributions* – we can be sure of what a word means to us only when we have managed to link it to the internal representation the speaker has used to form it. Otherwise, the word may keep its *linguistic referential meaning* without revealing the true conscious *and* unconscious intention of the one who said it. As mentioned in Chapter 5 Freud gave fascinating examples of all these processes in *The Psychopathology of Everyday Life* and *Jokes and Their Relation to the Unconscious*.

Furthermore, both the sound of words and their spelling can be tampered with to serve other purposes beyond their linguistic meaning. They can be split, rejoined with one another, altered by prefixes and suffixes, or augmentative and diminutives; words can be accented in an unexpected place, mispronounced, and otherwise transformed, including being preconsciously translated into another language as in Freud's example of forgetting the painter Signorelli's name. All these maneuvers bring with them complex motivations ranging from making a joke to betraying an unconscious intention. The conclusion seems obvious: the sounds of words can convey significant meanings or become like playthings which we use at times intentionally and at other moments without knowing what we are doing. Yet Freud demonstrated that even this tampering with the sound of words cannot escape the *internal determination* of mental processes. If we explore each instance of tampering well enough, sooner or later, we will find the *internal referent* – a representation, memory, thought, or scene – that gives meaning to the transformed sound of the word, or to put it differently, it will disclose the meaning of such a *psychical word* in the mind of the speaker.

I want now to sum up Freud's understanding of thought in relation to the spoken word. Nowhere does he offer a clear description of how he understands thought and its processing. The closest we have to a definition appears in his paper *Formulations on the Two Principles of Mental Functioning*, where he says: "It is probable that thinking was originally unconscious, in so far as it went beyond mere ideational presentations and was directed to *the relations* between impressions o objects, and that it did not acquire further qualities, perceptible to consciousness until it became bound to verbal residues" (Freud 1911, 221, my italics). In the *Proj ect* Freud had made it clear that thought processes create facilitations that must no be changed in order not to "falsify the traces of reality" (Freud 1950 [1895], 335 already established by the experience of satisfaction, which acts as the persisten motive for thinking processes. In that work he clearly established what woul remain his central conception of the intra-psychical function of speech: "Th indications of speech-discharge . . . put thought-processes on a level with percep tual processes, lend them [thoughts] reality and *make memory of them possible*" (pp 365–66). We have no other means of being aware of our psychic reality.

Freud's descriptions suggest that some perceptual representations remain uncon scious and, although they are associated to other representations, may not be par of the thinking process of establishing "*relations* between impressions of objects. Freud does not say so explicitly, but perhaps, together with thought processes, the contribute to the unconscious condensations and displacements typical of dream and defensive processes. All these unconscious processes will only reach conscious ness through speech. In *The Unconscious* Freud is more specific when he says tha such relations "which become comprehensible only through words, form a majo part of our thought-processes" (Freud 1915, 202). So far, we have thought processe that seem to be only unconscious while in this description there is a "major part" o thinking that depends on words. In his posthumously published *Outline of Psycho Analysis* Freud introduces a new conception: "The inside of the ego, which com prises above all the thought-processes, has the quality of being preconscious . . . I would not be correct, however, to think that connection with the mnemic residue of speech [*Sprache*] is a necessary precondition of the preconscious state. On th contrary, that state is independent of a connection with them" (Freud 1940, 162) The preconscious state is "something peculiar" governed by the secondary proces and Freud avows ignorance about the "shrouded secret of the nature of the psychi cal" (p. 163). He goes on to ask, "What, if this is so, is the true nature of the stat which is revealed in the id by the quality of being unconscious and in the ego b that of being preconscious and in what the difference between them consists? (p. 163). In brief, Freud knows that the *process* of becoming conscious require words but declares himself unable to ascertain the *nature* of such process.

Freud's idea that imagery represents a regression from verbal material to a *primi tive* mode of mentation calls for reconsideration. There is no doubt that durin analysis and as a result of the change in the use of the speech function there is significant increase in imagery, in particular visual imagery. The patient deepl involved in the analytic process brings up memories, events, scenes, thoughts fantasies dominated by sensory imagery, in particular of a visual type. This is a incontrovertible fact. Nonetheless to conclude from it that imagery is regressiv and primitive *in itself* must be questioned. We do not have enough data to clarif the role of imagery and the level at which it functions in everyday life and durin analysis. Several authors have studied imagery from particular points of view whi others have proposed a technical variation to explore imagery directly. As far as I am aware, however, the nature of imagery in analysis remains largely unexplored. I believe that we owe it to ourselves to find a richer description of imagery beyond the customary conception of it as regressive and primitive. Eva Lester comments: "Visual imagery aroused considerable interest during Freud's concentration technique but, following this, interest in imagery has declined and has remained low despite the 'primacy' retained by the dreams in the analytic practice and theory" (Lester 1980, 417). There is something surprising about this disinterest particularly because a large portion of our work consists in hearing the patient's description of his childhood experiences and present-day encounters with other people as scenes from his life. Furthermore, Roy Schafer has described how the analyst at work "builds up a temporally articulated internal image of the patient's world . . . The building up of this image of the patient is based on a series of partial introjections, emotional reactions, and revival of memories concerning oneself and the object. . . . The hypercathected internal image is thereby increasingly enriched, focused, hierarchically organized, and stabilized. It becomes a substructure within the analyst's ego" (Schafer 1959, 356). I agree with Schafer's description but can hardly consider that such an analytic function is nothing but a regressive process. In fact, as he says, it results from a multitude of perceptions and identifications that arise in the course of analytic treatment. My detailed examination of how Freud understood the structure of the psychic word and how he used imagery during analytic work has convinced me of this, at least: rather than primitive and regressive, the imagery we use for both processes is *progressive* in the sense that it conditions the verbal articulation of experiences and facilitates the work of the empathic imagination in its efforts to capture the patient's private reality.

I must now address the issue of translation. Freud said explicitly that in analysis the patient's words have to be translated for him to fully grasp what he means. My earlier description of the structure of the psychic word and Freud's description of the many uses of words in this chapter should have made that point abundantly clear. Freud uses the word 'translation' repeatedly and in relation to several aspects of mental functioning. Nonetheless he never offered any theoretical considerations about its psychoanalytic meaning. My perusal of the instances in which Freud uses the word and the concept of translation has led me to the bold but firm conviction that understanding Freud's theory of mind means to grasp that *we live our lives in constant processes of translation*. Sensations are translated into representations; bodily appetites are translated into 'instinctual representatives'; to satisfy a need we might have to name the representative, which is a translation of a translation; unconsciously registered representations must find their conscious translation by linking to words in order to achieve recognition; the patient has to translate the conscious scenes and thoughts in his mind into words for the analyst; the dream content translates the dream-thoughts into its deceptive imagery; the dream imagery must be translated to free it of defensive distortions; the analyst upon hearing the patient's words translates them into thoughts, images, and even sensations in his own mind and experience; to convey what she has grasped in the analysand's

communications she has to translate her inner processes into words for her patient
When symbols emerge during the session the analyst cannot take them at face
value. After some exploratory work she must translate them to fit the menta
context in which they have appeared. Repression, as Freud understood it, is the
defensive effort to isolate what could cause us pain by denying it translation into
words. We also carry out a certain type of translation, beyond words but also using
them, when we transfer the libidinal investment in our primary objects to the analyst or other people. In brief, speaking about psychical life always involves severa
translation processes; our *conscious* life depends upon the capacity to translate ou
internal realities into words: *we live our lives in translation.*

What is the relation between words and affects? Freud said explicitly that affect
are *attached* to representations and that they undergo an economic process of discharge when the patient experiences them as feeling. As I have noted repeatedly in
the various chapters and even in this conclusion, the problem resides in the absence
of a subject in Freud's theorizing. Breuer and Freud learned at the very inception
of their work that words without affect had no therapeutic effect. In fact, Freud
said that we must have more confidence that affects convey what is important
rather than trusting the simultaneous verbal expressions that may be deceptive.
find this *separation* unacceptable when I look at a moment of speech as the action
of a subject who is feeling and speaking at the same time. It is true that they belong
to two different types of processes and that they may be at odds with each other
if we describe them separately. Nonetheless, if analysis is to be possible, affect and
verbal expression must be part of the experience of the speaker at the moment o
speaking, even if defenses are at work and allow only partial consciousness.

The best confirmation I find for this in Freud's text is when the patients said to
him they had known all along what he had labored to bring to conscious light. H
also offers powerful evidence in the book on jokes and in his examples of everyda
pathology. In those writings Freud attributes the dynamic processes to the cross
purposes of conscious and unconscious *intentions* in the subject who makes a slip c
the tongue. The existence of the slip clearly indicates that it is the subject who kep
the unconscious intention alive. In other words, in actual life the *total subject* con
sciously and unconsciously remains connected to his past and present experience
and feelings, repressed or not. The feelings about what he is saying and to whom h
is saying them are there, whether consciously recognized or not. There were severa
factors that contributed to Freud's conception of affect as discharge. With regard to
its relationship to words, perhaps the most significant factor is his persistent focus on
substantives and the semantic components of words as he sought to find the 'solu
tions' to the mysteries of his patients' pathology. This point needs further elaboration

In *An Outline of Psycho-Analysis* Freud says, "We have no way of conveying
knowledge of a complicated set of simultaneous events except by describing them
successively" (Freud 1940, 205). Such events are the scenes, events, memories
have referred to all along in different chapters. They involve feelings as part c
their own configuration. Freud suggests that language presents its descriptions in
a temporal, directional, and linear sequence. This is factually true when languag

s separated from the speaking moment and looked at from the point of view of ts structural organization. The instance of speaking with another person also nvolves "a complicated set of simultaneous events" that includes the wish or need o speak to a particular person, the internal evaluation of what to say and what to uppress, the assessment of how the other is going to hear it, the wish to be heard n a particular way, and the evaluation of who the other person is in relation to he speaker. All these simultaneous factors are under the sway of powerful feelngs, such as the search for love, narcissistic self-investment, and self-protection. peaking, regardless of how neutral it may appear, is inevitably self-revealing, and ntends either to communicate or to avoid communication but cannot escape the eed to do something affectively with the person addressed by our words.

Speaking also encompasses complex simultaneous effects. Words affect the peaker/listener *simultaneously* at many levels: emotionally, somatically, intellectu-lly, when they awaken or create imagery, retrieve memories, and involve other nental activities. Invariably, as Freud has convinced us, words are placed in a vast ssociative network, both conscious and unconscious, that extends far beyond heir linguistic and idiosyncratic intended meaning. Psychoanalysis would not be ossible without this *multipotentiality* of the word, either spoken or heard. *This is the ifference between language as an objectively observable event and speech as an interpersonal ncounter.* When we speak we feel, and there is no way around this demonstrable act. Although Freud makes no mention of it, there is no way for us to speak enerically; after all we cannot help but size up the person of the analyst who has nstructed us to speak and, in the process, attempt to select under the sway of our lesires what we deem the best words *for her* and the *least harmful for us* at a given noment. Freud discovered this phenomenon when Dora forced him to recognize he presence of her transference on him.

Only in his last publication, *Constructions in Analysis*, did Freud note explicitly hat "analysis consists of two quite different portions, that it is carried on in two eparate localities, that it involves two people, to each of whom a distinct task is ssigned. It may for a moment seem strange that such a fundamental fact should ot have been pointed out long ago" (Freud 1937, 258). It is not strange to me fter reading all Freud had to say about his manner of using speech. He was intent n finding the 'solution' to the unconscious configurations in the patient's mind nd considered the patient as *his helper* in achieving his aim. His investment in the *emantic* component of words, necessary as it was for him to create psychoanaly-is, did not allow him to pay attention to the other components of the spoken xchanges with his patients. He held that words are deceptive and would not eveal what was really ailing the patient. He had to use them as a *means to an end,* hat is, to reach the depth of the unconscious.

He achieved his goal when he demonstrated beyond any reasonable doubt that ur unconscious is a core reality of our existence. Yet he left unattended the com-municative, affective, and conative components of words in his clinical and theo-etical work. This point is even more striking when we remember his assertion hat what brings about the needed clinical change in a patient is not intellectual insight, but "simply and solely his relation to the doctor" (Freud 1916–1917, 445). We confront this paradox in all of Freud's works: his life-long commitment to the talking cure that included the transference *and* the absence of explicit theorizing about speaking as a dynamic and interpersonal process between people.

In Freud's relentless pursuit of clues to how a patient had organized his internal reality we can observe a sort of detective in him. He wanted to complete the private *narrative* of the analysand's symptoms and pathological formations by following the associations that led a patient to create an internal construction of private beliefs or convictions supporting the narrative. With Fräulein Elisabeth he went a far as to send her to visit her sister's grave, just as a detective might take a suspect to the scene of a crime. I believe that this was a significant contribution to the understanding of psychopathology for a simple reason: the topographic theory of the mind of the 1900s or the structural theory of *The Ego and the Id* (1923a) are useful tools for an analyst to organize her conceptual understanding of the structure of the patient's difficulties, but they are far removed from the analysand's experience, which follows the narrative form. I wish here only to describe an observable process, not to enter into any controversy about factual or narrative truth. Such issues are beyond my present concern.

Freud mentions another function of words in *Remarks on the Theory and Practice of Dream Interpretation*, namely, the assistance they provide to the ego in dividing itself into a subject and object and locating itself in different positions, in clauses such as, "When *I* think what *I* have done to this man" or "When *I* think that too was a child once" (Freud 1923b, 120). These observations point to the fact that even in internal "speech" the spoken word functions as the only means we have to *identify ourselves and to objectify and make accessible to ourselves and others* our own thoughts, dreams, feelings, and wishes from the present and the past.

A final observation I would like to make concerns the fact that many of Freud patients, particularly after he became well-known, were foreigners – Europeans of different origins and Americans or British nationals whose mother tongue was not German. While Freud made a few scattered remarks about working with such patients, he never reflected systematically about the impact on analysis when the patient must speak a language that is not what he spoke in childhood or even in his contemporaneous everyday life. The same consideration applies to Freud analyzing patients in English.

My last task is to sum up how Freud, the man and the analyst, spoke with his patients. As I observed in Chapter 8 we don't really know how he talked to and with them. All we have is the *transcriptions* of words he reported having said to them. His tone of voice, feelings, and the manner in which he delivered his words to them cannot be retrieved. Here, I would like to draw some general conclusions on the subject of what he revealed in his writings about his working methods. repeat what he said to Kardiner with disarming honesty:

> I have no great interest in therapeutic problems. I am much too impatient now. I have several handicaps that disqualify me as a great analyst. One of

them is that I am too much the father. Second, I am much too much occupied with theoretical problems all the time, so that whenever I get occasion, I am working on my own theoretical problems, rather than paying attention to the therapeutic problems. Third, I have no patience in keeping people for a long time. I tire of them, and I want to spread my influence.

(Kardiner 1977, 68–69)

Freud's self-description is borne out by his publication about patients he treated. In each case he wanted to prove a theoretical point, and such an intention organizes the presentation. His mind was relentless when he was pursuing a theory, and he was absolutely determined to create a new science acceptable to his contemporaries. To the end he remained the well-trained scientist he had become in his early days.

As a clinician frequently he did not take his own advice; he talked about himself and his family with some patients; he discussed psychoanalytic politics with his trainees; he gave advice, books, and even a meal to Lanzer when "he was hungry." He used the objects he had collected in his office to illustrate some of his analytic points. He discussed literature and poetry with interested patients. He had no qualms about offering his patients lengthy indoctrinations, offering reassurance whether or not it was needed, encouraging the patient, or posing intrusive questions. In brief, he often did not follow the recommendations he gave to other practicing analysts. That is one part of the story; the other part is that his analytic intention to investigate unconscious motivations and narratives could not be deterred by the patient's efforts to keep secrets and to dodge what was painful or shameful. His clinical and theoretical mind could not rest until he had completed the *narrative* linked to the formation of the patient's symptoms, attitudes, and beliefs. He wanted to convince both his analysand and himself of the truth of their findings and constructions as a felt past experience. In fact, as he said in *Constructions in Analysis*, he was after the kind of conviction that made a clinical construction seem as real to both participants as the recollection of an actual memory.

Freud had an astonishing ability to listen and to associate to what the patients were saying in a dual mode: At one level he followed the associations and let them guide the progressive emergence of what they had to reveal, while at another level he was contextualizing what he heard within his existing theories and new theoretical elaborations. In that respect he enjoyed an enviable freedom of mind to use verbal expressions and grammatical functions in original ways; such innovations both deepened his understanding of the analysand's words and facilitated the creation of his own theoretical structures such as "*das Ich.*" His remarkable imagination and metaphoric capacity greatly enhanced his own associative processes in grasping the unconscious derivatives present in his patients' words.

To the list of these outstanding gifts I must add his constant disposition to learn from patients, to let them show the way, and to change his technique according to what he was learning from them. I believe that Freud's creation of psychoanalysis as a technical procedure stemmed from his flexibility in progressively modifying his first hypnotic therapies according to the responses of his lady patients; he continued to reflect on what they were teaching him about the conditions under which they would surrender their repressed secrets. It must be said, however, that Freud did not always display such adaptability in his clinical work when he was under the sway of his theoretical commitments and determined to demonstrate a point. I have described the painful situation with Dora when he failed to hear in her words that Dora was talking to him; meanwhile he was not exactly speaking to her or with her but rather speaking *for* Dora *about* herself in order to confirm his theories.

How did Freud communicate with us as his readers in his writings? Mahony's books (1982; 1984; 1986; 1996) offer a profound and detailed analysis of Freud's use of written language and narrative style, which illustrates his skill as well as his clinical and theoretical shortcomings. Freud's writings reveal his absolute mastery of German. In 1930 he received the Goethe Prize from the city of Frankfurt, given to people whose use of language honored Goethe's memory. His narrative style engages readers, involves them in the arguments, forces them to keep reading, to agree or disagree. In the end, they encounter something no writer had offered before: careful narratives of the inner workings, convolutions, desires, and detours of human beings' previously unknown unconscious life. Freud created a new narrative genre, that of the inner affective and experiential life we all harbor without knowing it. The clinical history as the personal story of the analysand's psychic life had entered the field of medicine. Soon it would expand to other fields, ranging from all varieties of psychotherapy to the analysis of literary characters and psycho-history.

Freud, the man who claimed that human beings live in the frame of two unknown realities, the external world and the unconscious, concluded that "internal objects are less unknowable than the external world" (Freud 1915, 171). We must offer him our gratitude because his dedicated clinical work and theorizing opened for the first time the closed doors of our most intimate life.

At the end of my long journey exploring his works, I would like to express my own gratitude to Freud. He made my efforts to learn about his involvement with words pleasurable, demanding, challenging, creative and, ultimately brought me to appreciate the profundity of his discoveries and the astonishing complexities he unveiled in our minds through the use of ordinary words.

Note

1 Excerpt from "East Coker," p. 23, from *Four Quartets* by T.S. Eliot. Copyright 1940 by T.S. Eliot. Copyright © renewed 1968 by Esme Valerie Eliot. Reprinted by permission of Houghton Mifflin Harcourt Publishing Company. All rights reserved.

References

Breuer, Josef, and Sigmund Freud. *Studies on Hysteria*. Vol. 2 of *Standard Edition*. London: Hogarth Press, 1893–1895.

Freud, Sigmund. Constructions in Analysis. Vol. 23 of *Standard Edition*, 255–69. London: Hogarth Press, 1937.

———. The Ego and the Id. Vol. 19 of *Standard Edition*, 1–66. London: Hogarth Press, 1923a.

———. Formulations on the Two Principles of Mental Functioning. Vol. 12 of *Standard Edition*, 213–26. London: Hogarth Press, 1911.

———. Fragment of an Analysis of a Case of Hysteria. Vol. 7 of *Standard Edition*, 1–122. London: Hogarth Press, 1905a.

———. Freud's Psycho-Analytic Procedure. Vol. 7 of *Standard Edition*, 247–54. London: Hogarth Press, 1904.

———. *Introductory Lectures on Psycho-Analysis*. Vol. 16 of *Standard Edition*. London: Hogarth Press, 1916–1917.

———. *Jokes and Their Relation to the Unconscious*. Vol. 8 of *Standard Edition*. London: Hogarth Press, 1905b.

———. *On Aphasia: A Critical Study*. Trans. Erwin Stengel. 1953. New York: International Universities Press, 1891.

———. *An Outline of Psycho-Analysis*. Vol. 23 of *Standard Edition*. 1938, 139–207. London: Hogarth Press, 1940.

———. *Project for a Scientific Psychology*. Vol. 1 of *Standard Edition*, 283–397. London: Hogarth Press, 1950.

———. Psycho-Analytic Notes on an Autobiographical Account of a Case of Paranoia (Dementia Paranoides). Vol. 12 of *Standard Edition*, 1–84. London: Hogarth Press, 1911.

———. *The Psychopathology of Everyday Life*. Standard Edition. London: Hogarth Press, 1901.

———. Remarks on the Theory and Practice of Dream Interpretation. Vol. 19 of *Standard Edition*, 109–21. London: Hogarth Press, 1923b.

———. Some Early Unpublished Letters of Freud. *International Journal of Psycho-Analysis* 50 (1969): 419–27.

———. The Unconscious. Vol. 14 of *Standard Edition*, 159–215. London: Hogarth Press, 1915.

Kardiner, Abram. *My Analysis with Freud: Reminiscences*. New York: W. W. Norton, 1977.

Lester, Eva P. Imagery and Transference in the Analytic Process. *International Journal of Psychoanalysis* 61 (1980): 411–19.

Mahony, Patrick. *Freud and the Rat Man*. New Haven, CT: Yale University Press, 1986.

———. *Freud as a Writer*. New York: International University Press, 1982.

Mahony, Patrick J. *The Cries of the Wolf Man*. New York: International Universities Press, 1984.

———. *Freud's Dora. A Psychoanalytic, Historical, and Textual Analysis*. New Haven, CT: Yale University Press, 1996.

Rizzuto, Ana-María. Metaphors of a Bodily Mind. *Journal of the American Psychoanalytic Association* 49 (2001): 535–68.

Schafer, Roy. Generative Empathy in the Treatment Situation. *Psychoanalytic Quarterly* 28 (1959): 342–73.

INDEX

psychoanalysts' use of spoken word 1–2, 178–9

Psychoanalytic Notes on an Autobiographical Account of a Case of Paranoia (Freud) 123

psychopathology, words and 75–80; agency issue and 76–7; intentions and 75–6; linguistic meaning and 79–80; memory lapses and 76–8

Psychopathology of Everyday Life, The (Freud) 13, 75, 181

pure metal, Freud term use of 101

Question of Lay Analysis: Conversations with an Impartial Person, The (Freud) 1, 106

Rat Man case, verbal communications with Freud and 148–58

reality principle 121–2

rebus 78

Recommendations to Physicians Practicing Psycho-Analysis (Freud) 103

reconstruction 90, 139–40, 156, 164, 178

regression concept 62–9; described 62–4; imagery and 64–9

Remarks on the Theory and Practice of Dream Interpretation (Freud) 108, 186

Remembering, Repeating and Working-Through (Further Recommendations on the Technique of Psycho-Analysis II) (Freud) 107

representational process 32–3; location and 127

repressed scenarios, translating into words 92–112; dream interpretation and 97–103; listening mode of analyst and 103–11; overview of 92–3; reflections and conclusions 111–12; theoretical conceptualizations and 93–7

repression 119–21; as defense mechanism 120; gaps and 119; kinds of 121; overcoming 39–41; spoken word and 39–40; topographic 127–8; translation and 119, 121

Repression (Freud) 120–1

repression proper 121

resistance concept 93–4

Rizzuto, Ana-María, works of: *Birth of the Living God: A Psychoanalytic Study, The* 3; "First Person Personal Pronouns and Their Psychic Referents" 5; *Freud, God, the Devil, and the Theory of Object Representation* 3; "Freud's Speech Apparatus and Spontaneous Speech" 4; "Freud's Theoretical and Technical Models in *Studies on Hysteria*" 4;

"Hypothesis about Freud's Motive for Writing the Monograph *On Aphasia*, A" 4; "Metaphors of a Bodily Mind" 5; Origins of Freud's Concept of Object Representation, The ('*Objektvorstellung*') 4; "Proto-Dictionary of Psychoanalysis, A" 4, 25; "Psychoanalysis: The Transformation of the Subject by the Spoken Word" 5; "Speech Events, Language Development and the Clinical Situation" 5

Rome Institute of Psychology 5

Rothschild, Salomon 86

Sachs, David M. 148

Sapir, Edward 6

Sappho (Daudet) 69

scenes: Anna O. case and 19–20; aphasia model and 37; Dora case, and imaginary 88–91; dream 55, 57, 67; Elisabeth von R. case and 48–51; Frau Emmy case and 21, 43; Freud use of 60, 173–4; of human interactions 174; meaning of 20; mental 76; Miss Lucy's case and 43–5; real or imaginary 12; representations and 173; *status nascendi* and 36; between superego and ego 174–5

Schafer, Roy 183

Scharman, Melvin A. 148

seeing, jokes and 85–6

sexual instincts 126

Sifneos, Peter 3–4

social play, jokes and 83, 88

Some Elementary Lessons in Psycho-Analysis (Freud) 114

speech, as living process 7

speech apparatus 26–31; components of 28–9; spoken word and 27–8, 37; structure of 27

"Speech Events, Language Development and the Clinical Situation" (Rizzuto) 5

Spence, Donald P. 148

Spitzer, Daniel 85

spoken word: body and, importance of 179; Breuer and 17–18; Doolittle and 143; ego and 14; function of 1; internal representations and 4–5; *Interpretation of Dreams, The* and 53–73; Lacan's linguistic approach and 5–6; neural/psychical structure of 4, 10; psychoanalysts' use of 1–2, 178–9; repression and, overcoming 39–40; speech apparatus and 27–8, 37; theoretical models of 114–15, 162, 163, 169